IN VINO
DUPLICITAS

Also by Peter Hellman

Chief! (with Albert Seedman)

When Courage Was Stronger than Fear

American Wine Handbook

The Auschwitz Album (with Lili Meier)

Heroes: Tales from the Israeli Wars

Shaping the Skyline

Fifty Years After Kitty Genovese (with Albert Seedman)

IN VINO DUPLICITAS

THE RISE AND FALL OF A
WINE FORGER EXTRAORDINAIRE

PETER HELLMAN

THE EXPERIMENT

NEW YORK

The Experiment, LLC, 220 East 23rd Street, Suite 600, New York, NY 10010-4658
theexperimentpublishing.com

The Experiment's books are available at special discounts when purchased in bulk for premiums and sales promotions as well as for fundraising or educational use. For details, contact us at info@theexperimentpublishing.com.

Library of Congress Cataloging-in-Publication Data

Names: Hellman, Peter, author.
Title: In vino duplicitas : the rise and fall of a wine forger extraordinaire
  / Peter Hellman.
Description: New York : Experiment, [2017]
Identifiers: LCCN 2017010305| ISBN 9781615193929 (hardcover) | ISBN
  9781615193936 (ebook)
Subjects: LCSH: Kurniawan, Rudy, 1976- | Swindlers and swindling--United
  States--Biography. | Swindlers and swindling--Indonesia--Biography. | Wine
  frauds. | Commercial crimes. | Wine industry.
Classification: LCC HV6692.K87 H45 2017 | DDC 364.16/3--dc23
LC record available at https://lccn.loc.gov/2017010305

ISBN 978-1-61519-495-7
Ebook ISBN 978-1-61519-393-6

Cover and text design by Sarah Schneider
Author photograph by Dan Sagarin

Manufactured in the United States of America

First printing August 2018
10 9 8 7 6 5 4 3 2 1

To Peter Thustrup.
We met as strangers one late morning more than thirty years ago at his Paris rare wine shop. An hour later, we were sipping a wine of his, a 1947 Meursault, at a nearby bistro. And so we bonded. Wine can do that.

Contents

Author's Note

This book grew out of a seemingly minor story about the withdrawal of twenty-two lots of wine from an auction in New York in spring 2008. Over the next eight years, I filed dozens of stories in print and online about the making and unmaking of the wine counterfeiter who was the source of those wines. All appeared in *Wine Spectator*. Those stories would become this book's bedrock. Without the support and reach of the magazine, the tale might never have found critical mass. *Wine Spectator* did for this story what the *Washington Post* did for Woodward and Bernstein reporting on Watergate and what the *Boston Globe* did for the reporters who pried open the molestation scandal that later became the basis for the movie *Spotlight*. I am not so foolish as to think that a tale of fake wine is on par with presidential or priestly misdeeds, but the outcome is similar: Without a publication willing to stay with the story, it's not going to reach readers, and the wheels of justice might never start to turn. Google is a wonder. Still, the implosion of print journals since the late 1980s, ranging from the loss of magazines like *Life* to the diminished page count of *The New York Times*, makes me appreciate all the more deeply the value of those publications that remain strong and still get printed on paper.

Introduction

I was about to cross Boulevard Raspail in Paris when a silver Renault pulled over. The driver leaned across to open the passenger-side window. His friendly eyes locked on mine. He was in a fix, he told me in good English, without even asking me if that was what I spoke. He was returning from a menswear trade show in Deauville, where he represented the Giorgio Armani line. Somebody had stolen his wallet. Now he was almost out of gas. He needed just a little cash to pay for a couple of liters to get himself home.

Too bad for this fraudster, I thought. He'd picked the wrong guy to be his mark. He wasn't going to scam me. I was about to turn away when he asked me if I was Jewish. The appropriate answer was that it was none of his business. Yet I nodded.

He pointed to a small Star of David dangling on a chain strung from the cigarette lighter on his dashboard. Looking back, I'm confident he could have produced a Saint Christopher's medal or a Muslim crescent moon and star.

Seeing that I was not reaching for my wallet on his behalf, he said, "OK, no problem, sorry to bother you. Enjoy Paris!" He started to roll his window up and then, with a sudden bright smile and arch of the eyebrows signifying that he had a great idea, he rolled it back down.

"Hey, your sweater size is medium, right?" Reaching to the back seat, he grabbed a garment bag bearing the Armani logo. The pale blue sweater within was a sample left over from the show, he explained. He would be getting new samples for the next season's show, and he no longer needed this one.

"It's cashmere," he said. "Top quality, double-thick Armani. At Barneys in New York, you'd pay six hundred dollars. You'll look great in it."

He thrust the garment bag out the window. "I don't want any money from you," he said. "It will make me feel really good if you accept it. Americans saved my father's life in World War II. He was badly wounded by the Germans in 1944 and he was operated on by your army surgeons. Saved his life. Please take this sweater as a token."

My hands, as if on puppet strings, took the bag.

As this generous-spirited stranger started to roll up the window, I felt a pang. How wrong of me to be gifted with an Armani cashmere sweater and give nothing in return!

"Hold on," I said, tapping the window to get his attention. From the wallet in my back pocket I pulled out a hundred-franc note—about twenty dollars in those pre-euro days. "This will get you a little gas."

He grabbed the money. Up went the window and he sped off. Not even a thank-you. I sensed that he was already scanning the pedestrians, looking for his next American.

Inside the zipper bag was a cheesy polyester rag, nasty to the touch. I pitched it into a trash can. Unexpectedly, I felt admiration for this now-departed master of manipulation. He'd pushed buttons in my psyche even as I was aware that he was doing it, yet I was powerless to disconnect. It was a performance worth the price of admission.

Push the right buttons in people who think they are too savvy to be fooled, as the master counterfeiter who is the subject of this book did repeatedly, and what is billed as the rarest of wines can be sold to marks for a far higher price than the rarest cashmere. The wealthy collectors who spent millions on those fake wines were canny fellows in their businesses. Yet, in the hands of this unlikely con man, they did as I had done: They responded to his perceived generosity by opening their wallets.

✻

The average price paid for a bottle of wine in America hovers around eight dollars. For that price, you'll get a perfectly decent weeknight sipper. Made to an exacting industrial standard, it will reliably taste the same from one vintage to the next and, even if supposedly dry, will probably carry a hint of sweetness. For twenty dollars, you'll expect to get the benefit of better grapes, more selective harvesting, and more attention paid in the winery. Over twenty dollars, the wine should have the potential to develop extra character as it ages. At this level, the wine in your glass ought to make you think as well as drink. Hit the fifty-dollar mark, and be confident that the producer has overlooked no detail or expense to make the very best wine she can. Unlike a fine garment, whose quality you can see and touch right down to the seaming, the bottle tells you nothing about the care that went into making the wine within. A seven-dollar bottle looks and feels no different from a seven-hundred-dollar bottle. Its label, possibly featuring a cute animal, could well be more eye-catching than a "serious" label.

So, until you inhale the scent of the wine and get to know it in your mouth, there's no way to judge how the winemaker might have gone the extra mile to make the best possible wine, or how costly it was to do that. Two examples, one each from Bordeaux and Burgundy:

On a perfect late summer afternoon in Bordeaux (the same day on which Katrina was inundating New Orleans), I was standing on the steps of Pape Clément, a turreted and gabled château that was once the home of the first French pope. Its imposing proprietor, Bernard Magrez, dark-suited even under the strong sun, was staring out at a far corner of the vineyard, where a team of workers were busily doing . . . what? It was too early to start harvesting. Magrez explained that a famed vineyard consultant, Michel Rolland, known as the "flying winemaker," had recommended that the height of his vine trellises be raised several inches in order to allow more sunlight to filter between the leaves. That would help ripen the grapes. That was the job these workers were doing.

But were they changing the trellising just in that corner?

Most of the vineyard would be done, Magrez answered. The cost, in a country where vineyard labor is paid very well, would be daunting. Of course, no banner on Pape Clément's label will ever shout, "New and Improved!" Nobody who purchases Pape Clément will have any way of knowing about its proprietor's investment in trellis raising. The best Magrez can hope for is that consumers will savor the wine just a wee bit more than if he had not made that investment, even if they don't know why.

Several years later, on a February morning after a light, wet snow had fallen, my mud-caked shoes were planted at the base of the shallow slope of Clos de Vougeot, one of Burgundy's most renowned vineyards. This particular plot belonged to Domaine Faiveley, one of more than eighty owners in Vougeot. With me were Erwan Faiveley, fourth-generation head of the domaine, and Bernard Hervet, general manager. Higher up on the slope, gravelly, porous soils drained rather than retained water. Down here, the soil was mostly clay, which retained water. It was slurped up by the lower rows of vines. The result was plumped-up grapes that yielded unacceptably dilute juice compared to the more intensely flavored grapes from higher up on the slope.

Faiveley's solution was to create a new drainage system to keep the vines from sucking up excess water. Like the raising of Pape Clément's trellises, it was an act of expensive TLC that customers would never know about. But the cost was built into Faiveley's Clos de Vougeot, priced at $150 or more. Owners of properties of lesser repute would be unlikely to bear the financial burden of doing what Magrez and Faiveley did.

What about bottles that cost far more than Pape Clément or Clos de Vougeot? Surplus cash needs to be parked somewhere, and a wine cellar filled with orderly arrays of rare and renowned bottles is an excellent place to put it. Those bottles lie in wait to be ceremoniously uncorked to mark a happy event or to impress a guest. Meanwhile, they appreciate in value as they slumber. Consider 1945 Château Mouton Rothschild, a Bordeaux beauty made for the long haul after a hot and dry summer when France was stretched thin from war and occupation. Baron Philippe de Rothschild, proprietor of Mouton, had fled to London while the Germans inhabited his château and returned only as the grapes were ripening that year.

Do certain grapes know when it's a season to celebrate by giving their all? The crest of Mouton's 1945 label is embellished with a delicately drawn *V* for victory to mark the German surrender five months earlier. Of this wine, decades after the vintage, the great British taster Michael Broadbent wrote, "The power and spiciness surges out of the glass like a sudden eruption of Mount Etna."

In 1950, Sherry Wine and Spirits (now Sherry-Lehmann), a wine shop catering to a "silk stocking" clientele on Manhattan's Upper East Side, sold 1945 Mouton Rothschild for $2.25 per bottle. Sixty-five years later, while wandering in the duty-free zone at Charles de Gaulle Airport, I spotted a bottle of that same wine in a locked glass sales case. It was priced at 25,000 euros, or about $28,000. One of the perks of having bought the wine for $2.25 per bottle "way back when" was that you could be confident that it was real. Not so with any bottle of 1945 Mouton offered for sale today, not least one on sale at a duty-free shop.

Honest wine dealers and auction-house specialists assume that such a legendary bottle is guilty until proven innocent.

Ten bottles of well-credentialed 1945 Mouton were the highest-priced lot in the twenty-thousand-bottle auction from the cellar of billionaire Bill Koch at Sotheby's New York in May 2016. They sold for $343,000 to a phone-in bidder. The highest price ever paid for a single bottle auctioned by Sotheby's was $310,700 for a jeroboam (equal to six regular bottles) of 1945 Mouton sourced directly from the château and sold in New York in May 2007. Had it been sourced from anywhere else, the price would almost certainly have been lower.

Some collectors set their sights on price appreciation. They store their precious bottles as if they were bars of gold, hoping to unload them at auction when the market is strong. Other collectors are, first and foremost, attracted to the arcane nature of old French wine. Any wealthy sap can drop a bundle on a condo overlooking an azure sea, a bejeweled Rolex, or a Ferrari. Buying a case of obscure bordeaux or burgundy from a favored vintage elevates the possessor into a cultured priesthood.

Unlike the oceanfront pad, the burglar-bait wristwatch, or the sex-bomb sports car, these bottled treasures are baffling to many people. What exactly is it that makes them so desirable? Can that moldy bottle of ancient La Tâche or Château Latour, born in a year that in human terms would now mean residence in a nursing home rather than the cellar, emitting a whiff of barnyard when the crumbly cork is pulled, actually give more pleasure than a ten-buck bottle of spunky zinfandel that smells fresh and tastes fruity? Whatever the deal is, ownership must be a sign of a person of highly refined taste.

The most fervent collectors are seeking dalliances with the elusive bottles that will make the earth move. Their hope is that one such elixir, shared at a well-laden table with others who are equally passionate, will do a thing that we all hope to do, but can't: defeat the ravages of time. It will do this not merely by allowing them to hold on to life as elders in a desiccated state, but by offering up deeper pleasures than callow youth provided. For these acolytes of very old bottles, wine rapture won't replace erotic encounters of their youth, but it might be the next best thing. And afterward, the bedsheets won't need washing.

I once read in a British wine magazine an account of a tasting of many vintages of champagne undertaken in the depths of a limestone cellar in Épernay in the heart of bubbly country. The tasters, old-timers all, sipped from dusty bottles, each one older than the one before. They discussed the merits and shortcomings of each vintage until they came to the last and oldest. It was the 1914 vintage, harvested mainly by women and children. Most able-bodied men had gone off to the nearby battlefront to defend against the invading Germans. That October, the thunder of artillery could be heard as the grapes were picked. A lifetime later, the tasters in the cellar contemplated this still-alive champagne made in the early days of the Great War.

For this, there were no words. Only the tears of grown men.

When I was in my midsixties, I had the privilege of tasting a 1914 champagne, rated as one of the great vintages of the last century. Because Champagne is at the northern limit of where wine grapes can ripen, great years were few and far between. (Global warming is changing that.) The wine was served on the terrace of the Pol Roger champagne house in Épernay on a gentle summer evening. At ninety-seven years old, this wine was weightless yet vivacious, more spirit than flesh. I didn't shed tears, but I did try to imagine the lives of the women and children who made the wine while their fathers, husbands, and sons endured the front, hoping to stay alive while defending the home soil, its dips and rises covered with vines. And because of that old bubbly, I felt in the back of my mind, or maybe in my heart, an awareness of my own parents whom I had recently lost and the parent that I am who will one day be lost. At that future date, unknown but certain to arrive, maybe that 1914 Pol Roger will still be a survivor, still evoke a shimmer of memories for another person privileged to sip it.

For French men and women who care deeply about their wine (not all do!), a great old bottle is an expression of the spirit, yes, but also an expression of their soil, a particular piece of French earth. As it loses its youthful bloom of fruit and the edge of testy tannins, a wine of exceptional character morphs through one aging phase, then another, until all that's left are essences of the soil of *la belle France* that nurtured it and a burnished glow in the mouth and memory. The French say of such a wine, "*Nous l'avons bu avec grande émotion*": "We drank it with great emotion."

We Americans have no way of feeling that precise emotion, any more than we can feel the collective pulse of a French crowd quicken when it sings a full-throated "Marseillaise." Think of how an impromptu version of that anthem drowned out a German drinking song in the movie *Casablanca*! And how, for their part, the French could never feel the same tingle that we feel from hearing and watching Whitney Houston's soaring rendition of "The Star-Spangled Banner" at Super Bowl XXV (thank you, YouTube!). No matter how we savor a stupendous French wine, it still issues from foreign soil. It nurtured them, not us. When these French folks drink the identical wine, they know it's been birthed by the home soil. It's family.

The French are adept at putting highly elusive sensory aspects of wine into rational form. I learned that early in my wine-buying days. In 1976, I was poking around in the windowless, frigid brick storage cube behind Town Wine & Spirits in Rumford, Rhode Island. This was where the Fishbein brothers, Stanley and Elliott, serious wine merchants both, stored their higher-end inventory. In a corner, hidden at the bottom of a pile of boxes, I found a case of top-end white burgundy: Corton-Charlemagne, vintage 1964, made by Drouhin, a domaine known for refined, long-lived wines.

"Holy smokes! How long has *that* been there?" said Stanley.

Most white wines older than a decade would be on their way down. This one had the possibility of being alive and well. My wine-buying buddy Bob Wool was with me, and we negotiated a price for the case on the spot. Six bottles each. Leaving Rumford, we stopped at a picnic table under the shade of a few trees at the edge of a high school athletic field. For wineglasses, we made do with clear plastic cups. My memory of that Corton-Charlemagne is of a wine both severe and sumptuous. In that era, I thirsted for butterball California chardonnays, so I wasn't attuned to this linear, firm-spined Burgundian model. I did intuit that this was a liquid for grown-ups. If I was going to be one, I had better pay attention to what was in my plastic cup.

Visiting Beaune a few years later, I knocked at Drouhin's cellar door on tiny, charming Rue d'Enfer. Fifth-generation owner Robert Drouhin, a reserved yet friendly man, appeared. He was as leanly elegant as his wine that I'd found in Rumford. Even without an appointment, he generously acted as my tour guide around the firm's Roman-era cellars. When I told Drouhin about my memorable half case of his 1964 Corton-Charlemagne, his pale blue eyes engaged me with sudden interest.

"Nineteen sixty-four was a highly unusual vintage," he said. "As the wine got older, the secondary aromas were never replaced by the tertiaries."

Drouhin's obscure reference was to the aromatic evolution of the handful of wines, mainly red but a few white, built for the long haul. The phases were laid out by the venerated French enologist and master taster Émile Peynaud (1912–2004). In the primary phase, the fruit character of the grapes is in the forefront. The second phase is composed of wine aromas derived from fermentation. The third phase reveals an array of nuances that develop only after the wine rests for years in bottle. Very slow oxidation via the cork may add to those nuances. *Bouquet*, as in a mix of differently scented flowers, rather than *aroma*, which could be the scent of one flower, is the term of art for what the nose inhales and appreciates at this stage. This late-arriving set of sensory vectors represents full maturity. If the bones are good, as they were in that 1964 Corton-Charlemagne, the wine becomes handsome rather than pretty. Think late-career Katharine Hepburn.

Beyond good bones, there is the winemaker's goal of consorting with magic. "We try to give our wine the liberty to develop freely over time," says Pierre-Henry Gagey, wine director at Domaine Louis Jadot, which makes age-worthy wines throughout Burgundy. "What moves me is when, after ten or twenty years in bottle, a wine develops an extra dimension that comes not from us but from the soil. This can only happen when we do *not* utilize all the available modern technology, which can only gum up these magical processes. We are here to express something that is beyond our control. We need to pay attention to conserve the magic."

The best red bordeaux, if properly cellared, can deliver full-on pleasures for even longer than the best burgundy. On my sixty-fifth birthday, a generous friend and the most insightful taster I know, a Swede named Peter Thustrup, gifted me with a birth-year bottle of Château Latour, one of the five greatest wines of the region. Its virility, I'm not ashamed to say, might have been greater than my own. By bordeaux standards, it wasn't even that far along. In the late 1960s, Michael Broadbent, who got the wine department of London-based auctioneer Christie's up and running after World War II, sought out northern English and Scottish country houses dug under with naturally dank and eternally chilly cellars. Here was preserved fine bordeaux purchased by the gentry in the previous century. Some current older owners, quite possibly preferring whiskey to wine if their doctors permitted them to indulge at all, were quick to take up Broadbent's offer to sell their long-ignored treasures at Christie's. His report on an 1870 Lafite tasted prior to a 1971 auction: "The cork was sound, the level high, the colour so impressively deep that it could have been mistaken for a 1970; nose flawless, the bouquet blossoming in the glass. . . . Thank goodness the 13th Earl of Strathmore, who had originally bought it, didn't take to it."

The top rung of red burgundy does not live as long as its bordeaux equivalent. But it can come close. Romanée-Conti is a wine that (so say the chosen few who get familiar with it) doesn't deign to unveil all its endowments for two decades or more. And then it holds on . . . and on. In 2002, Broadbent sampled the 1865 Romanée-Conti at a tasting in San Francisco hosted by venture capitalist and maximum collector Wilfred Jaeger. The 138-year-old wine had a "sweet, low-keyed, virtually faultless bouquet despite showing a bit of age, opening up fragrantly after only 15 minutes and holding well. . . . In remarkable condition."

Imagine how it would feel to discover, possibly after heaping praise on one of those bottles, that you had been deceived by a cunningly accurate counterfeit. And not only had you been fooled by the labeling on the bottle and the branding on the cork—suppose, even more dastardly, a faker highly alert to nuances of wine taste could concoct a close approximation of the authentic wine. In Burgundy, where more than 1,300 officially named parcels of vineyard each produce a wine that the owner swears is capable of individual nuances and quirks, fakery is looked upon as ultimately appalling. Laurent Ponsot, a fourth-generation Burgundian winemaker who fought a long and costly battle against the counterfeiting of his own wines, compares the deceit to the shock of a man learning that his wife, whom he held in reverence and believed was faithful, has cheated on him.

I hate to think of the destruction that would be wrought on my own forty-year-old memory of the scent and taste of the wine that first seduced me if I were to learn that it was a liar in a glass. The setting was a fancy New Year's Eve dinner on the beach at Tryall, a resort in Jamaica. In my guise of journalist, I attended as the guest of Clive Davis, then president of Columbia Records. *The New York Times Magazine* had assigned me to profile Davis, and I had wangled an invitation to do "research" by joining him at Tryall. The table for fourteen diners was set on fine linen. An upside-down pig sizzled on a spit. Moonlight dappled the splendid scene through the soft rattle of palm fronds. Between each pair of place settings, a bottle of wine was set.

The wine ignoramus lifted his glass. The aroma lofting from it was rich, dark, spicy, come hither. At first sip, those aromatics became liquid. They seduced every private place in my mouth.

I scribbled down a few facts from the label: "Château Mouton Rothschild, vintage 1959, Baron Philippe de Rothschild, Propriétaire á Pauillac." This wine, then sixteen years old, would have been near its dark-fleshed prime, although I had no way of assessing that, or even of knowing that a bottle of wine could have a prime. Back home in New York, I learned that 1959 Mouton, like the victory vintage of 1945, was on its way to being a bordeaux legend. It was way out of my price range, but I did own the memory of its smell and taste, and I still do.

My wise friend Peter Thustrup once said that owning Picassos, as his father did, means paying constant insurance premiums, but owning the memory of high-value wine won't cost you a damn thing.

That 1959 Mouton is a wine that the central actor in this book counterfeited multiple times. One customer who bought it was a software mogul and wine collector named David Doyle. He purchased nineteen bottles for $2,234 each and eleven magnums for $6,406 each. In an affidavit, Doyle's associate, Susan Twellman, wrote that this single counterfeiter "has severely damaged the rare fine wine market. . . . Authentic wines are now viewed with suspicion and have become severely impaired in the marketplace, making future recovery of investments in these rare fine wines questionable."

Fueled by dot-com spoils in the hands of the newly rich, prices of the most sought-after wines soared at the beginning of this century and took a not-very-long breather in the wake of the 2008 financial crisis. Rare wines are not like rare animals. Humans can intercede to breed creatures such as pandas and gorillas in refuges or zoos when the animals are threatened with extinction. Rare wines can't reproduce. Once the cork is pulled on a survivor, its remaining life span is measured in minutes. It could be the last bottle on earth.

So counterfeiters had a strong incentive to get to work. They had the comfort of knowing that they were not likely to be caught. Certain merchants and auctioneers, happy to make an expensive sale to credulous rich people, looked the other way when suspicious bottles came into their hands. Serena Sutcliffe, long the global head of Sotheby's wine department, bitterly complained for years that law enforcement authorities had no interest in investigating a problem that threatened to become a pestilence. Although never publicly stated, the law enforcement view seemed to be that if ultrarich collectors wished to spend outlandish amounts of their money on wine, they had better damn well be sure it was authentic prior to purchase. Cops as well as government prosecutors couldn't be bothered with wine counterfeiters. They had worries enough, what with terrorism, drug cartels, and Wall Street misdeeds.

But the ground shifted with the case at hand. For the first time, the US Justice Department targeted a wine counterfeiter for criminal prosecution. Credit for that largely goes to a quintet of diverse actors. First was a Kansas-born billionaire and self-proclaimed "hick" and "hoarder." Second was that Burgundian winemaker who felt cuckolded by the faking of his wines. Third was a successful Los Angeles civil lawyer and dedicated collector of French wines who speaks not a word of French but devotes countless non-billable hours to detecting indicators of fraud on wine bottles. Fourth was a handsome young assistant US attorney who was crazy about wine. The civil lawyer called him simply a "wineola." Fifth, partnering with the fourth, was a veteran, crusty FBI agent with no real interest in wine who prepared for this case by reading *French Wine for Dummies*.

If not for these five determined actors, this masterful, mysterious, gentle-natured counterfeiter might have gone on polluting the reputation of the finest wines that French soil and its winemaker servants combined to produce.

Nobody need pity the rich guys (women victims are few and far between) who lost a bundle buying wine that turned out to be fake. They won't be reduced to taking out payday loans. And for those of us who don't have their kind of money and never will, that ungainly German word *schadenfreude* applies: In their own arenas of enterprise, these rich guys know how to call the shots, yet they were manipulated by a very young man of infinite persuasion.

Still, no collector, whether of modest or unlimited means, should have to lose faith in the prized wines that he owns—or was tempted to own. Is that wine in a handblown bottle from another era, its label seemingly stained by decades of hibernation, the real thing or a skillful fake? If I, for one, ever again have the chance to taste the wine that first seduced me, I'll wonder: Is this really the darkly scented elixir that was created in the perfect summer of 1959 in the vineyards of Mouton Rothschild? Or was it made in a canny counterfeiter's kitchen?

That weasel of doubt is the depressing legacy of Rudy Kurniawan.

CHAPTER I

Becoming Dr. Conti

A camera recorded Rudy Kurniawan, twenty-six years old but looking young enough to be carded, as he attended a Christie's wine auction in Los Angeles, a catalog of fancy wines in his lap. The rare Asian among older white males, he wore a caramel-colored leather jacket, zipped up almost to the neck. His straight black hair is of modest length, and his sideburns just brush his ears. His eyes are dark and sharp behind black-rimmed eyeglasses. The auctioneer had just gaveled down a prize lot of wine that might have been made many decades ago by a callus-handed French farmer who would have been gratified to get a buck per bottle. In this year of 2003, somebody in this room had just bought it for thousands of dollars. Kurniawan turned to the person on his left. "Dude," he said, "I drank that wine on Thursday night. Now I feel bad. Can I refill the bottle and put the cork back in?"

Kurniawan flashed a smile and chuckled to himself.

Seekers of pulse-quickening wine often come by their passion not gradually but by epiphany. At a certain moment, the contents of their glass whisper intimacies straight to their soul. Most likely, the transformative wine is well-aged bordeaux or burgundy. In Kurniawan's case, he claimed it was a "cult" Napa Valley cabernet sauvignon called Opus One, vintage 1996. To qualify as cult, a wine needs to be ultra-ripe, ultra-high-priced, and, because demand often exceeds supply, a bitch to acquire. If you want it direct from the winery, you may have to go on a waiting list—or even go on a waiting list to get on the waiting list.

A *Wine Spectator* review written four years after the vintage described 1996 Opus One as "bold, rich, and leathery, delivering tiers of currant, mineral, spice and sage." Kurniawan ordered the bottle in 1999 or 2000, so the story goes, at a family dinner to mark the birthday of his father, who was visiting from Indonesia. They were gathered at a restaurant at Fisherman's Wharf in San Francisco, but when asked in 2006 for the restaurant's name by a *Los Angeles Times* reporter, Kurniawan could not remember, despite boasting a guillotine-sharp memory for any experience connected to wine. Released at $125, 1996 Opus One was probably double that price or more on the restaurant's wine list.

Something about that bottle clicked open a previously inactive sensory circuit in Kurniawan. Wasting no time, he embarked on an informal crash course, learning all he could about wine. He began to show up at wine tastings at shops in and around Los Angeles. A refreshingly young entrant into an older crowd's game, he was high-spirited and able to turn on strong emotional connectivity in others.

Because Indonesians of Chinese ethnicity are scarce at West Coast rare wine tastings, Kurniawan was easy to notice and remember. Tapping into a shadowy family fortune, he bought a bounty of very expensive wine. His corkscrew was hyperactive. Elite Napa Valley reds, like that Opus One, came first on his shopping list. The more difficult they were to get, the more eagerly Kurniawan sought them. He also fancied muscle-flexing, amped-up Australian reds. As is common with wine novitiates, it was that wallop of flavor rather than a caress that he was looking for.

Kurniawan sped on to high-end bordeaux, then began a deep engagement with the intricacies of burgundy. In those early days, he was buying copiously from Woodland Hills Wine Company, a shop with a deep inventory of high-end wine located in the San Fernando Valley. Kyle Smith, whose family owned the shop, invited Kurniawan to become a member of a tasting group of burgundy buffs calling themselves BurgWhores. They were tasting wines at price points that required wealth, and Kurniawan seemed to have it. Being a member of BurgWhores gave Kurniawan entrée to a world where he quickly rose to a starring role. It wasn't only that he stepped up with trophy bottles. He had a puppy-dog talent for charming his fellow BurgWhores. Where he and his money came from, nobody knew. He was a one-off.

What he tasted, he precisely remembered. If the wine was a multi-grape blend, he seemed to be able to pick out each variety by its character. In his classic *The Taste of Wine*, Émile Peynaud suggested a simple way to explain the difference between average wine tasters and the truly gifted. It's done by analogy to what the ear hears: Go to a room adjoining one where people are gathered and hold up a fine crystal wineglass. Strike the edge of the bowl with a fingernail or a spoon so that it pings. In the other room, the least sensitive listener hears only an unknown sound. One level up, a more discerning listener identifies the sound as the pleasurable ping of crystal. The gifted listener, hearing the same ping, says, "That vibration corresponds to the note E."

She has perfect pitch. Kurniawan has it for wine.

More books have been written about wine than about home gardening. Wine newbies often try to learn more by reading about it. Kurniawan, too, opened books, and he sucked knowledge from more experienced tasters. First and foremost, however, he educated himself by incessantly tasting. Émile Peynaud argued that to be successful the taster must "proceed by intuition . . . without the aid of reasoning." With this approach, "the study of details and deductions aren't necessary. Contact with the organs of smell and taste alone suffice to . . . unveil [a wine's] identity. Either we get it right away, or we don't."

To get it right away was Kurniawan's gift. "I've seen Rudy nail ten out of twelve burgundies that he tasted blind," the wine auctioneer John Kapon of Acker Merrall & Condit tells me. Rajat Parr, a San Francisco sommelier and winemaker, says that after observing Kurniawan at a tasting, "I was very, very impressed. He identified most of the wines blind." Jefery Levy, a film producer and screenwriter who drank with Kurniawan (and spent two Christmas Eves with Kurniawan and his mother), says flatly of his friend's tasting savvy, "He was almost always extremely, unbelievably, insanely correct."

So correct that Levy became suspicious. Kurniawan was pulling off his tasting feats at restaurant wine dinners. Was he "flipping somebody in the kitchen a thousand bucks" to tip him off on what wines were being poured supposedly blind? Levy decided to test Kurniawan at his own home, where he could set up a foolproof blind tasting. "I tried to trick him in all sorts of crazy ways. I served him wines from Bordeaux, Burgundy, Italy, Spain, California. Either he would get the country, the year, the maker, or he would get very close." Reaching for an explanation of Kurniawan's tasting chops, Levy references method acting: "It's about sense memory," says Levy. "You try to get emotions going based on memories in your life. Rudy had a sense memory, but it had to do with his nose and taste buds."

Levy calls Kurniawan a wine "savant." He could remember individual wines in the way Dustin Hoffman's "Rain Man" could account for every card in a deck at a Las Vegas blackjack table. Étienne de Montille, a winemaker from Volnay who knew Kurniawan, calls him a "UFO." Being perceived as both a savant and a UFO could only be helpful to Kurniawan when he trotted out unicorn-rare bottles. Had he lacked those qualities, people might have had more suspicions about him and the source of his wines.

Kurniawan declared himself a guardian of authenticity. He boasted a sharp eye for tiny details on the label, branding on the cork, or neck capsule of a trophy bottle confirming that the wine within was real or gave it away as a fake. He told the British wine writer Jancis Robinson, "When I go to restaurants and drink great wines, I'm very careful to ensure that the empty bottles are trashed and the labels are marked so they can't be reused." The opposite was true: Rudy was very careful to ensure that empties were returned to him with labels unmarked.

A false bottle, Rudy wanted you to know, was bad enough. What really ignited him into pyrotechnics of outrage was false taste. Allen Meadows, America's leading burgundy critic and writer of the wine review *Burghound*, recalls a dinner at a Los Angeles restaurant to which Kurniawan brought a special bottle. But when Kurniawan tasted the wine, Meadows says, he fumed: "'Goddamn it, I am angry! I am going to get my effing money back!' And he defaced the label because he said he didn't want anyone to refill the bottle."

At another dinner, Kurniawan cut back on the drama, possibly for the benefit of a Burgundian notable at the table, but still questioned a bottle's authenticity. The Burgundian was Jeremy Seysses, an Oxford-educated member of the family that owns Domaine Dujac, an elite winery in Morey-Saint-Denis. The restaurant was Osteria Mozza in Los Angeles, always a favorite of the wine crowd. "Rudy is a year younger than me," says Seysses, whose mother and wife are both American. "We drank and talked well. Rudy was into art. This was not a dinner where wines were being put into competition. At one point, the sommelier presented Rudy with a bottle, definitely one which he had brought. There was a very discreet exchange, one not meant to draw attention, but it was clear that

Rudy was saying the bottle wasn't right. He rejected it. What was the point? Was it to draw me into the group that saw that he was careful to guard against fakes? He did not overact the part."

As Kurniawan's reputation as a taster and bon vivant grew, he was also rapidly building an inventory of pricey wine. Combing the websites of fine-wine dealers in the United States, the UK, and France, he bought what he wanted, apparently free of budget constraint. At auctions on both coasts, he became known as a bidder who would raise his paddle and keep it raised until all others had lowered theirs, no matter how high the price soared. The priciest wine auction of the early twenty-first century, on a per-bottle basis, was the sale of the blue-chip burgundy and bordeaux wines of the late tobacco heiress Doris Duke, which had slumbered in New Jersey and Hawaiian cellars since the 1930s. In 2004, they were sold by Christie's for the then-record price of $3.77 million. Kurniawan was there. And he was buying.

Kurniawan boasted, early on, that his mysteriously wealthy family back home sent him an allowance of $1 million per month. In some months he spent more than that on wine purchases alone. In a buoyant market for fine wine, he could expect to resell what he didn't keep for more than he had paid. And buoyant the market was. Between 2003 and 2006, *Wine Spectator*'s Auction Index rose by 54 percent. In the first half of 2007, the index rose by another 7.4 percent. That surge correlated precisely with the period when Kurniawan was trading most aggressively.

Kurniawan had a knack for gaining the trust of wealthy collectors, whether they were corporate kingpins, investment bankers, Hollywood types, or real estate moguls. When these collectors gathered to share their treasures, Kurniawan was always the last to arrive. He was forgiven because he always brought fabulous bottles, often oversized. The key to an outsider's entrée into these rarified tasting circles is pinpointed by Wilfred Jaeger, the physician turned venture capitalist who was already a noted collector when

Kurniawan was still a boy: "If you brought a great wine, you got invited."

Even at the end of a wine-drenched evening, Kurniawan could be counted on to pull out one more special bottle. "A few of us lingered to talk about the evening," an attendee posted on the Mark Squires Bulletin Board on RobertParker.com, a wine chat site, after a dinner at now-closed Campanile in Los Angeles. "As is so often the case, Rudy Kurniawan went to his car and came back with his customary generosity: Rousseau Chambertin 1923 [both appellation and producer are supreme, the vintage excellent]. . . . A silky kiss all through the mouth, attack to finish. Masterpiece. Thank you, Rudy." And after another splendiferous bacchanal, that same taster wrote on eBob: "Thank you again and again and again. If you were a girl I'd marry you." The next morning, the admirer reconsidered: "After some sleep, I still don't think you are pretty enough to marry. But you're still the best." To which another reader replied, "While I can't marry Rudy, either, can he adopt me?"

Even knockout wine could not have been enough to inspire this lovefest. It also had to do with Kurniawan's manner of pouring it. Kurniawan avoided lording it over the recipients of his costly bounty. He wanted you to share the pleasure, and did not seek gratitude. And so gratitude is what he got.

"Rudy not only showed up with the goods, but he was so passionate," says Vincent Cariati, who bumped into Kurniawan in 2002 while shooting footage for a documentary (stillborn) about cult winemakers in Napa Valley. Kurniawan wasn't part of the plan, but Cariati was drawn to him and made eight hours of footage of him. "He really loved wine and engaging in conversation about it. At the time, there was not a hair of thought that this guy was anything less than genuine because he was giving so much at every level. He would walk into a restaurant with these beautiful bottles, and nothing was off. Nothing to make me second-guess. He satisfied all the receptors that any human being uses."

Kurniawan could be thoughtful in small ways. Daniel Posner, a wine dealer in White Plains, New York, still remembers a small courtesy done years ago. "Each holiday season, I send out greeting cards to my regular customers. The only one who *ever* sent me back a thank-you was Rudy."

Not only thoughtful, but always a generous host. Samantha Sheehan, proprietor of Poe, a tiny gem of a Napa Valley winery, remembers her first dinner with Kurniawan from a time when she knew little about wine: "My brother, Trevor, who was wine-brokering, called me to say that a friend, Patrick [Stella, a son of the artist Frank Stella], had flown in from New York. They were going to dinner the next night with Rudy. I said, 'That's my birthday! You have to spend it with me. I want you to get me an invite.'"

The dinner hosted by Kurniawan was at wine-friendly Mozza. The details are graven in Sheehan's memory. "Rudy wore an Hermès jacket with his name stitched into the lining and on his wrist was a magnificent Patek Philippe watch. He had brought his mother. She wore a beautiful gray cashmere sweater and she was covered in diamonds. It made such an impression on me. She was like a Chinese princess."

Later, Sheehan was invited to a Kurniawan-hosted dinner attended by an executive of champagne maker Louis Roederer: "There were seven of us at the table. Rudy opened a 1917 Roederer. No bubbles were left, but it had essences of apricot and peach." It was hard to imagine that Kurniawan could top that. But top it he did, with the first commercial vintage of Cristal, Roederer's elite bottling. Sheehan found these wines to be "beautiful and incredible."

Sheehan recalls a deep-into-the-night bacchanal at the New Jersey home of a major collector. Rudy did not attend, but a bottle so rare that it could have been sourced only from him was uncorked. It was a several-decades-old bottle of the *grand cru* Clos Saint-Denis, a grand cru red burgundy from Domaine Ponsot, one of the region's most admired producers. In the early hours of the morning, Sheehan found the bottle in the bushes in the backyard. It was still half full.

❧

Details about Kurniawan's early life are elusive. His Indonesian passport states that he was born in 1976 in Jakarta. His Chinese name is Zhen Wang Huang. Owing to ethnic frictions between the Chinese (less than 2 percent of Indonesia's population) and the native Muslims, Chinese parents often also gave their children Indonesian names. Rudy Kurniawan is a name borrowed from a badminton champion in a country where the sport is popular. Kurniawan's mother's Chinese birth name is Tan Lee Woen, although, like her son, she goes by an Indonesian-sounding name: Lenywati Tan. The family is said to have inhabited a walled compound in Jakarta, but there is no confirmation of that claim.

Kurniawan arrived in California in or about 1993. He graduated from California State University, Northridge. He told some people that he was on the college golf team, but the school's longtime coach has never heard of him. As an accounting major, he was an A student, but his student visa precluded him from getting a regular job. He picked up part-time work at a golf pro shop until he was questioned about an expensive Japanese-made driver that had gone missing from inventory. Kurniawan walked out of the shop and was not seen again. This was a time in his life, apparently, when his million-dollar allowance had yet to kick in.

While a student, Kurniawan lived in a Pasadena apartment with one of his three older brothers, Andy Suryanto, who had also come earlier to the United States to study. They were joined by their mother in 2001. In a letter that year to US immigration authorities, Kurniawan stated that only his mother and not his father, Makmur

Widjojo, is listed on his birth certificate "because of their Chinese ethnicity even though they were born there [Indonesia], thus their marriage was not recognized and I am born out of wedlock."

Anti-Chinese rioting and violence, ignited by financial crisis, broke out across Indonesia in 1998, not for the first time. By then, Kurniawan was safely in California. In his application for asylum in the United States, Kurniawan wrote, "My family are Chinese and Christians [his birth certificate designates him as Buddhist], and to the Muslims in Indonesia, we are the enemy and must be removed or completely destroyed. I am vulnerable and only death awaits me in Indonesia." Unlike his mother, Kurniawan was denied asylum. In 2003, he ignored an order to leave the United States, which he claimed had been sent to his previous address. With his mother and brother Andy, he had purchased and moved into a five-bedroom, white stucco house located at the end of a cul-de-sac off Naomi Avenue in Arcadia, a city east of Los Angeles that lies under the immense southern slope of the San Gabriel Mountains. Home to the Santa Anita racetrack, Arcadia in recent years has attracted a thriving Chinese American community, earning it the nickname of the "Chinese Beverly Hills." (Its population in 2010 was fifty-six thousand, of which 59 percent was Asian.)

An early triumph for Kurniawan was his partnership in purchasing a barrel of prize wine with Matt Lichtenberg, a Hollywood business manager whose clients include comedians Will Ferrell and Larry David. While still a fledgling wine geek, Kurniawan probably met Lichtenberg through the tasting group BurgWhores. In May 2002, Kurniawan, dressed in jeans and a checked sports shirt, arrived in a black SUV at the Hospice du Rhône auction held in Paso Robles, midway up the California coast. The purpose of the nonprofit Hospice du Rhône is to promote Rhone style wines wherever they are grown on the planet. (Other than wordplay, the event had nothing to do with the famed Hospices de Beaune charity auction held each November in Burgundy.) Kurniawan was just in time to bid on a single barrel of vintage 2001 red wine donated by Sine Qua Non, a Central Coast winery with a fanatical following. SQN's bottlings are known for their full-throttle intensity and their distinctive, one-of-a-kind labels created by coproprietor Manfred Krankl. Demand for SQN far exceeds supply, so would-be purchasers of new releases must first put their names on a waiting list. Years may pass before they are invited to make a purchase.

Kurniawan did not have to wait. Never lowering his paddle until his was the last in the air, he purchased the barrel for $25,000. The young wine, a Rhône-style blend of grenache, syrah, and mourvèdre, was divided among twenty-four bottles, fifteen magnums, and six double magnums. The label states that the wine was "produced and bottled exclusively for Rudy Kurniawan and Matt Lichtenberg by Elaine and Manfred Krankl of Sine Qua Non, Ventura, California." The wine bears the name Rudy Matt Cuvée in quaint lettering, the *R* and *M* printed in bright red.

For a young man who three years earlier knew nothing about wine, the branding of Rudy Matt Cuvée was a coup. Kurniawan was then already dabbling in wine sales. His access to a supply of bottles from legendary French vintages had other dealers scratching their heads. Some of Kurniawan's offerings had not surfaced in the rare wine market for decades, or ever. Then again, nobody had seen a wine dealer quite like Kurniawan—ever. Most wine professionals have developed their expertise by working in restaurants, or in the wine department of an auction house, or in wine shops, or for importers or distributors. Not Kurniawan. He had no more traditional credentials to be a wine dealer than Donald Trump had to be president. That lack of credentials may have added to his mystique as a young man who seemed to have shamanic powers of making incredibly rare wine appear. Adding to the intrigue was that the true source and amount of his family wealth could not be nailed down. The story most often told was that the family controlled the sales of Heineken in parts of Asia. There may have been beer enterprises in the extended family, but not Heineken. When in 2006 a *Los Angeles Times* reporter asked Kurniawan the source of his family's wealth, he responded: "I don't talk about my family."

Kurniawan had to do more than merely dangle his purported treasures in front of collectors. He needed to ingratiate himself into their circles. That he did with charm and generosity, always ready to uncork precious bottles and pour the contents liberally wherever there were wealthy people who might become clients. Who would not invite a guest who was sure to arrive bearing treasures from his cellar of the wine gods? Who among them would not be eager to buy some of those very same bottles from Kurniawan, given the opportunity and the means?

Curiously, although Kurniawan was welcomed into the homes of wealthy collectors, he rarely invited any of them to his own home. One person who was invited in, when Kurniawan was still new to wine, was Kyle Smith, interviewed in a French television documentary about Kurniawan. "He said to me, 'When you see all the bottles around, don't run away. My mom thinks I'm spending twenty dollars per bottle on them.'" Smith estimates that the bottles he saw averaged out at more like "four to five hundred dollars."

In lieu of that unavailable hospitality, he blazed the restaurant circuit. A favorite spot was Mélisse, a hotspot for big spenders on wine. According to sommelier Brian Kalliel, Kurniawan began bringing up to ten guests there in 2001 or 2002. The bottles he bought were priced at "anywhere from five to twenty thousand dollars." Kurniawan instructed Kalliel to return all the empties and their corks, saying that his mother liked to save them.

Wherever he dined, Kurniawan was quick to reach for the check, and he tipped generously. Often, he rounded up to the nearest thousand: To a $709.04 bill at Cut by Wolfgang Puck in the Beverly Wilshire Hotel, Kurniawan tipped $290.96, adding up to a clean $1,000. The next day, at Vietnamese-themed Crustacean, also in

Beverly Hills, Kurniawan added a $1,027.73 tip to a $1,972.27 check, charging an even $3,000.

Kurniawan's youthfulness was in his favor. "We tend to hang around older gentlemen, so it was nice to see a young guy with this kind of passion," says Paul Wasserman, Los Angeles–based son of a Burgundian *négociant*. Wasserman, steeped in Burgundian lore since childhood, mentored Kurniawan in his earliest days of learning about wine, although he claims that because of his student's fast learning curve, the mentorship was soon reversed, at least when it came to the wines of Bordeaux. It bothered Wasserman that when Kurniawan hosted private dinners at restaurants that were both trendy and wine-friendly, he would get a check for "more than others would be charged." The restaurateurs knew that Kurniawan would pay the bill without questioning the amount or asking for a discount.

One didn't need to be a wine buff to be disarmed by Kurniawan. "He was the nicest, kindest client I ever had," says Jerry Meyer, a Los Angeles–based interior designer catering to high-budget clients, hired by Kurniawan to work on a new home he had just bought. "He was very polite and very funny." But Meyer acknowledges Kurniawan's "eccentricities," which included being two or three hours late for meetings. "He'd always come over in a different car—a Bentley, a Ferrari, a Range Rover. And then he'd fall asleep in the middle of the meeting. I'd go over and shake him awake." At Hermès, Kurniawan's preferred outfitter, Meyer sat with Kurniawan's mother while her son ordered a half dozen custom suits—all lined with Hermès' signature scarves. Each suit required four scarves.

Wealthy clients, Meyer acknowledges wryly, "can afford to create their own realities." Reality for one Meyer client, as described in a 2008 article in the *Robb Report*, was to have him individually decorate each of seventeen bathrooms in a fifteen-thousand-square-foot Bel Air, California, house. At first, Meyer could find only sixteen. "Then I remembered, there is a small bathroom in the projectionist's booth in the home theater," Meyer explained. "Union rules require that a projectionist must have immediate access to a bathroom." Kurniawan's Arcadia house, while ample for himself, his mother, and brother Andy, did not comport with his claim of family wealth back in Indonesia or with the lifestyle of the rich collectors he now mingled with and sold wine to. In July 2005, he purchased a new six-bedroom house in the gated community of Bel Air Crest in the hills above the 405 freeway. The price was $8 million, financed by a $6 million mortgage. Kurniawan and his mother were to move in once radical remodeling was completed. Meyer got the job through one of his clients who purchased wine from Kurniawan.

Kurniawan, eager to show off the new digs even while renovations were underway, planned to throw a party. He and Meyer shopped at Gearys in Beverly Hills, which the decorator calls "an old-line, important store" specializing in home decor and watches. Meyer was there to advise his young client on selecting table settings for the party.

On Gearys' second floor, Kurniawan put $30,000 on his American Express black charge card for table settings. On the way out, he spotted two Patek Philippe watches in a display case. One was in white gold, the other rose gold. He bought both of them.

But the party planned for the new house was canceled by decree of Kurniawan's mother. Her feeling was that the festivities would fall too close to the death of Kurniawan's brother, Andy Suryanto. Andy, two years older than Rudy, lived with his mother and brother and had dabbled in small businesses. In a 2005 Friendster post, Andy wrote: "I live everyday to enjoy life, appreciate what I can get and give what I can share. Life is beautiful!......)" He listed his favorite books as "The Bible, How to get an Asian girl for Dummies, How to survive in this world for dummies, etc." According to a police report, Andy died of an apparently self-inflicted gunshot to the head at a hotel on September 12, 2005.

For a time, remodeling of the Bel Air Crest mansion went forward. Although the house was turnkey ready when Kurniawan purchased it, Meyer says "it was torn apart—walls, ceilings, and roof." Kurniawan's mother was slated to take the second-floor master bedroom suite. Plans were drawn up for special floor-to-ceiling shelving for her collection of several hundred Hermès Birkin handbags. (Named for British singer and actor Jane Birkin, these roomy accessories are regularly offered at auction. One sold in Hong Kong in 2015 for $221,000.) Three upstairs bedrooms were to be combined into Kurniawan's bedroom. Work was also begun on converting the twelve-car garage into a temperature-controlled champagne cellar—one of four wine cellars planned for the premises.

One feature that Meyer didn't foresee being altered was the in-ground, mosaic-tile-lined swimming pool and Jacuzzi directly behind the house. But the designer failed to account for the verdict of a feng shui consultant, introduced to him as Master Dragon. While the ancient art attempts to harmonize nature and human activity (it translates as "wind-water"), feng shui is mainly focused on the home and workplace. Master Dragon arrived one Saturday with Kurniawan and his mother. Holding a compass-like instrument, he walked around the four sides of the pool and Jacuzzi.

His verdict: When the pool and Jacuzzi were empty, the feng shui was acceptable, but when filled with water, they were too close to the house.

Not an insoluble problem, according to Kurniawan. He decided to move the pool back from the house. Meyer pointed to the steep hillside dropping off at the rear of the property. Relocating the pool close to it would not be advisable. An earthquake, or even a heavy rainstorm, could send the pool collapsing over the precipice.

Feng shui won out. The next time Meyer visited the house, the pool had been moved to the rear of the lot. "Because of where it was, the foundations had to be dug down sixty-five feet," says Meyer. By moving the pool rather than doing away with it, perhaps Kurniawan envisioned that one day his guests would lounge about while sipping great wine.

Other new custom features of the house included remote-controlled shutters with wiring threaded through their hinges and a custom-wired Lutron "whole house" lighting system that could be operated from a master switch with one touch. Kurniawan purchased a grand chandelier that had originally hung in a grand hotel. It was to be mounted over the staircase ascending from the foyer. At Meyer's suggestion, Kurniawan commissioned a glass artist in San Francisco to create sconces to complement the chandelier. An in-wall safe had been preinstalled in the house, but Master Dragon frowned on it. At his direction, a second safe was installed—one for American dollars, the other for foreign currency.

All the money and effort sunk into the mansion was for nought. When financial problems closed in on Kurniawan, work stopped, and multiple tradesmen, unpaid for their work, filed liens against him. He and his mother never moved in.

But before that happened, Kurniawan's career moved up a signif-icant notch in December 2005 when he attended a tasting of twenty vintages of Domaine de la Romanée-Conti (DRC) La Tâche at L'Au-berge Carmel in Carmel-by-the-Sea, California. The guest of honor was Aubert de Villaine, coproprietor of DRC and Burgundy's most venerated winemaker. Kurniawan arrived by private jet. His party included Paul Wasserman, John Kapon, and Kapon's girlfriend. They had reportedly attended a Lakers game in Los Angeles the pre-vious evening. Almost three dozen attendees each paid $2,995 for the weekend of food and wine.

On hand was Bruce Sanderson, a *Wine Spectator* editor whose tasting beat is Burgundy and Italy. In the impressive roll call of La Tâche vintages presented, expectations were especially high for the 1934 and 1962 vintages, considered to be exceptional. But in his *Wine Spectator* report on the event, Sanderson wrote, "I was less enamored with this pair than others at my table." Were these vintages contributed by Kurniawan? La Tâche from 1962 was one he sold often, even as it was almost impossible to find from other dealers. "There was some discussion about the provenance of some of the wines, mostly about whether they had been recorked and topped off with a different vintage," Sanderson told me eleven years after that weekend. "At some point, somebody mentioned that Rudy [then twenty-nine] was the foremost expert on Pétrus labels [Bordeaux's priciest wine]. Rudy slept through much of the dinner."

Dozing at the table was something that Kurniawan did often and well. Jeremy Seysses remembers witnessing this the first time he sat with Kurniawan. It was at La Paulée, a bacchanal devoted to burgundian wine, long celebrated in Meursault at harvest's end and now in New York as well. "Rudy was asleep holding a wineglass without spilling it."

In 2006, as work went forward on his new mansion, Kurniawan's future looked bright. By year's end, he was striding atop the fine wine auction market as both buyer and seller. In just two mega-auctions that year, New York auctioneer Acker Merrall & Condit sold seventeen thousand bottles of "Rudy wine" for just over $35 million, including the auctioneer's commission of about 20 percent. The sales were known as Cellars I and II. The first was held in January at the wine-centric restaurant Cru. It fetched a handsome $10.6 million. The second, that October, stretched over two days at Café Gray in Time Warner Center, overlooking the southwest corner of Central Park. Cellar II brought in $24.69 million—a record for a single wine auction. Though his name was absent from the catalogs, it was an open secret that Kurniawan was the consignor—that is, the owner of the goods who had placed them with the auctioneer to be sold. At both auctions, a jovial Kurniawan mingled with the crowd.

Cellar II stands at the apex of wine auctions, Acker style. "The scene was very different from the arid salesrooms of Christie's and Sothebys in London where the nearest thing to sustenance is the auctioneer's glass of water," blogged Robinson in early 2007. "Kapon worked against a backdrop of white coated chefs . . . cooking up lunch, steam and lip smacking aromas rising up in the increasingly fevered atmosphere as prices continued to exceed already robust estimates."

In a phone interview with Kurniawan, Robinson was startled to hear that the vast sea of wine he had sold at the two Cellar sales "constituted just one third of his collection." And Kurniawan elaborated on what happened after his father's birthday dinner after he ordered the life-altering Opus One. Kurniawan wasted no time in scooping up every bottle of the wine he could find: "The next thing I knew, I had two hundred bottles," he said. He said he opened "five or six different similar bottles in one night, trying to see the difference between them." Soon, in a regimen of intensive home-schooling, he was doing the same thing with other kinds of wine. And he expanded into auctions. "I bought aggressively," he told Robinson. "I never say, 'Give me two bottles.' I say, 'How many cases do you have? Twenty? I'll take them.'"

Much of the wine Kurniawan sold at the two Cellar sales was standard auction fare: age-worthy wines, mainly French, from readily available vintages. He had bought these wines from a wide range of domestic and European dealers and auctions, including at Acker itself.

Sprinkled like a fancy grade of white powder among the great bulk of fine but not exceptional lots on offer were the Kurniawan specialties: regular bottles, big bottles, and cases of wines from mythic vintages. Kurniawan himself was addicted to these bottles, opening them constantly at home and sharing them generously elsewhere. By getting intimate with their scent and taste and volume in the mouth, he was gaining the precise knowledge of vintage and vineyard character that he could use to impress potential customers. But for all the camaraderie he shared with these wealthy people, Kurniawan remained an outsider.

They were American citizens from birth, while hanging over him was a deportation order. They had wives, children, lovers. He went home to his mother, conversing with her in languages strange to them. That linguistic divide was impressed on Jefery Levy one post-midnight as a limo took him and Kurniawan and other drinkers to a Manhattan restaurant: "Rudy is on his phone and he is arguing in a different language. When he was done, I asked him who he was talking to. 'My brother in Asia,' he said. 'He needs to send me my allowance for this month.'"

"One's relationship with the native language is similar to that with the past," the author Yiyun Li has written. "Rarely does a story start where we wish it had, or end where we wish it would."

Being the youngest brother in the family was part of Kurniawan's story. In a scene in *Sour Grapes*, a 2016 documentary film that contrasts Kurniawan's frenetic wine world with the eternal serenity of Burgundy's vineyards, Kurniawan's big brother Dar sits across from him at a table of wine carousers. Little brother is the life of the party, while Dar seems reserved. His expression suggests (at least to me) that he is wary of the persona that Rudy has created for himself. And that he had better not misstep. In another brief, boisterous scene, possibly at a different dinner gathering, Kurniawan is asked if he is "independently wealthy." At first, he deflects the question, but suddenly answers: "No. I'm broke. I scam people." The others at the table cackle and Kurniawan joins in. Just as he did at the Christie's auction, wondering out loud if he could refill an expensive bottle and recork it, Kurniawan has declared a truth, confident that those around him at the table will take it as a joke.

❦

Beginning about 2002 and until spring 2008, as Wall Street plunder and heady real estate values made many Americans rich or richer,

Kurniawan fed the hunger for oldest and rarest wine, cost be damned. How had he, still in his twenties, managed to acquire this seemingly limitless lode of *introuvables*? Kurniawan offered plausible, if unprovable, explanations. Early on, he claimed to have bought the cellar of a wealthy family in Florida. But even a very large private cellar could not keep on giving at the rate that Kurniawan was selling.

And so a new, more intriguing story began making the rounds: Kurniawan had acquired, possibly with a partner, a huge trove of old French wines in Europe. It was dubbed the "Magic Cellar," or as Acker's John Kapon called it, "THE Cellar." Its lineage was said to go back more than a century to a time when the then-dominant French retail wine shop chain, Nicolas, purchased large quantities of the finest French wines directly from the most renowned vineyards. Barrel-aging and bottling took place in Nicolas' own cellars. The firm held the wines patiently. When Nicolas' cellar masters deemed these glories of French soil to be mature, they were proudly released as the holiday season approached. And they were priced affordably. Those were the days when the bourgeoisie could afford to put a bottle of an aristrocratic bordeaux such as Château Latour or a stellar burgundy such as La Tâche on the table.

Nicolas lavished special care on its annual holiday catalogs. Each year, a different artist was commissioned to illustrate them. Draeger, a French printer specializing in high-quality art images, produced the catalogs in lush colors. Satisfying the French predilection for clear-cut tiers of quality, the holiday wines were divided into "regular," "exceptional," and "prestige" categories. The highest tier was sure to quicken any collector's pulse. Amazingly, as late as the 1960s, Nicolas still offered 1868 and 1869 vintages of Château Lafite Rothschild at prices that now look laughably low: one hundred francs, then about twenty dollars.

Nicolas required that proper respect be accorded to its prestige-level bottles. The catalog specified that the wine had to be decanted at the firm's depot before it was home-delivered in an insulated basket. This service was available only in Paris and its immediate suburbs. Under "Conditions of Sale," the catalog stated, "VERY IMPORTANT ADVICE: Due to the rarity of these reserve wines under our deluxe tariff, we will only accept orders for immediate consumption and not for cellaring. We will reduce orders that appear to us as exaggerated." Nicolas expected that corks would be pulled on these rarities in the season they were sold.

These wines bore a "Réserve Nicolas" strip label around the neck of the bottle and a circular red "Établissements Nicolas" or "Selection Nicolas" stamp on the main label. A rear strip label, lettered in white on a black background, instructed: *"Ce vin doit être décanté"* ("This wine must be decanted"). Many of Kurniawan's rarest wines carried these markers, supporting his claim that the "Magic Cellar" drew its strength from old Nicolas stock.

The century-old Nicolas headquarters and cellars commanded the left bank of the River Seine at Charenton-le-Pont, south of Paris. This was once the busy depot for wines in large casks barged up from vineyards in the South. One free afternoon in Paris, I made an impromptu visit to Charenton-le-Pont, where an employee kindly showed me where a passage led into a deep cellar that once contained the firm's choicest wines. So smoothly had the cellar entrance been sealed up after the French surrender in 1940 that during World War II the Germans never discovered it. Similar strategies to hide the pride of French vineyards were carried out all over occupied France.

The Nicolas empire was purchased from the founders' descendants by cognac giant Rémy Martin in 1984 and resold four years later to beverage producer Castel. In 1995, Castel signaled a change of emphasis in wine marketing by creating a category called "Les Petites Récoltes" ("the Little Bottlings"). In the same year that Castel bought Nicolas, the historic Charenton-le-Pont property was sold off. Headquarters were moved to a sterile location in an industrial area near Orly Airport. Management abandoned the tradition of nurturing the pride of French vineyards in its own cellars and sold off its precious old stocks to a large Bordeaux négociant. The archive of holiday catalogs was discarded save for one set rescued by a junior employee. Luckily, many customers who received the catalogs were loath to discard them. They are now collectibles.

"What Rudy did was brilliant," says Paul Wasserman. "He exploited the fact that few people knew much about Nicolas' former wine practices. It was rumored that in the old days the wines had been periodically refreshed and resealed with unbranded corks. That gave Rudy license to sell wines with blank corks."

And to sell wines that might give the impression of being more youthful than they had a right to be.

Wasserman was puzzled that many bottles from long-ago vintages sold by Kurniawan still had pristine labels. No stranger to Burgundian cellars, he knew that decades-old labels typically develop at least traces of discoloration and mold. Wasserman asked the Burgundian expert Bernard Hervet why so many of Kurniawan's Nicolas cellar labels had escaped blemish. Hervet responded that it was probably because, unlike French cellars, American cellars tend to be dry. Once the wines arrived here, the mold and staining that humidity causes was reduced. "Rudy was great at exploiting this kind of fog," says Wasserman. "Very early on, he exhibited this 'catch me if you can' craftsmanship. He would test people with different bottles. I think he did it very cautiously in the beginning. I was then on Rudy's side. I had a total suspension of disbelief."

Few collectors, especially those new to the game, actually *knew* what the real thing should taste like. "It's surprisingly easy to fob off flawed or inauthentic wine," says Wilf Jaeger. "At a certain point, people have drunk too much and they are not paying attention."

Even if they are paying attention, and do question a wine, they are unlikely to "kill the buzz" at a festive table, as Allen Meadows puts it, by calling out the suspect bottle. And, as Jeremy Seysses of Domaine Dujac notes, if you are the guest of honor at a dinner at which your own wines are being proudly served, "it would be humiliating to your host if you let on that you suspect a fake." And so the fakes have a best friend whose name is courtesy.

Any kind of sensory intrusion may alter the intricacies of wine judgment. The venerated chef Fernand Point (1897–1955) of the Rhône Valley restaurant La Pyramide long refused to serve cocktails to his clientele because, in their aftermath, "after one cocktail or, worse yet, two, the palate can no more distinguish a bottle of Château Mouton Rothschild from a bottle of ink!" Madame Point, overseer of the dining room while her husband was in the kitchen, was equally adamant about any such interference. The writer Joseph Wechsberg tells of overhearing her nix a caller's request for a reservation, solely because the caller, in a previous visit, had smoked between courses—this in an era when cigarettes and even cigars were pervasive in other dining rooms.

Wine, like a swivel-hipped running back, can be difficult to get a grip on. It is also ready to play tricks on experts and amateurs alike who have had no cocktails, aren't smoking, and are stone sober. Controlled experiments by behavioral economists and psychologists have shown that when subjects are given two wines to taste and are told that one is expensive and the other is cheap, the former is more often preferred. Only after picking their favorite do the subjects learn that the two wines are identical. That result is based not only on preferences expressed in words. According to brain imaging done during the tastings, the subjects' "pleasure centers" light up more actively as they taste the supposedly more expensive wine.

A similar experiment was done in an English port and sherry house long before brain scans, but was just as persuasive. It was conducted on a trio of self-anointed, very senior "experts" by T. G. Shaw, an Englishman who worked in the wine trade. As laid out in his 1863 book, *Wine, the Vine, and the Cellar*, Shaw secretly had several glasses of sherry drawn directly from a single cask. He then asked the trio, "whose opinion was regarded as law," to weigh in on which sample they preferred. After "tasting, and retasting, and much profound thought," the elders pronounced their verdict: "Although similar, one possessed rather more of this, or that, than the other."

Shaw doesn't reveal whether he informed the tasters that the wines were identical. His bottom line still holds true today, and Kurniawan knew the truth of it: "In wine-tasting and wine-talk there is an enormous amount of humbug."

Humbug isn't always the root cause of being made to look silly over wrong wine judgments. Wine importer Kermit Lynch, in his memoir, *Adventures on the Wine Route*, recounts a blind tasting of a pair of old bottles put on at dinner by the owner of Domaine de Chevalier, a prestigious property in the Graves region of Bordeaux. Both wines issued from the château, the owner said, but which vintages were they? Clearly, one bottle had "aged as one would wish oneself to age. It still had spirit and vigor," Lynch writes. The other bottle "belonged in a rest home, if not the morgue." Guests made the obvious guesses: The wonderful wine was from a great vintage, the other from a loser.

So it came as a shock to learn that both bottles were from the same superb 1928 vintage. The stark difference in the glass was the result of one bottle having rested all along in Domaine de Chevalier's cellar, while the other had been purchased from a négociant who had apparently mishandled the wine. Most likely, too-warm cellaring was the culprit. The lesson of Lynch's story is that storage conditions are a game changer, and must be factored into appraising old wine.

Dr. Patrick Farrell, one of just over four hundred men and women to hold the British credential master of wine, tells of a blind tasting he witnessed in the state of Georgia at which an experienced taster mistook a bottle of Robert Mondavi Woodbridge merlot for Château Pétrus, the world's most famous merlot-based red wine. The cost of the Woodbridge bottle was probably under eight dollars, while the Pétrus was many multiples more. Truly, a humiliating mistake for the taster, and a clarion warning to others who think they cannot be fooled.

Even the world's most powerful wine critic was badly fooled by a blind tasting of wines already familiar to him. That was the reckoning for Robert Parker in October 2009, when he led a blind tasting of fifteen red wines from the 2005 Bordeaux vintage before one hundred enthusiasts who had paid $795 each to attend the event at a Manhattan hotel. Parker had highly rated all the wines three years earlier in his journal, the *Wine Advocate*. When the wines were unveiled at tasting's end, it turned out that Parker had failed to correctly identify any of the wines. And he had mistaken Château l'Eglise Clinet, a Pomerol that he had rated tops among the 2005s in his newsletter, for Château Cos d'Estournel à Saint-Estèphe. Not only are these two châteaus physically distant from each other, but the wines are made from different grape varieties. The contrast should have been clear-cut, but Parker missed it. And that put him in good company: Harry Waugh, a legendary British taster, having once been asked when he had last mistaken a burgundy for a bordeaux, famously responded, "Not since lunchtime."

Kurniawan, with his virtuoso nostrils, might have avoided at least some of the mistakes that tripped up Parker that evening. He was especially respected for his ability to navigate the most intricate category of all: red burgundy. Unlike red bordeaux, which can be blended from as many as five different grapes (cabernet sauvignon, merlot, cabernet franc, petit verdot, and malbec), red burgundy is built from one grape only: pinot noir. Bernard Magrez, Bordeaux-born and owner of numerous châteaus in the region, once told me that he was envious of the Burgundians. "We need several grape varieties to make our wine," he said. "In Burgundy, they need only one for white, one for red."

The flavor profile of wine made from one variety could be expected to keep to the straight and narrow. Instead, red burgundy is quicksilver and moody, nuance in motion. It's an elixir that has foiled many a taster. The network of the Côte d'Or's 1,300 individual *climats*, stretching for thirty-five north-south miles, is dauntingly complex—far more so than the division of Bordeaux into many fewer designations. Each Burgundian vigneron swears by the individuality of the vines he or she tends. Nobody can know them all, certainly not Kurniawan, who never set eyes on Burgundy. In the end, it was his imprecise knowledge of a particular domaine's history that tripped him up. It happened amid extreme merriment, one spring evening, in New York.

The mistakes that he made, minuscule and highly arcane, upended his life. Also upended would be the practices and pleasures of seekers after rare old wine.

"Rudy took the innocence away from what we do," says Allen Meadows. "I'll be pissed off at him for that for the rest of my life."

CHAPTER 2

Underside of
an Auction

The phone rang just after five o'clock on a Friday afternoon. It was April 25, 2008, and I wasn't thinking about wine, least of all counterfeit wine. "There's an Acker auction that starts in an hour at Cru," said wine dealer Geoffrey Troy. "Something unusual is supposed to happen. You should get down there." Troy knew that, as a freelancer, I wrote regularly for *Wine Spectator*. He smelled a story.

Thirty years earlier, Troy had made the leap from the trucking business started by his father to wine. His shop, New York Wine Warehouse, located in a former foundry in an industrial section of Queens, New York, under the shadow of the Fifty-Ninth Street Bridge, is entered via a windowless black door. A block away is the unkempt edge of the East River. The place feels like Mafia body-dump land. You can buy budget wines from Troy, but his specialty is the high end. Some dealers may be tempted to sell expensive wines with less than sterling provenance, especially to customers who won't know the difference between real and fake. Troy has a reputation for doing the opposite. "If one person poisons the village well, we'll all be poisoned" is his adage.

With his last-minute call, Troy was alerting me to Ponsot poison.

In that spring of 2008, the aggressive Wall Street brokerage firm Bear Stearns had already imploded—an aftershock of the pricking of the bundled-mortgage bubble in the previous year. Wall Street had taken little notice of the darkening sky. It had dished out $32 billion in bonuses at the end of 2007. Huge sums were still being "doled out to twenty-six-year-olds to perform tasks of no obvious social utility," as Michael Lewis put it in *The Big Short*. Why not blow a million or so of that on wine? So long as the stock market still floated on automatic pilot, the wine auction market, on the rise for seven years, remained stubbornly strong, and no auction firm was stronger than Acker Merrall & Condit. Its third-generation leader, John Kapon, a man proud to be both dissolute and disciplined, had personally wielded the hammer at the marathon Cellar I and II sales in 2006. That year, Acker vaulted from fourth place to the top of the global wine auction market. Without Kurniawan, it would not, could not, have happened.

The restaurant Cru, the scene of that evening's auction, was a deceptively low-key presence at the base of a Fifth Avenue residential building in Greenwich Village, just north of Washington Square Park. The small Cru logo on the entrance awning was easy to miss. As a French adjective, *cru* means raw or blunt (as in crude). As a wine noun, it most often refers to classification: The thirty-two best wines of Burgundy are designated grands crus, while the five greatest châteaus of Bordeaux are *premiers crus*. A murderer's row of those wines awaited guests at the restaurant. The markup was quite gentle on these wines, but they were still priced out of the reach of normal diners who didn't care to spend a week's or a month's paycheck on a single bottle.

Within Cru, the decor was glitz-free. Diners perched on straight-backed, untufted black banquettes. Scant art graced the wainscoted, buff-toned walls. Chef Shea Gallante's menu, touching French bases with an American hand, was not overly elaborate. The spotlight was saved for the wine list—actually two lists, one each for reds and whites. They totaled 4,500 selections, backed up by an inventory of 150,000 bottles. Eighty percent of it was burgundy. Another restaurant might proudly own a few bottles or a case of, say, Domaine Dujac Chambertin, a difficult bottle to procure at any price owing to tiny production and high demand. Squirreled away in Cru's cellars were thirty cases of Dujac Chambertin. Kurniawan claimed that the wine list "looks like my phone book."

Cru was owned by Roy Welland, son of a math professor, who inherited his father's way with numbers. Taking up the game of bridge in his early twenties, he soon won multiple championships in the United States and Europe. Welland made his fortune as an options trader. "Roy's brain could program winning options strategies before computers could," says Robert Bohr, who was Cru's wine director. Welland's gigantic personal wine collection doubled as Cru's wine list.

As a go-to spot when high rollers were in a mood to drink stupendous wine, Cru's main rival was the East Side restaurant Veritas. Its wine list also drew from the personal collection of its coproprietor, home textiles entrepreneur Park B. Smith. Reflecting the two owners' contrasting preferences, Veritas was where you went for ripple-muscled Rhône Valley reds, while lovers of filigreed burgundy headed for Cru. With their wine lists heavily weighted to expensive bottles that scared away just plain folks, both Cru and Veritas were humming in that spring of 2008. Neither was fated to survive for very long.

Kurniawan purchased bottles aplenty at Cru. They were emptied with a cluster of wine buddies, mainly clients of Acker and auctioneer Kapon. "Rudy would host these unbelievable meals—they wanted the single best of everything: caviar, Alaskan crab legs, the best beef," says Bohr. "At three AM, we'd send out for bacon-wrapped Crif dogs from the East Village." (Smoked then deep-fried, these hot dogs got their name from the attempt of one partner to say the name of a former partner, Chris, while chewing a hot dog: "Crif.")

Bohr recalls how Kurniawan's gang once gathered at Cru over four consecutive nights—"twice for dinner, twice after dinner." The checks, picked up by Kurniawan, totaled $80,000. In retrospect, Bohr believes that Kurniawan's largesse served him well when it came time to sell wine. "These were guys who ran hedge funds and other extremely wealthy people. Yet they weren't necessarily secure in their wine expertise. And they were suspicious of sommeliers who were not in their wealth class. But Rudy was different. He was one of them."

That four-night binge began one midnight in early October 2004, when Bohr got a call at home from the restaurant. Kapon was on the line. "John told me that Rudy and Allen Meadows were having a heated debate over which was better—the 1942 or 1943 La Tâche." Could Bohr keep Cru open for them so the issue could be settled?

La Tâche is one of six red wine grands crus owned by the Domaine de la Romanée-Conti, a winery nestled under the shadow of the village church in the sleepy Burgundian commune of Vosne-Romanée. At the apex of the domaine's holdings is Romanée-Conti itself, a four-and-a-half-acre vineyard producing about five thousand bottles annually of the single most expensive wine on earth. As far back as 1733, the wine sold for five to six times as much as Burgundy's next most expensive wine. Right behind Romanée-Conti, or even neck and neck in many vintages, is La Tâche. It's only after twenty years or so, say the few with the experience to make a considered judgment, that Romanée-Conti reveals a marginally greater completeness that allows it to nose ahead of La Tâche. Surviving bottles from vintages during the German occupation are exceptionally rare, yet Cru's cellar held multiples of both La Tâche 1942 and 1943.

After claiming that he was normally "too lazy to post," Kurniawan did write at length on the Mark Squires Bulletin Board about that four-day marathon that included the dueling La Tâches. The day had kicked off with an Acker-sponsored tasting of fourteen white burgundies, led by Allen Meadows. Then came a date with

1990 red burgundies at a private home. "Then I called Cru and Robert Bohr gladly welcomed us even though they are closed for the night. I believe its 12 am by now. There were 7 of us. Upon arrival I ordered '42 and '3 La Tâche to start."

Kurniawan found the 1942 bottle to be "sweet, ripe and rich on nose and palate, yet missing the classic fragrance, complexity and purity of La Tâche. A little clumsy. Nonetheless, a very good La Tâche." The 1943 bottle was "sweaty and slightly singed. . . . Palate is quite dense and meaty though. Purer and deeper than the 42 but not as fat. The wine evolved and showed much better in the glass after 2 hrs or so. Still not the best bottle I've ever had."

More DRC wines were dispatched from Cru's list, capped off by the 1971 Romanée-Conti ("always one of my fav. Rc. OHH La LA"). "Of course, it's 3 am and time to go BUTTTTT, Robert [Bohr] generously pulled the cork on the great 1990 Chave Cuvée Cathelin [a prize red, pure syrah, from Hermitage in the Northern Rhône], , , oh man......what can I say - Let's drink it."

The "head to head" of the 1942 and 1943 La Tâches was repeated five more times. "Each time the 1942 won out," says Bohr. Their price in 2004 was "so low that they were like . . . *free*."

How much would "free" have been in dollars? "About fourteen hundred dollars per bottle," says Bohr. Looking back on that battle of the wartime La Tâches, Bohr says, "It was a shit show—one of many nights that our entire garde-manger [cold pantry] was full of empty bottles." He says that Cru's service staff vied for the chance to work those marathons in order to share very liberal tips.

Bohr oversaw many "shit shows," but he draws a line between himself and the deep-pocketed participants. He is proud to come from a New Jersey family of "military people and tradesmen." He took out loans to get through New York University, where he was a protégé of former president John Sexton. He gets it that there isn't much sympathy among today's drinkers for the excesses that went on at Cru before the financial crash. "I only ask for a little bit of empathy and compassion from those who weren't there," Bohr says. "A lot of people, me included, were probably insufferable because we were in the midst of a hedonistic time period. A lot of fast money was being spent."

And spent, some would say, egregiously. In that same month of the La Tâche showdown, Acker convened an event called "The Top 100 Wines of the Century"—although the actual number was 144 wines. They were consumed by forty paying guests at four of New York's top restaurants: Daniel, Cru, Per Se, and Veritas. Kapon called the event "the greatest celebration of fine wine the world has ever seen." The cost was $25,000 per person.

⁂

As I arrived at the Acker auction thirty minutes into the bidding wars, the fast money was chasing lot forty-two, a pair of bottles of 1959 Dom Pérignon Rosé champagne. The first vintage ever of DP Rosé, it was never commercially released, according to a catalog note. The story being touted was that the shah of Iran had bought—or had thought he was buying—the entire production of 1959 DP Rosé. This bounty of bubbly was to be consumed at the celebration in Persepolis of the 2,500th anniversary of the founding of the Persian Empire by Cyrus the Great. Dom Pérignon's cellar master could not be blamed for holding back a stash of this debut superb vintage in the Dom Pérignon cellars.

The two bottles being offered were estimated to sell for between $5,000 and $7,000. After a fierce bidding duel, auctioneer John Kapon tapped his hammer at $70,000. With Acker's commission, the tab for the two bottles came to $82,000. At that price, they pulled away from the realm of what even the superrich and their A-list guests were likely to consume. Anyway, well-stored bordeaux and burgundy from 1959, a magnificent vintage across France, could still be glorious. Rosé champagne, probably not so much.

Acker's catalog billed this sale as "An Important Selection from the Cellars of Robert A. Rosania Including a Most Comprehensive Offering of the Finest and Rarest Champagne." Rob Rosania is a compactly built, room-dominating New Yorker who grew up in an Italian American, born-again Christian household. He is not ashamed to say that his family twice had to resort to food stamps when his father was unemployed. Rosania made a fortune in real estate. His vast wine collection has always been dominated by bubbly. In his introduction to the catalog, Rosania wrote that his first champagne experience was either a 1937 or a 1934 Krug (one of the great champagne houses, favoring a rich, full-on style): "I couldn't believe how incredible it tasted—what citricity and pitch the wine had, although I didn't even know what those words meant then." (Rosania defines *citricity* as the grapefruity acidity that enlivens the bubbly. *Pitch* is, as he later put it to me in an email, the "wine's ability to elevate on the palate.") Savoring that old Krug, Rosania wrote, "I knew then and there that I had to have more, and the rest is a blur, as I had an insatiable appetite to understand them all."

Rosania's champagne sold that evening for an impressive $2.6 million. But this auction would be remembered less for that than for just twenty-two lots of Domaine Ponsot red burgundies that would not be sold.

As Jancis Robinson has noted, the traditional British-bred way of conducting wine auctions is decorous and dull. At art or furniture sales, bidders can usually eyeball the works being sold. Not so at wine auctions, where the goods normally remain hidden away in temperature-controlled storage. Nothing much happens at these old-style wine auctions beyond the auctioneer's drone as dark-suited attendees sit in rows, eyes on their catalogs. From time to time, they silently raise their paddles.

Kapon, once an aspiring rap and hip-hop music producer, disdains the decorum that imposes dullness in the sales room. So long as he presides, alcohol-fueled merriment is abetted. "John was the first one to break it out," says Jefery Levy. "It was like a giant fun party with an auction." Choice wines from Acker's own inventory and from consignors are poured generously. Attendees are encouraged to bring and pass around their own trophy bottles. As Kapon conducts the bidding, he habitually keeps a trio of stemware perched on the front edge of the podium: one each for white, red, and (most frequently refreshed) champagne. His focus on selling wine does not waver.

Kapon's nickname for Rosania is "Big Boy." The reference is to his extroverted personality, not his size. A bundle of exuberance at this auction, he cruised the room wearing a purple, windowpane-patterned cashmere sports jacket. Bohr offered Rosania's friends pours from a magnum of 1928 Château Pétrus that Big Boy had supplied. Noticing that my eyes were on the bottle, Bohr kindly offered me a pour. Except for some nineteenth-century madeira, it was by far the oldest wine I had ever sipped, and it filled my mouth with a deep and tranquil richness. It seemed to push away the noise in the room.

Had Pétrus, a humble little farm of special repute in the prewar era, actually gone to the expense of acquiring extra-large bottles, labels, and corks in order to bottle magnums of the excellent 1928 vintage? Nobody still alive knows for sure. And, as good cheer reigned at Cru, nobody cared. I, for one, believed I had been privileged to know the true taste and texture of 1928 Pétrus. Of course, I wanted to believe.

Late in the auction, Rosania heaved a jeroboam of 1945 Bollinger champagne into a special cradle that held it at a forty-five-degree angle. (In champagne, a jeroboam holds four regular bottles, not six.) He raised a saber. *Thwack . . . thwack.* The third swing sliced off the neck of the bottle as the crowd cheered. And cheered.

"Shut the fuck up!" called out Kapon, who still had many more lots to sell. He had good reason to be snappish. Twenty or so minutes earlier, at the midway point of the auction, he had paused the fast-paced action.

"We've got a little unusual situation here," he announced. "At the request of the domaine, and with the agreement of the consignor, we're withdrawing lots four hundred fourteen through four hundred thirty-four." These were all the Ponsot lots listed in the catalog. "I guess there were a couple of inconsistencies there, so we had to pull 'em."

"Fuck you!" yelled a person in the room, abruptly deprived of the chance to bid on wines estimated to sell for up to $60,000 per case. (Was the *f*-word ever loudly heard in the whole history of British wine auctions, begun by Christie's in 1766? Here at Acker, it was heard twice.)

Acker had just been been blocked from the chance to earn a substantial commission. Had the Ponsot lots sold at their high estimates, the auctioneer stood to net about $150,000.

At auction's end, I asked Bohr to point out the consignor. Kurniawan's social norm, I later learned, was to be a circulator, perpetually in contact with collectors. But now, he was hanging back. He seemed to be looking inward. Normally, I identify myself as a journalist when I'm looking for quotes, but not this time. Best to let him assume I was a collector—maybe one who had hoped to bid on some of his withdrawn lots.

"Hey, Rudy, what happened with those Ponsot wines?"

His eyes, behind black-framed eyeglasses, took me in. He seemed to be sifting his memory, trying to pinpoint where he might know me from.

"We try to do the right thing, but it's burgundy," he said. "Shit happens."

Kurniawan did not say more. I scribbled his words in the corner of a page of my catalog.

Just how much shit had happened, and where it would lead, nobody yet had any idea. Maybe not even Kurniawan. But he surely foresaw that questions would be raised about where he had sourced the withdrawn bottles.

In retrospect, when it came to old burgundy, this auction turned out to be deeply layered with deceptions that would only slowly be peeled away. They started with Kapon's mid-catalog introduction. Printed in boldface, it introduced a collection of mythic burgundies from an unnamed consignor, although Acker regulars knew that it was Kurniawan. Besides the twenty-two Ponsot lots, there were dozens more from two other elite Burgundian domaines: Armand Rousseau and Georges Roumier.

Kapon's text painted a tempting picture of how he had managed to wangle uber-rare vintages of these three domaines from the owner of "'THE' Cellar, responsible for a countless number of my life's greatest wine experiences." In this rendition, Kapon and the owner "got to talking about Rob's [Rosania's] upcoming sale, and it took me about a month thereafter of begging and pleading (i.e., can I please have some Roumier, Rousseau, and Ponsot PLEASE! Please, please, please, please), but finally he acquiesced. Praise the Lord!"

Kapon's overheated prose hid a cold truth: That spring, Kurniawan was a laggard debtor who owed millions of dollars to Acker and a coterie of its wealthy clients who had loaned him the money. The proceeds from that evening's sale of his wines were intended to partially pay down his debts. The Ponsot lots, estimated to fetch three quarters of a million dollars, were counted on to help Kurniawan dig out. Instead, Laurent Ponsot had rendered them unsalable.

Bidders for the Rousseau and Roumier offerings from "THE Cellar" might have felt their enthusiasm dampened had they known the Ponsot lots were to be withdrawn. But Kapon withheld that announcement until the other lots had been offered. As it was, many sold for handsome prices: Six bottles of Roumier's 1962 Musigny sold for $45,980. A case of 1949 Rousseau Chambertin went for $72,600.

A jeroboam of the same wine fetched $50,820. Yet many of those lots were also suspect, even if the domaines that supposedly made them had not protested, as Ponsot had done. Some bottles bore the stickers or stamps of two long-established overseas retailers, ostensibly conferring a level of trust that they had been impeccably sourced.

But that trust was open to question. Neither Berry Bros. & Rudd, the London dealer founded in 1698, nor Nicolas, founded in 1822 and the stated source of so many of Kurniawan's rarest wines, appears to have sold certain wines emblazoned with their logos. Case in point: those 1949 Rousseau bottles. All bore a circular Berry Bros. & Rudd sticker stating, "By Appointment to H. M. the Queen, Wine & Spirits Merchants."

Alun Griffiths, BB&R's wine director at the time, searched for the old Rousseau wines in his firm's modern computerized records and in a handwritten ledger from an earlier era. He found that "it does not appear that these wines have been through our hands." And he further noted that the circular stickers on the bottles shown in catalog photos of the Rousseau lots are a design "introduced in the 1990s." They superseded the stickers that would have been used for the 1949 vintage.

As for that jeroboam of 1949 Rousseau Chambertin, Griffiths commented, the purchase price was "a lot of money so I very much hope the wine is up to it!"

Finding nothing in his own records, Griffiths decided to query Domaine Rousseau about those modern shoulder seals on the 1949 Chambertins. The one person able to answer authoritatively was the late Charles Rousseau, then the octogenarian head of the domaine. Rousseau had begun working at the domaine with his father, Armand, in 1959. The response received by Griffiths was that Rousseau "thinks the wines are definitely genuine and even recalls sticking the seals on himself. How and why he obtained the seals is a mystery, but he has a clear recollection so it appears we can safely say that these are genuine."

Ponsot cast a cold eye on that response. "I talked to Rousseau's son, Eric," he says. "He knew that his father was eighty-five. Can you believe somebody's memory is accurate at that age? I am not very close to my own father, but I know that at eighty-five he would have the sense to know what he didn't remember."

Before Charles Rousseau weighed in, an employee of Domaine Rousseau told me that he had examined the photos of the domaine's wines in the Acker catalog. There were tiny details of the labels that he questioned. But after Charles Rousseau vouched for the labels, this employee recanted his initial concerns. Rousseau, a hugely admired icon of Burgundy who did not want to think unpleasant thoughts about counterfeits, died in 2016, in Burgundy, at age ninety-three.

Besides the 1949 Chambertin in question, other Rousseau lots fetching nosebleed prices included a case of 1962 Chambertin sold for $80,000 and four bottles of 1945 Chambertin sold for $32,000.

"This could be the last one on earth," said Kapon from the podium. Up for sale was a single bottle of Roumier's 1935 Musigny. That was only Roumier's second vintage of an appellation that wine writer Hugh Johnson says can be "the most beautiful, if not the most powerful, of all red burgundies." So little is produced that Roumier ages the wine in a custom-made, extra-small barrel. Clive Coates, a British authority on burgundy, writes of Roumier's Musigny: "It is a pity there is so little of it. I have sampled it ten times in cask for every occasion I have met it in bottle."

Yet in a career far briefer than Coates', Kurniawan was able to offer thirteen vintages of Roumier's Musigny ranging from the debut 1934 to 1978. In all, twenty-seven bottles of these wines were snapped up for more than $100,000 before adding the buyer's premium of 21 percent.

Two months after the Acker auction, I queried Christophe Roumier, current head of the domaine, on his opinion of these bottles, in particular the ones that would have been made by his grandfather. He responded that he "found no indication of a fake label. But photos are not enough to reveal details. My sense is that the labels [from] 1949 and 1959 are looking far too clean, unspoiled, and unscratched more than forty years after. . . . [I]t is hard to believe, but who can tell? I also feel that too many bottles of Musigny are appearing at sales, when we know that our yearly production cannot exceed six hundred bottles. But again, who can tell? As long as the bottles (capsules and cork) look untouched, and the labels look exactly as they should, I can testify to nothing."

Roumier did not mention, and I did not know, that in the previous January he had been guest of honor at a private dinner in New Jersey at which wines purportedly made by his father and grandfather were served. Hosting the six-course meal, attended by several persons knowledgeable about burgundy, was a billionaire named Don Stott, a high-volume buyer of trophy burgundy. Stott had aggressively bought Roumier lots, many consigned by Kurniawan, at previous Acker auctions. According to Douglas Barzelay, a collector who was at Stott's table that winter evening, neither Roumier nor other guests believed that the majority of the wines were authentic. Of the "eleven or twelve" wines tasted from Cellars I and II, Barzelay estimates that "roughly 70 percent" were "clearly fraudulent."

And perhaps not even Kapon was rock-certain that all the lots from "THE Cellar" he offered that April evening were the real thing. Many previous Acker catalogs were more sparsely illustrated than this one. It featured page after page of full-color photos of the rare wines on offer. Was Kapon putting prospective bidders on notice to look very carefully? If they did, they would have found numerous details to question, even if they were not privy to what the winemakers knew. Why did labels on purportedly very old bottles look brand-new, as on the 1949 Roumier Bonnes-Mares or various vintages of Rousseau Chambertin Clos de Bèze? Dazzling white was not the norm for labels on bottles that had spent decades in a damp cellar.

And wasn't it puzzling that the heavy deposit in the neck of 1929 Ponsot Clos de la Roche suggested that the bottle was indeed very old, yet the label looked new, as if an octogenarian's face were smooth as a child's? Why were there no photos of any of the six Clos Saint-Denis lots, none younger than 1971? Ponsot acolytes, who for sure had never before seen these vintages, would have been highly curious to study the absent images.

Despite the withdrawal of the Ponsot lots, that evening's sale of Kurniawan's Rousseau and Roumier lots helped to draw down his debts to Acker and other lenders, but not by nearly enough. Three weeks after the auction, Acker would quietly file a lien on dozens of artworks owned by Kurniawan in a belated attempt to secure his loans. As with wine, this boyish-looking collector had an eye for what the art market found highly desirable. The encumbered works were by, among others, Andy Warhol, Robert Indiana, Richard Prince, Ed Ruscha, Damien Hirst, and one of China's highest-priced artists, Zhang Xiaogang.

Seven months after the Cru auction, Acker would further tighten the screws on Kurniawan. It would obtain a signed "confession of judgment" in a debt proceeding in a New York court by which Kurniawan legally admitted that he owed Acker $10.4 million.

That would be a staggering reversal of fortune for the man whom Kapon called "this century's greatest collector on the planet." Kapon claims never again to have sold any wine consigned by his former friend, drinking buddy, and best client. Christie's New York, on the other hand, would sell Kurniawan's wines multiple times after Acker abandoned him, without revealing the name of the consignor.

Not all proprietors of French wineries, especially Burgundians, were troubled upon discovering that fakes of their own wines were being put up for sale. Quite the opposite. If certain collectors, as careless as they were wealthy, insisted on spending wads of cash on unpedigreed bottles that turned out to be counterfeit, well, *tant pis*. It was their folly. Laurent Ponsot, however, rejected that position.

Within minutes of my own late arrival at the Cru auction that evening, Ponsot, a fine-featured man with sharp blue eyes and, as he would later describe it to me, "Jesus-length" sandy blond hair entered the restaurant and slipped into a seat at a corner banquette. Amid much mirth, he remained poker-faced. Few in the room recognized him or knew why he had come.

CHAPTER 3

The Man from Morey-Saint-Denis

I love my babies. When your children
are attacked, you defend them.
—Laurent Ponsot, April 2008

The first time Laurent Ponsot saw a fake bottle of his own wine,
he was in a shop in Kuala Lumpur, Malaysia. It was labeled Clos
de la Roche 1990, an excellent vintage of his flagship wine. "It was a
crude copy, but I said to myself, 'This is super!'" he later told French
newspaper *Libération*. "Lower-end brands don't get copied. The ones
they copy are the Breitlings or Rolexes!"

He was raised in a village known for centuries to lovers of fine
red burgundy. Yet Morey-Saint-Denis is so tiny and sleepy that it
long had no post office. Old labels of his family winery list its address
as "Morey-St. Denis par Gevrey-Chambertin"—the next village to
the north, which did have a post office. The Ponsot family home,
stone-built and steep-roofed, is nestled into a vine-lined hillside high
up on the middle of the Côte de Nuits, the northern portion of the
Côte d'Or and the most exalted source of pinot noir on earth. Ponsot
was born in 1954, directly above the family wine cellar. He retains
pleasant childhood memories of winter evenings whiled away in the

living room where his grandfather, Hippolyte, sat in front of the fireplace, pen in hand, signing the labels for his wines, one after another.

"In those days, we had no television," his grandson says. The domaine's origin goes back to Ponsot's great-uncle, William Ponsot. His name was given in an era when British names were in vogue in France. William was born in Saint-Romain, another sleepy Burgundian wine-growing village that lacked the fame of Morey-Saint-Denis. He settled there after returning from the Franco-Prussian War in 1872. The family owned restaurants in major railway stations in northern Italy, where Ponsot wines were first sold. The childless William passed on the domaine to his cousin and godson, Hippolyte. This Ponsot became a lawyer and diplomat in the Middle East while keeping his attachment to the home soil. The family's principal vineyard holdings were in Clos de la Roche, one of thirty-two grands crus that constitute the Côte d'Or's top vineyards. Although Morey chose to append the name of the Clos Saint-Denis vineyard to its name in 1927, the village's largest and best-known grand cru vineyard is Clos de la Roche. Among its eighteen proprietors, Ponsot is the largest, owning almost nine out of a total of forty-two acres.

Hippolyte returned home for good in 1922. It was still the era, troubling to him, when the region's grape growers, or vignerons, were just that and no more. Their job was not to undertake the bottling and marketing of the fruit of their vines. That was the job of the large négociant firms, based mainly in Beaune and Nuits-Saint-Georges, which paid the growers fast money that might be sorely needed to finance their next vintage. The négociants "raised" the wine in tank and barrel, blending different lots to get their signature taste and style.

No matter how lovingly the vigneron tended his vines or how distinctive (in his eyes) to their soil his grapes might be, his fruit, along with that of others, ended up being subsumed into the négociant's branded bottle to be sold in markets near and far. It was a rational system. The little grower tucked away in a sea of vines on the Côte d'Or intimately knew the quirks and moods of his own vines in sickness and in health, knew how to coax out of them the most wine-worthy grapes. But he had no expertise in the fine points of vinifying wine and no hope of packaging and marketing his wine so that it reached the shelf of a wine shop in London, Manhattan, or Buenos Aires. But it could arrive there, blended with other parcels, bottled under the label of a négociant with global reach such as Louis Latour, Joseph Drouhin, Louis Jadot, or Joseph Faiveley. The name of the négociant on the label might be printed larger than the vineyard name—even a name as great as Clos de la Roche.

Beginning in 1932, Hippolyte broke with local tradition and stopped selling his new vintage to négociants. He made the wine himself. A handful of other growers began to do the same. Hippolyte was also an early advocate of creating strict new regulations to guard the authenticity of Burgundy's individualistic vineyard sites. The plan called for detailed controls to ensure that a bottle of wine actually came from the appellation named on the label. Methods of tending the vines, limits on yield per vine, and even communal tasting panels that could reject wines judged not up to snuff (they rarely did) were all to be required.

Previously, all the grapes in that bottle labeled as Clos de la Roche need not have been harvested in the named vineyard, or even within the village limits of Morey-Saint-Denis. The important thing was for the wine to conform to how the négociant wanted Clos de la Roche to taste. Loyal customers of the brand preferred it that way, just as Coke loyalists don't want their quaff to taste like Pepsi. Loyalists to the soil, a particular terroir, felt otherwise. They were aware that their Clos de la Roche would not be the same from one year to the next. Those differences, which could be dramatic, were welcomed in the same way that parents welcome different personality traits in their children. Despite opposition of the négociants, *appellation controlee* in Burgundy was enacted in 1935 and 1936. The victors were led by a small squadron of growers that included the Duc d'Angerville and Hubert de Montille in Volnay, and Hippolyte Ponsot in Morey-Saint-Denis.

Hippolyte's son, Jean-Marie Ponsot, advanced the cause of better burgundy in his own way, experimenting in the 1960s with different clones of the pinot noir grape to identify their particular aromatic and flavor profiles. (A clone derives from a particular "mother" vine with desirable flavor or productive attributes.) Different clones could produce strikingly different wines even when grafted onto the same vine. Jean-Marie's clonal selections remain in use at the family domaine as well as in faraway vineyards. He also expanded his domaine's production to include Chambertin and Latricières-Chambertin, both grands crus. These vineyard parcels were not owned by Ponsot but farmed under the tenant system called *métayage*, or sharecropping. In return for tending the vineyard and making the wine, Ponsot shared the vintage in equal quantities with the landowner, who apparently preferred the pleasures of Paris to the quiet life among the vines.

Interviewing Jean-Marie Ponsot was no pleasure, according to the British wine writer Remington Norman. During a domaine visit in 1990 or 1991, Norman found him to be "a bluff, gruff, inflexible man of unequivocal views which, as is so often the case, are restated rather more than is necessary for their portent to be fully appreciated." Yet his wines were, "fortunately, neither as direct nor as abrupt as his manner." In fact, Norman found the style of the wines to be "above all for finesse and elegance." The lesson would seem to be that the personality of the winemaker and his wines need not be a match.

Jean-Marie's only son, Laurent, chafed at growing up in a village that moved only to the rhythms of the vine. And since his relationship with his difficult father was no incentive to stick around, he left Volnay while still a teenager. In Nice, he got a business degree, then headed to Paris, where he built a successful travel agency themed to active sports touring. His own high-energy outlets included scaling the summit of the Matterhorn, where more than five hundred climbers have given up their lives. The climb is daunting even in summer, when blinding snowstorms can hit. Ponsot did it in winter.

Badly injured in a 1988 auto accident, Ponsot climbed no more mountains. But he did take up flying, and earned international and acrobatic licenses. At ground level, he has a passion for driving fast cars and motorcycles. With his wife, Claude, Ponsot has crossed America on his Harley-Davidson. In a nod to his love of this country, he arranged for the wedding of one of his sons to be held in Las Vegas.

Ponsot wasn't the only young Burgundian asserting his independence from the vine. Other heirs to multigenerational domaines also elected to escape the intense monoculture of the Côte d'Or, which is ruled by the vine. One was Erwan Faiveley, heir to a major domaine in Nuits-Saint-Georges. His grandfather Georges was the largest Burgundian exporter in the 1930s. Georges was also a cofounder of the Confrérie des Chevaliers du Tastevin, founded in 1935 to boost the fortunes of the ailing wine business. Yet Erwan Faiveley at first wanted none of it. He struck out on his own to be a banker.

Another was Étienne de Montille, whose father was the revered Volnay winemaker and pioneering estate bottler who turned away from selling his wine to négociants. Étienne de Montille bolted from the sleepy village of Volnay for California while still a teenager and later became a banker. His career was successful, but he still returned to Volnay, ready to bond with the family vineyards. De Montille's younger sister, Alix, trained both as a lawyer and as a chef in top French restaurants, but journeyed home to become a winemaker. She and her brother now make a range of white wines called Deux Montille (in spoken French, it sounds the same as de Montille).

Yet a fifth to stray was Jean-Marc Roulot, fifth generation of his family firm in Meursault. Roulot migrated to Paris to become an actor before returning. His wife is none other than Alix de Montille. A sixth is Frédéric Mugnier, who was a professional pilot. But the day came when, like the other prodigals, he returned home to the vineyards.

As Erwan Faiveley came to understand, "You think you own the vineyards, but you learn that the vineyards own you."

The vineyards that Laurent Ponsot owned called him home in 1981, as they had called his grandfather in 1922. Under his direction, the commercial reach of the domaine's wines was dramatically widened. By 1990, they were sold in forty countries in Europe, Asia, and the Americas. Clearly, Ponsot was a canny businessman. But he was also a passionate defender of the wines and the soil they issued from. His job was to get his wines in bottle, as he once put it to me, with "the greatest possible respect for authenticity."

⚜

One of the first to be puzzled by Acker's offering of Ponsot rarities was Douglas Barzelay, a retired, prominently mustached New York lawyer and true believer in the sensory virtues of mature burgundy. Unlike many recently arrived big-ticket buyers at wine auctions, he has had old wine on his mind for decades. As Kurniawan would do much later, he first focused on the châteaus of Bordeaux, then moved on to the more intricate landscape of Burgundy. He has long coordinated the domestic chapters of the Confrérie des Chevaliers du Tastevin, whose members have no agenda other than to sit together to enjoy good food and even better burgundy and to raise their voices in song.

Clos Saint-Denis is one of the lesser-known grands crus of Burgundy. Its tiny village is described by Remington Norman as the "rather somnolent filling in the sandwich of which the outside pieces are Gevrey-Chambertin and Chambolle-Musigny." Yet the vineyards are not without pedigree. They go back at least to the twelfth century, getting their name from a nearby religious college that owned them. The soils of Clos Saint-Denis, yielding a modest 1,900 cases among all producers in an average year, give a wine that is not showy, yet can be satisfying: gentle, harmonious, but with sneaky fullness. Ponsot calls Clos Saint-Denis "the Mozart of the Côte de Nuits."

One of ten proprietors in Clos Saint-Denis, Domaine Ponsot farms just 1.5 acres. Its production under the family label is less than two hundred cases. The wine rarely comes to auction. When it does, its price is always dear. In 2015, three magnums of the 2009 vintage, called Cuvée du Centenaire, sold for $1,960 each. For burgundy collectors looking for worthy yet obscure rarities, Ponsot's Clos Saint-Denis fits the bill. As a collector, Doug Barzelay had long sought out Ponsot wines. Yet he had never come across any of the domaine's Clos Saint-Denis so ancient as these. Neither had his fellow collector and Ponsot fan Michael Rockefeller. The same for wine merchant Geoffrey Troy and leading burgundy critic Allen Meadows.

So it was a jolt to Meadows to discover a bottle of 1959 Clos Saint-Denis on the table of a Los Angeles restaurant one April evening in 2008. The dinner was hosted by John Kapon and Rob Rosania to preview a select few of the prize wines to be offered at the upcoming Cru auction in New York a few weeks later. Mostly, Rosania's champagnes took pride of place at the dinner as they would at auction. But there were also some red wines. The Clos Saint-Denis was served side by side with a Ponsot 1959 Clos de la Roche, which a couple from Denver had brought. But Meadows' eyes were on the 1959 Clos Saint-Denis.

"I said, 'Wow! I've never had this even once,'" Meadows told me. "As soon as I got home, I looked in my notes. Sure enough, the oldest Ponsot Clos Saint-Denis I'd seen was vintage 1985. Then I called Doug. He had seen the catalog and he was already on it. For him, too, 1985 was the oldest vintage of the wine he'd seen."

In the aftermath of the dinner, Kapon posted a perfunctory comment on the 1959 Clos Saint-Denis in his blog *Vintage Tastings*, in an entry titled "Big Boy Does Los Angeles." The same note would appear in the auction catalog. Kapon described this Clos Saint-Denis as having "oats and brown sugar in its nose, also having classic bouillon, garden, carth, and dirt. Citrus, earth and 'caramel' . . . were present in this tangy wine, and Allen was all over its 'lemongrass' quality, and it was just that!"

"Lemongrass" is not an aroma or taste attribute common to red burgundy. By finding it in this Clos Saint-Denis, Allen Meadows may have been hinting that he had suspicions about a wine he had not come across in all his decades of burgundy tasting. Perhaps, if this wine were poured earlier, one of the other experienced tasters at the table might have questioned it. But this bottle was the fifteenth wine of the tasting, the first eleven having been champagnes. At this stage, all those bubbles must have blurred the critical acuity of all at the table. And if the tipplers weren't blurred yet, they would be by the time the next dozen wines were poured. Kapon remembers "waking up the next morning still drunk." Due to catch a flight back to the East Coast for yet another tasting marathon, Kapon elected to skip it.

To be fair to those who were at the table, that false 1959 Clos Saint-Denis could have been cunningly close to the real thing. The bottle itself may have actually been old and appropriately encrusted with sediment. It may have contained a portion of lesser burgundy from 1959. That abnormally warm growing season imparted dark color and muscular flavor to the wine. Quite possibly, the wine had been kicked up by a precisely calibrated transfusion of fruity and energetic California pinot noir. That would be a product that could fool even an experienced taster of old burgundy, the more so when those at the table are primed to find pleasure, not fakery. In such a situation, Meadows told me, "You don't want to kill the buzz."

Checking the winery's website, Meadows and Barzelay confirmed that the domaine first produced Clos Saint-Denis in 1982. That was the year in which Laurent Ponsot's father, Jean-Marie, contracted to farm a parcel of the grand cru owned by the Mercier family of Domaine des Chézeaux. Ponsot was at his desk, three days before the auction at Cru, when Barzelay called to alert him to the impending sale and to inquire whether there was some way the Ponsot label might appear on vintages of Clos Saint-Denis going back to 1945—the oldest being offered in the Acker catalog.

"It's a good thing I was sitting down, or else I would have fallen over," Ponsot says.

Barzelay ventured one possible explanation for how pre-1982 vintages of Clos Saint-Denis might authentically exist: Could Ponsot's father or grandfather have purchased grapes from those earlier vintages from other proprietors? If so, that fruit could have been vinified at the domaine and the Ponsot label affixed to the bottlings. But Ponsot shot down that theory.

The opportunity offered to his father in 1982 to sharecrop the Mercier holdings, not only in Clos Saint-Denis but in two other choice vineyards, had been the impetus for Laurent Ponsot to abandon Paris for his home village. "My father told me that the work was going to be too much for him, and he didn't want to take it on," Ponsot says. "I was having my life outside the winery then, but I said, 'OK, I'll come back.' And so, 1982 was our first vintage from Clos Saint-Denis."

Ponsot studied the full-page color photos of the wines in Acker's online catalog. They were sure to quicken the hearts of unsuspecting collectors hungering to own iconic burgundy unavailable anywhere except from "THE Cellar." Ponsot saw only fakery.

One photo showed twelve bottles of 1962 Clos de la Roche, each topped with a bumpy, dull red, wax capsule. Ponsot knew that the only time the domaine used wax to seal the crown was in the winter of 1985, when he used red wax to reseal the oldest bottles in his home cellar. Some of those bottles were sold at a charity auction in London. But unlike the wax crowns in the Acker photos, Ponsot's rewaxed bottles, some of which remain in the domaine's cellar, are smooth instead of bumpy, bright red rather than dull red. Another tip-off that all was not well with this 1962 Clos de la Roche as shown in the catalog: The label stated "Cuvée Vieilles Vignes," an "old vine" designation that Ponsot says was debuted only years later. Pasted on the necks of all these bottles were "Réserve Nicolas" strip labels, the lettering white on a shiny black background. The Nicolas provenance might have inspired confidence in prospective bidders—except that Ponsot insists that his family never sold its wines to Nicolas. Disconcertingly, most of the Nicolas stickers looked fresh and new.

Turning the page, Ponsot got another surprise: a full-page photo of a single bottle of 1929 Clos de la Roche. The bottle looked its age, with heavy sediment adhering to its glass neck, an indicator of decades of lying on its side. The wax capsule was badly faded and cracked. The label stated, *"Mis en bouteille au domaine"*—bottled at the property.

That, says Ponsot, could not be. "My grandfather did not bottle his wine at our domaine until 1934."

One more error: Some Clos de la Roche importer's strip labels seen in the photos bore the name of Alexis Lichine, an importer who never dealt with the family. One importer strip label is correct: "Robert Haas's Vineyard Selections," Ponsot's longtime American importer.

Expertly counterfeited wines—both the bottle and the wine within—are hard to "convict" beyond a shadow of doubt. Here, as offered in the Acker catalog, was the rare open-and-shut case. Ponsot turned thumbs down on the full array of thirty-two bottles and six magnums of Ponsot Clos Saint-Denis. He did concede that a few of the Clos de la Roche examples might be real. Acker's estimated prices for these lots ranged from $7,000 to $9,000 for one bottle of the 1945 Clos Saint-Denis to $30,000 to $50,000 for six magnums of the same wine. The single bottle of 1929 Clos de la Roche was estimated at up to $18,000 before the buyer's premium.

Ponsot authorized Barzelay, a client of Acker and friend of John Kapon, to call the auctioneer on his behalf. Barzelay informed Kapon that Ponsot wanted all twenty-two lots bearing his family's name to be withdrawn from the Cru auction. "John was clearly not happy about this, though he agreed to do it," says Barzelay. "He did not, however, want to make any announcement ahead of the sale."

Ponsot was scheduled to be guest of honor at a wine dinner in Philadelphia on the weekend after the sale. Taking no chances that the lots in question might be sold despite Kapon's assurances, the winemaker sped from Burgundy to Zurich and grabbed a flight to JFK in New York, then taxied straight to Cru. The next day, a tense lunch meeting was convened by Kapon at Jean-Georges, one of the city's finest restaurants, located in the Trump International Tower overlooking Central Park. The others at the table were Ponsot, Kurniawan, and Barzelay.

"After the usual salutations, I asked the question I had in mind," Ponsot says. "'Where are these bottles coming from? Can you give me the source?' At that moment, I saw Rudy looking down at his plate. He said, 'I buy so many bottles, I don't remember where I got all of them from.'"

That response did not sit well with Ponsot. "It was bizarre that someone can have in his hands eighty-four bottles of very old Ponsot. I myself had never known of so many very old bottles supposedly from my winery in one place. How could you not remember where they're coming from—especially if you paid a lot of money for them? If I had bought a Maserati, I would remember the details of that."

John Kapon had a different view. Unlike Ponsot, he wasn't surprised that Kurniawan couldn't remember where he bought Ponsot fakes. "It's tough for Rudy to figure out where he bought something, because he had so many sources," Kapon told me in the aftermath of the sale. "He was the biggest buyer of wine in this century." That claim wasn't hyperbole. Kurniawan was a wine shopaholic who often sent out a barrage of orders on a single day.

In the four-year period ending in 2008, Kurniawan charged $40 million worth of wine on his black American Express card. The heaviest charges were at New York Wine Warehouse—more than $3 million.

On the morning after the Cru auction, I called Mitch Frank, news editor of *Wine Spectator*, and told him about the withdrawal of the Ponsot lots. He assigned me to write a story about it. Laurent Ponsot agreed to be interviewed. But I needed to be in contact with Kurniawan to learn if he had had any luck in figuring out where he had bought the faux Ponsots. John Kapon supplied me with Kurniawan's email address.

After several messages went unanswered, Kurniawan called me. "I have a pretty good idea of where I bought [the Ponsots]," he said. "I will be working directly with Laurent. We want to get to the bottom of this. My goal is that I just want the market to get healthy." He declared his love for burgundy, even more than bordeaux. "I love how when it gets very old, it gets to be the color of the veins in an old lady's arm."

Nothing in his words or tone struck me as false.

✶✶✶

After the debacle at Cru, Kurniawan's high visibility in the upper reaches of the wine world dimmed. For a time, Kapon still defended him. He, like Ponsot, expected Kurniawan to pinpoint the source of the withdrawn bottles. When time passed without any explanation forthcoming, the auctioneer backed away. Ponsot was more patient. He continued to give Kurniawan the benefit of the doubt. Given a little more leeway, perhaps Kurniawan would eventually come up with an explanation of where he had sourced the fake wines. And that would lay the blame elsewhere.

"I wasn't yet sure if Rudy was victim or predator," is how Ponsot put it.

About his own role, Ponsot was clear: "Some of my own colleagues were happy to see their bottles sell at huge prices. I told them that they were probably fakes but they didn't react. I could have done the same. If I had said nothing, the Ponsot image would have still been big. But it is not enough to leave things as they are. What I decided to do is not for fame. My will is to respect our authenticity of *all* the appellations we have in Burgundy. People are only a tiny link in the chain. We are connected to the geological universe under our soil. I will not see it abused. I'm not the richest man, but I will spend my money to find the people who did this."

After the post-auction lunch, Ponsot returned to Burgundy following a stopover in Greece. There, he awaited news from Kurniawan. After three weeks passed with no word, he wrote:

> Dear Rudy,
>
> It was a pleasure for me to meet you and to have a chance to talk over an excellent lunch when I was in New York. I look forward to seeing you, if possible, when I am next in Los Angeles, from July 17 to 19. I would like to follow up on our discussion at lunch, as I remain committed to finding whoever is the source of the counterfeit Ponsot wines.
>
> As you promised, will you please e-mail me the information of who sold you these wines? I will then be responsible to deal with them.
>
> With warm regards,
>
> Laurent Ponsot

Three weeks later, Kurniawan wrote back:

> I am responding to you the second time and hopefully you
> get this. Again, I am very excited and would love to have
> dinner and wines with you in July. The wines I bought
> from the cellar of Pak Hendra in Asia.
> Cheers,
>
> Rudy

"I was happy to have an actual name, but I'd never heard of this person," Ponsot says. "And when you say Asia, it's quite wide. I've been selling to many countries in Asia since 1982, and so I know that market quite well."

Eager to learn more about Pak Hendra, Ponsot flew to Los Angeles for a dinner with Kurniawan on July 19, three months after the Acker auction. The restaurant was Il Grano, known for virtuoso Italian fare and a deep wine list. It was chosen by Ponsot, who did not want Kurniawan to control the venue. "He was surprised that I knew the place, where he knew the chef-owner." Kurniawan arrived with a selection of bottles meant to display his connoisseurship. Ponsot picked two. First to be opened was a wine unique to his domaine: Clos des Monts Luisants, a rare, barely two-acre outpost of white burgundy vines on slopes where red wine rules. It is made from *aligoté*, a grape once commonly planted in the region but ripped out almost everywhere in favor of chardonnay. Ponsot's great-grandfather planted this aligoté in 1911. Each October, Ponsot's website explains, the sea of red wine vineyards surrounding Clos des Monts Luisants turns rusty ochre, while the aligoté's leaves turn silvery. In French, *luisant* means "glistening." Rare as white Clos des Monts Luisants is, the vintage that Kurniawan brought, 1975, made the bottle even rarer.

Next, Kurniawan uncorked wine royalty: La Tâche. The vintage, 1955, was excellent, although *Wine Spectator* rated the wine a barely acceptable eighty points, finding it "a bit lean, very intense, and slightly acidic." Both wines, in Ponsot's opinion, were real.

"Rudy would not have dared to bring fakes," he says.

Outwardly, it was a pleasant meal, yet both men had reason to feel tension. Ponsot sensed that dinner date was "less comfortable" than the first time they had met at Jean-Georges in New York. This time, Ponsot was determined not to leave without the information he sought. As they sipped the Monts Luisants, Ponsot thanked Kurniawan for providing him with the name of Pak Hendra.

"Now you must give me more details about this Mr. Hendra."

Kurniawan fumbled for a scrap of paper and scribbled down two telephone numbers, which he said were for Pak Hendra. Both were in Jakarta, Indonesia—not a city known as a reliable source of very rare burgundy. That name and two phone numbers, Kurniawan claimed, were all the information he had concerning the source of the faux Ponsots.

Before they parted, Kurniawan asked Ponsot for a favor. Would he be willing to come to Kurniawan's wine storage warehouse to check the authenticity of some of his old wines? As he often did, Kurniawan was declaring himself a defender of real wine. Perhaps Ponsot might have done that, but not until the matter of the twenty-two lots of faux Ponsot was settled. Back in his office in Morey-Saint-Denis, Ponsot dialed each number. The first went unanswered. The second sounded like a fax number. From friends in Asia, Ponsot later learned that *pak* means "Mr." in Indonesian and that Hendra is as common a name as Smith is in English-speaking countries. In effect, Kurniawan had provided him with a name that was the equivalent of "Mr. Smith" in a country with a population of nearly 250 million.

"My friends who are collectors in Singapore told me that if anyone was selling such rare Ponsot bottles anywhere in Asia, they would have known about it," Ponsot says. "In any case, my feeling was that these bottles had never seen Indonesia.

As to where he now thought Rudy should be placed on the predator-or-victim spectrum, Ponsot says, "The percentage changed—not to the good."

Though quick to spot the flaws in the Acker catalog photos of the faux Ponsots, the winemaker was impressed by the expertise that went into fabricating them. Undoubtedly, these were genuine old burgundy bottles, handblown rather than machine-molded and heavier than modern examples. Had those very bottles lain in the cobwebby corner of an unknown Burgundian cellar? If so, how had they been transformed into Ponsot look-alikes? And who had done it?

One of Ponsot's strategies, as he sought the source of the Kurniawan bottles, was to try to be on hand wherever old burgundy was being poured. If he detected a fake, he would try to track down its maker. Perhaps it would be the same one who made Kurniawan's fake versions of his own wines. Even if Kurniawan was involved, Ponsot did not think that Kurniawan was himself the maker. His fakes were too good for a relative neophyte to have concocted without expert help.

Ponsot attempted to persuade key fellow winemakers to establish a communal image bank of wine labels, capsules, and bottles. That resource could be referred to when the authenticity of a bottle was in doubt. But that effort fell flat. "Maybe it could happen in Bordeaux, but Burgundians are too individualistic to cooperate like that," he told me. "They want to keep their information to themselves."

Ponsot tried another tack. He contacted the French government consumer fraud watchdog agency. Its name could be fodder for a Monty Python skit: La Direction Générale de la Concurrence, de la Consommation et de la Répression des Fraudes ("General Directorate for Competition, Consumption, and Repression of Fraud"). Along with prosecuting more common scams, such as the faking of Chanel bags or Hermès scarves, the DGCCRF issues recalls on such items as toxic finger paints and potentially allergenic dresses. It also investigates wine fraud. But it wasn't responsive to Ponsot's plea for help in finding out who had faked his bottles.

"I was told that without proof that a wine labeled with my name was fake, the agency wouldn't do anything," he says. The agency's preferred method was to monitor activities in wineries, thereby detecting fraud at the source. The agency had done that at Labouré-Roi, a long-established Burgundian négociant specializing in selling wines to airlines and cruise ship lines. Labouré-Roi's misdeeds included adulterating vats of better-quality wine with cheaper stuff, and then pasting stickers on the bottles that falsely claimed wine-fair prizes. If Ponsot could have fingered a facility where fakes of his wine were being made, the DGCCRF might have investigated. But he couldn't.

Ponsot had one more idea: Why not create a fund to help cover the cost of his investigation, including travel to Asia and legal fees, which would eventually mount to six figures? Each wine collector who contributed to the fund would be entered into a raffle. The winner would receive a methuselah (equal to eight regular bottles) of Ponsot's top bottling, Clos de la Roche, Vieilles Vignes. In a superior vintage, its market price could exceed $5,000. Ponsot abandoned that idea, but not the investigation.

For all the intensity of his effort, the search had thus far been fruitless. Ponsot compared himself to Don Quixote, tilting at windmills, although minus the companionship of a Sancho Panza. His travel expenses, mainly from trips to Asia, where he sought to unravel mysteries shrouding Kurniawan and his mysterious family, mounted. But he was looking in all the wrong places.

CHAPTER 4

The Auctioneer

I am a drinker, occasionally even a drunk.
If there is anyone who drinks more old wine than
me on a yearly basis then I need to meet you.
—John Kapon

From 2005 to 2008, years of pocket-jingling exuberance in the wine market, John Kapon and Rudy Kurniawan prospered together. Neither could have done it without the other. If not for Kapon, Kurniawan might never have cut a swath through the upper reaches of the New York wine world as he had already done in California. If not for Kurniawan, whose transactions through Acker Merrall & Condit mounted to tens of millions of dollars, Kapon might have lagged in breaking out of the second tier of wine auctioneers. Or maybe never made it out. As the trophy wine market suddenly cooled in the aftermath of the faux Ponsot affair in April 2008, coinciding with forebodings on Wall Street, it seemed that just as the duo of Kurniawan and Kapon rose together, they might sink together.

As a skinny senior on the wrestling team at Manhattan's elite Collegiate School, Kapon was unbeaten in New York State, but not because he was the strongest. "John never stopped looking for advantage," according to his paternal uncle, wine educator Ron Kapon. "You could win by pinning your opponent or on points. If John was winning twenty to zero, he wanted to win thirty-five to zero." The teenager worked evenings in the family wine shop on Manhattan's Upper West Side. At the time, his long-term goal was to be a hip-hop and rap producer. Fresh out of New York University, he tried but failed to negotiate a music production deal with Columbia Records. Abandoning hope of a music career, he began working in the family shop full-time.

Pondering the career path he did not take, Kapon told me in 2012, "Did the world lose an earlier Eminem?" He shrugged and answered his own question: "I traded the rhyme for the vine."

Acker Merrall & Condit started in 1820 as a grocer, and it remains one of Manhattan's oldest continuously operating retail businesses. In 1912, 75 cases of imported anchovies, 225 cases of canned mussels, and 50 cases of wine en route to the firm went down with the *Titanic*. In a 1930s newspaper ad, Acker trumpeted "good, sound, honest wine at sensible prices," including 1929 Château Margaux for $2.38 per bottle and Paul Jaboulet Aîné's 1929 Hermitage La Chapelle for $1.70. Those were piddling prices for France's greatest wines at a time when the cover price of *Fortune* magazine was one dollar. Kapon's grandfather became a partner in Acker shortly after the repeal of Prohibition. He bought out his partners in 1963 and was later succeeded by his son Michael. In 2011, Michael passed the CEO mantle to John, the only one of his three sons to be involved in the family business.

His father was a stern taskmaster. "In any company, you need somebody whose word is law," the elder Kapon, age eighty, told me. "My father yelled at me a lot," John Kapon says, but he remembers his pride at becoming a wine merchant: "I was my father's son."

Through most of the 1970s, New York was on the rocks financially and in just about every other way. Asked to name the city's main growth industry, locals pointed to illegal drug sales and corporate moving services relocating financial firms from Manhattan to the suburbs. The side streets of the down-at-the-heels Upper West

Side were dotted with dope dens, and shattered car windows lined the curbs. Heroin was in higher demand than fine wine, and Acker was just scraping by. "My father would put bottles of Romanée-Conti in his holiday gift packages, because he couldn't sell the stuff," Kapon says. (With Acker's 2016 holiday season price of the 2002 Romanée-Conti at $13,995 per bottle, the wine wasn't likely to go into gift bags.) By the time Kapon was out of college, the neighborhood's decline had bottomed out, but Acker remained an unsung local bottle shop.

Wine auctions were illegal in New York until 1993 owing to a ban enacted at the behest of the retailer wine shop lobby, which did not want competition. The ban was lifted only when a new law authorized wine auctioneers to open for business so long as they were either a licensed wine retailer or partnered with a wine retailer.

Michael Kapon was one of the first to put a toe into the auction arena, working with an experienced general auctioneer in 1995. And then he quickly retreated. "My dad felt it was more trouble than it was worth," John Kapon says. "He felt that if we were to ever do any more auctions, we should do it on our own." Eventually he convinced his father to let him give auctions another try. But he would do it his own way.

At age twenty-six, Kapon tried his hand at an auction by partnering with Phillips, a two-hundred-year-old firm that lent gravitas to upstart Acker. That auction was held in Phillips' East Side galleries in 1997. Kapon was not impressed by the methods of traditional auctioneers. "I'd listened to the lectures of these guys, who didn't have any new ideas, and I'd just be shaking my head inside my head," he says. He had an idea of his own that he hoped would give Acker a leg up against the likes of entrenched Christie's and Sotheby's, each founded in London centuries ago. "Back then, auction houses charged fifteen percent commission to both buyer and seller, but it was pretty obvious that sellers needed money and buyers had money. So we changed the whole landscape of the industry by setting the seller's commission to zero. Today, no seller anywhere pays fifteen percent commission unless he's living under a rock."

Acker's first auction under the new policy was held at the Park Lane Hotel on Central Park South in early 1998. "We whipped it up on short notice with wines sourced from our existing client base," Kapon says. "We were really scratching and clawing. It was more L [loss] than P [profit]."

The infant auction house's zero commission for sellers attracted new clients, including a free-spending few who morphed into an informal drinking club headed by Kapon. They dubbed themselves the "Twelve Angry Men," although the number of members was fluid. What were they angry about? Sifting for an explanation, Jefery Levy explains, "Sometimes you bring a very nice bottle of wine to a dinner, and everyone else brings a shit wine. So you get angry."

Nobody brought shit wine to a Twelve Angry Men dinner.

Most extroverted of the group was Rob Rosania. "I knew John when he was just a guy who ran the local wine shop," he tells me. "But it was clear to me that he had a different level of personal passion as opposed to just business passion. And he was a very hard worker. In what other major auction house is the owner also the auctioneer?"

Besides "Big Boy," key Angry Men ranks included Levy ("Hollywood" Jef), investor Ray Tuppatsch ("King Angry"), and real estate and banking mogul Edward Milstein ("the Punisher," also known as "Airplane Eddie," probably because he owns one—handy for trips to Burgundy, where he co-owns a négociant firm). Milstein denies being an Angry Man, but he makes appearances in Kapon's online diary, *Vintage Tastings*. There was one part-time Angry Woman: Wendy Agah, who works behind the scenes as a consultant with some of Acker's biggest customers and collects wine with her husband, James Agah, a sometime attendee at Angry Men sessions. Rudy Kurniawan was dubbed "Dr. Conti" (Romanée-Conti is his favorite wine) and "Mr. Forty-Seven" (his favorite bordeaux vintage).

By 2004, the Twelve Angry Men were in peak tasting mode. They had pockets deep enough to pay for crazily expensive wine and physical constitutions strong enough to drink a lot of it. They scorned the polite atmosphere of traditional auctions. "What would you do if you were a young wine collector—go where it was boring or where it was exciting?" asks Rosania. Kapon limned the ground rules for the Twelve Angry Men sessions in a December 2004 blog post: "Each month someone has to host and take everyone out to dinner, whether it be at a restaurant or in their home. The host picks the theme and sets the table accordingly with the three (or more) bottles that he is bringing, and then everyone else brings a bottle (or two) as well. One little thing the host has veto rights on any BYOB, which has certainly caused a few ruffled feathers. Believe me, it sounds a lot simpler than it ends up being!"

The group tasted not genteelly but prodigiously and ruthlessly, setting trophy bottles against each other, at least a dozen at a single sitting that lasted deep into the night. Kapon somehow always managed to jot down notes on each wine tasted, posting them in *Vintage Tastings*. Wine folk accustomed to respectfully savoring a fine old bottle or two over a sedate dinner were lucky to be spared Angry Men marathons. From the outside, they seem to have been more like cockfights, ending with the winner strutting. But these tasters saw it differently. Rosania argues, "People convince themselves they know the great wines, but until you taste two great wines side by side, measuring their character in tandem, *you don't really know.*"

Kapon puts it more bluntly: "Education is inebriation." But he was highly disciplined about that education. Extreme stamina was also required. One weekend in 2011 in Chicago, Kapon blogged tasting notes on one hundred wines uncorked over three consecutive nights, twenty-two of them after a Saturday auction. On Sunday morning, he was up at 5:30 AM to catch a flight to New York so that he could attend a wine lunch at Thomas Keller's restaurant Per Se. There, he sampled twenty-nine vintages spanning sixty years of Château

Margaux, one of the five Bordeaux grands crus. "The great wines, you have to give them a piece of yourself," Kapon says. "You have to really study them, and it's a physical exercise. Wine is meant to be tasted before it is consumed. It's really a science of taking small sips and chewing it like food. You process everything. You smell it like a lover, and taste it when it's gone." Has any one person ever made love to as many wines as Kapon did that weekend in Chicago and New York?

Kapon believes that he met Kurniawan at a wine dinner in Los Angeles in 2001 or 2002. Each was an outsider, each in a different way. Kapon was still on the periphery of traditional wine auctioneering and content to stay an outsider. "If you call Acker, you will never get the daughter of a rich man answering the phone," he once said—a comment not likely to have endeared him to his glossier competitors at Christie's and Sotheby's.

Kurniawan, always bearing rare "lumber," as magnums or larger bottles are called, was welcomed into the unstuffy, hard-living midst of the Twelve Angry Men. (In blog posts, Rosania, also a bearer of big bottles, sometimes signed off on his wine comments as "Lumberville.")

In Los Angeles, Kurniawan was also a member of an informal group called Deaf, Dumb, and Blind (DDB). The game plan was that at each dinner, one member would present a dozen wines with no hint as to grape variety, region, or vintage. Each taster was challenged to sift his taste memory to try to nail the wine. DDB was said to be the brainchild of talent manager Matt Lichtenberg, with whom Kurniawan bought the barrel of wine that became Rudy Matt. Blogging about a DDB event in 2003, Kapon wrote, "I have always been welcome when in town, almost like an honorary East Coast member, and whenever Dr. Conti is going to open at least a dozen bottles, it is usually worth making an extra effort to be there." Of a baker's dozen wines tasted, Kapon awarded his top mark of ninety-nine points to a 1955 Leroy Chambertin, calling it "one of the greatest wines I have ever had." One point behind was a "plum and chocolate" 1982 Pétrus boasting "subtly strong t n a" (not tits and ass but tannin and acid).

Kapon tried to work up enthusiasm for three other prize bottles from the DDB—but faltered. One, from a classic Burgundy vintage, was Romanée-Conti 1937. Kapon found this bottle to be "sour and oxidized," dismissing it as "close to a DQ" (disqualified). He awarded it a score of "92+?" That may seem high, but not in the context of Kapon's usual scores, which cluster around ninety-five. Another, even older, vaunted vintage of the same wine, 1929 Romanée-Conti, "kicked off a big marijuana debate" based on its aromas: "band-aid, leather, garden, iodine and a pinch of oxidation"—a taste profile that would send many a wine buff scurrying out to the local liquor store for a substitute bottle of Yellow Tail. Kapon scored that wine ninety-five points and noted, "Rudy found my score excessively low." The third wine was Roumier's ultra-rare 1962 Musigny. Kapon judged it to be "impure and a little stewed" and rated it "90+?"

In retrospect, Kapon's tepid reaction to this trio of ostensibly mythic bottles was on the mark. Time would tell that they were very likely fake. All three were offered, five years later, at the faux Ponsot auction. Their provenance was "THE Cellar." At that sale, a single bottle of 1929 Romanée-Conti sold for $29,000, a six-pack of 1962 Roumier Musigny for $38,000, and a bottle of 1937 Romanée-Conti for $29,040. In his catalog notes for these three wines, Kapon waxed enthusiastic, upping his scores from those assigned at the DDB dinner. Each now received ninety-eight points.

In Kapon's high-energy, low-decorum *Vintage Tastings* notes, wine and sex frequently shack up, as in his reaction to a 2000 red burgundy, Emmanuel Rouget's Vosne-Romanée Cros Parantoux: "Ceramics, leather and spice paved the way for 'sweet flowers,' which shortly became 'good snatch,' which shortly became 'latex sex.' Geez, I can't take myself anywhere."

A few bottles later comes Ponsot's 1990 Clos de la Roche Vieilles Vignes. It's so alluring that Kapon invents a new acronym for it:

"WILF. As in a Wine I'd Like to F lol." He ends the note by switching to a metaphor: "This was a Ferrari tire fresh off the pavement, thick as a brick and then some." One of Kapon's most vivid blog posts recounts an epic evening in Las Vegas in 2005. After an Italian wine dinner hosted by wine critic Robert Parker at Valentino in the Venetian Hotel, "We ended up in Rudy's hotel room for the real tasting of the night. . . . I arrived just in time for a swallow of 1962 La Tâche out of magnum. Damnit! When Rudy starts opening up bottles, you have to move quickly."

More bottles were opened, few of which Kapon can "effectively review . . . except one, one wine which became a nuclear bomb for the evening, destroying every wine in the room once it was open, and changing my personal history of wine forever." It was 1945 Romanée-Conti. "I hate to deal in absolutes . . . but this wine took the cake and proceeded to eat up memories of the dozens of other wines that I have had that could contend for the elusive title of Best Wine I Have Ever Had. The aromas, the texture, the flavors, the finish, all of its components were flawless, and the wine was amazingly fresh but decidedly and deliciously mature as well."

Fully buzzed, Kapon cruised into the bathroom and placed his glass atop the toilet while peeing. "CRASH! My glass of 1945 Conti slipped off the toilet tank top and crashed to the ground. What kind of place has slightly curved toilet tank tops, so slight that you cannot even notice until your glass of 1945 Conti slips off of it! . . . Disappointed but unfazed, I emerged from the bathroom unscathed to the delight of the crowd who roasted me quite well."

Kapon awoke the next morning "still hammered and feeling noticeably drunk. I took a quick look around me to get my bearings, only to find myself sleeping next to Rudy on his bed! I must have crawled in at night since Rudy was kind enough to let me stay sleeping on his couch. . . . I gathered myself and quickly headed down to my room, scaring a few small families in the process (let's just say that I wasn't exactly prim and proper at the time)."

No matter how dissolute his nights, Kapon kept his sights on raising Acker to the auction market's top spot. One way to draw in more bidders was to convert his auctions into occasions to eat, drink, and be merry. Acker wasn't the first to use a restaurant setting. Another New York–based auctioneer, Zachys, did it in 2002 at Daniel, New York's grandest French restaurant. But Kapon followed suit soon after, booking top restaurants spacious enough to host an auction. Once Cru opened in 2004, it became his favorite venue. High-value wines were poured nonstop. When Kapon took a break from selling, he glided among his guests like a sommelier, offering pours, as in, "Would you like to taste the 1991 Comte de Vogüé Musigny or the '82 Billecart-Salmon Blanc de Blancs out of magnum?" (Yes, please.) Kapon had figured out that when wine is flowing, you're more likely to raise your paddle and bid higher than if you stayed dry. In 2005, Acker's sales of $18.7 million put the firm in fourth place among all auctioneers, far behind pacesetter Christie's at $41.9 million. The next year, fueled by Kurniawan's Cellar I and Cellar II auctions at Café Gray, Acker leaped to first place with sales up a startling 222 percent to $60.25 million. Ever the iron man, Kapon remained at the podium hour after hour at the record-breaking $24.7 million Cellar II sale, personally gaveling down all 1,458 lots.

"Before those two sales, John was selling some very nice stuff, but it was smaller consignments—onesies and twosies," says Barzelay. "The reality is that Rudy was integral to the leap that his business made."

Even as Kapon's business soared, he could not ignore an intensifying drone of negative murmurs about the infiltration of counterfeits in the fine wine market. He was riled by comments made at a Napa wine symposium by a former Sotheby's wine specialist named David Molyneux-Berry. The subject was old magnums of Pomerol's Château Lafleur. Production at the tiny property barely crept over one thousand cases, but what the wine lacked in volume it made up for in long-lived intensity of aromatics and flavor. (Just the scent of the

2000 Lafleur, offered by Bill Koch at a 2017 lunch on his rear terrace and vivifying the languorous Palm Beach air, was enough to make my eyebrows feel like they were lifting to my hairline!) Once obscure, the château's wines became a darling of collectors after being praised to the sky by Robert Parker. Lafleur was owned by two elderly sisters, Thérèse and Marie Robin, who lived together at the château their entire lives. Their chai (where the wine rests in barrel), according to Parker, also housed "a bevy of ducks, chickens, and rabbits." The residency of those animals neither upset Parker, himself raised as a farm boy, nor caused the wine to suffer. Parker awarded the 1947 vintage one hundred points, writing, "It is the only wine that has ever brought me to tears."

One of the sisters had told Molyneux-Berry that only five magnums of the 1947 vintage had been bottled. She had also told that to a French wine critic, Michel Bettane, who had told it to Paul Wasserman. Yet a Manhattan retailer, Royal Wine Merchants, sold eighteen magnums between 1998 and 2008, according to records subpoenaed by Koch in a lawsuit against Royal. Additionally, between 2004 and 2006, more than half a century after the vintage, fourteen *more* magnums were sold by Acker, most if not all consigned by Rudy Kurniawan. At the Cellar II auction, six of those magnums were sold for $25,891 each.

Was the old lady's memory accurate? If so, could a négociant, possibly in Pomerol-loving Belgium, have bought 1947 Lafleur in barrel and bottled more magnums in its own facility? Precise answers to that question are long out of reach. Not in doubt is the fact that in the caution-to-the-winds era that lasted until the spring of 2008, Acker hawked a bounty of old vintages of small Pomerol properties, notably Lafleur and Pétrus, which for decades had been effectively extinct in the larger marketplace.

Kapon took the measure of the situation, as he saw it, in a fierce broadside posted on the "eBob" bulletin board on August 15, 2007.

Greetings from Hong Kong everybody.
Anyone want a case of 1947 Lafleur in magnums?

Seriously, guys, everyone needs to relax a little bit. Fake goods are nothing new to the world, and like it or not, unfortunately, luxury goods will always be counterfeited. . . . Wine is now officially a luxury good, and there will be counterfeits. . . . If you are not confident that something is real, there is a simple solution: don't buy it. If you do not trust the merchant you are dealing with, then don't deal with that merchant. . . .

What should not happen now is a modern day version of the Salem witch trial. Rudy's collection was the most extraordinary to come to auction ever. Period. Why do you think it was successful? Because it was loaded with fake wines? Quite the opposite. I personally have had HUNDREDS of these types of wines from his collection with HUNDREDS of America's greatest collectors AND critics in public forums. If you were not there for any of these dozens of occasions over a period of four to five years, it is easy to say, 'Yeah right.' There are more doubting Thomases and members of what I call 'The No Joy, No Luck Club' than believers and always will be . . . unless you were there, whether it was once or fifty times. . . . There will be lemons here and there. What Rudy did do is drink this stuff at an enormous rate. For five years he educated himself as to what was right and what was not. He probably consumed $10 million of wine on his own, much of it opened for many other people as well. He, in essence, became more of an authority than most people in the world, someone that I often turn to when I have questions. He was fortunate to be able to have the means to do that, and when those means became a little tighter due to other investment opportunities and personal reasons, he chose to thin out his collection. This was never the plan.

Rudy worked very hard to make sure he was offering only what he thought was authentic. That's why he put his money where his mouth was and gave a money back guarantee on EVERY bottle. . . . To this day if anyone has any problem with any wine that came from him, he will take it back. What more can you ask for? He is an honorable person, one of the most passionate wine lovers on Earth, one of the people that makes the wine world truly great.

Even as Kapon fiercely defended Kurniawan, he had to know that troubles were roiling Kurniawan's world. Only four months earlier, just before an auction in Los Angeles, Christie's had been forced to withdraw six magnums of 1982 Château Le Pin, a Pomerol produced in even smaller quantity than Lafleur and in high demand. Their consignor was Kurniawan. Kapon also knew all too well a closely guarded secret: Significant numbers of wines purchased at Kurniawan's record-breaking Cellar II auction the previous October were now being returned as buyers took advantage of a ninety-day money-back guarantee on problematic bottles. Kapon had refunded their money, and it was up to him to get Kurniawan to reimburse him. Still, Kapon had invested too much in Kurniawan, drunk too many mind-blowing wines provided by him, and sold too many wines that were not returned, to allow himself to confront the unthinkable: that Kurniawan might be a con man.

Eight months after his ringing defense of his friend and best client, Kapon was forced to withdraw the Ponsot wines from the podium. Laurent Ponsot had nailed them as counterfeits, and Kapon had to bow to that judgment. Whatever his private thoughts, the auctioneer outwardly held to the belief that Kurniawan himself was a victim of an as-yet-unidentified counterfeiter. "For a period of time, he was the biggest buyer of fine wines in the world," Kapon told me in the aftermath of the auction. "He was buying at whatever price, and setting the bar for the market. It's easy to look back after the Ponsot episode and say he should have been more careful. It's not a problem that is unique to him and to us. Nobody was thinking there were any issues with his cellar. He did an amazing series of dinners for the biggest collectors on the planet and everyone was blown away by the wines. One of the scariest things is that they could be that good, the tastes so good."

Some of the wines may have tasted "so good" because they *were* the real thing. Some invitees to dinners cohosted by Acker and Kurniawan before auctions featuring his wines still believe that he did serve many authentic treasures at the table and then substituted fakes at the auction: Kurniawan's version of "bait and switch."

Should Kapon have been expected to distinguish reliably between real and fake decades-old bottles? He prides himself on being alert to tiny variations in labels and branding on corks. Beyond those physical markers, he puts highest priority on what his own well-honed sensory radar tells him about authenticity. As Brian Orcutt, a New York–based wine consultant, put it to me in the aftermath of the "faux Ponsot" auction, "John's method of authenticating a bottle is to destroy it." In other words, it's only by tasting the wine that he can feel confident as to whether the liquid is true or false.

So Kapon is willing to overlook issues with the labeling on the bottle or the way the cork is branded if they are trumped by true taste. Or, at least, how he perceives true taste at a given moment. The pitfall in relying on true taste, even when a taster is as experienced and focused as Kapon, is that wine, especially old wine, refuses to hold still for its close-up. In *The Compendium*, his handsomely produced tome of twenty years of tasting notes, Kapon himself refers to the mutability of apparently identical bottles as the "Pandora's box of the fine-wine world. I have had many different impressions of the same wine, sometimes from the same case!"

Even so, Kapon trusts his tasting judgment, built on a foundation of thousands of tasting notes, more than he does label or cork branding, which can contain irregularities or just plain quirks. "I had a couple of DRCs [Domaine Romanée-Contis] with a collector, and the stamping on the corks was not quite right," he told me after the Ponsot auction. "And yet they were mind-blowing." Kapon is correct not to insist that every detail of a bottle be consistent with those from other vintages. Allen Meadows points to a "Vieilles Vignes" ("Old Vines") label on a bottle of Ponsot's Clos de la Roche from a vintage that Laurent Ponsot had not planned to so designate. There is no formal definition of *vieilles vignes*, but it generally refers to vines whose roots go deeper than those of young vines and presumably extract more nutrients from the soil, a characteristic reflected in more intense and complex flavors in the wine. When Meadows queried Ponsot, he explained that the printer had made the mistake of putting "Vieilles Vignes" on some of the labels. Rather than have the job done over, Ponsot used the labels.

And then there was the baffling case of the label with the missing honeybees, first mentioned to me by Allen Meadows. Decades ago, a customer of Maison Joseph Drouhin, the distinguished Burgundian domaine, was perplexed by a change in the labels of the latest vintage of the domaine's flagship wine, Clos des Mouches, which is made as both a red and a white burgundy. In French, *mooches* are flies, although in local usage, *mouches à miel* refers to honeybees, which have always been abuzz on the Clos des Mouches label. This customer had noticed that one or more honeybees were missing on the labels of the wine he had received. Robert Drouhin, proprietor of the domaine, checked with the printer. The plates used for the old label, it turned out, had become worn. A few of the honeybees no longer printed up sharply. So the printer simply knocked them off the lithographic plates. Drouhin decided that the look of fewer honeybees made for a better label design. Bottom line: What looked like it might be a fake label was simply an updated label.

"Years ago, the market was run by 'buyer beware,'" Kapon told me in the aftermath of the stillborn Ponsot sale. "If you didn't like the wine you bought, it was tough shit. And Rudy was the guy that changed that. He would give you your money back. He was really a wine lover and buyer, first and foremost. His passion always came across."

Passion was all to the good, but what about provenance? Kurniawan had assured Ponsot that he would locate the source of the fake bottles. As time passed, his silence got louder.

"When a cellar gets as big as his and when you're not a great record keeper, the point is that it's hard to know which bottle comes from where," Kapon told me several months after the Ponsot sale. "I did ask him for a name for who sold him the Ponsots and I got that, although I wouldn't share it. He told me he gave it to Laurent. Other than that, I haven't really spoken to Rudy. It's discouraging that more hasn't come to light. He was planning to sell more wines with us, but we decided not to do it until he got his house in order."

Had Kapon considered the possibility that the true source of the faux Ponsots was not a collector, not the marketplace, but Kurniawan himself?

"I really can't see Rudy doing that," Kapon said. "That would be . . . *criminal stuff.*"

CHAPTER 5

Collapse of the Con

The term *confidence man*, or simply *con man*, was probably first applied to a dapper Manhattanite named William (also known as Samuel) Thompson who, in the mid-nineteenth century, struck up conversations with strangers on city streets. Sometimes announcing himself as an old acquaintance, he acted surprised when he was not remembered. At a certain moment, he would ask: "Have you confidence in me to trust me with your watch until tomorrow?" Quite a few of these strangers, cannily made to feel guilt at having no recollection of this nice chap, felt that the right thing to do was to honor his request. Thompson's downfall came when one victim recognized him on the street two months after he had been persuaded to "lend" him his gold lever watch then valued at $110. "Officer Swayse, of the Third Ward, being near at hand, took the accused into custody," according to a July 8, 1849, report in the *New York Herald*. It was headlined, "Arrest of the Confidence Man." Within weeks, a quickly thrown-together play called *The Confidence Man* opened at the Chambers Street Theatre.

The news reports about Thompson probably caught the eye of Herman Melville, then living in New York, whose final novel, published 1857, was called *The Confidence-Man*. It is set on a Mississippi

River steamer bound from St. Louis to New Orleans, departing on April Fools' Day. Aboard is a con man who, in various guises, scams one passenger after another. The psychological ploy he most often uses on his victims is akin to Thompson's: a convincing backstory capped by some variation on the question, "Do you not trust me?" "Do you not have confidence in me?"

In David Maurer's 1960 classic, *The Big Con*, the particularity of this genre of criminal is dissected: "Although the confidence man is sometimes classed with professional thieves, pickpockets, and gamblers, he is really not a thief at all because he does no actual stealing. The trusting victim literally thrusts a fat bankroll into his hands. It is a point of pride with him that he does not have to steal."

Kurniawan was from the same tribe as Maurer's con man. He was aided by his quicksilver charm—the starting point for any kind of con. That quality allowed him to pick holes in the reticence of moneyed people. His tasting acuity and wine literacy were impressive yet never off-puttingly pompous. Most of all, it was his generosity that unlocked the caution of his victims. The wildly expensive wine that he poured was often real. Or, if it was not, the recipients wanted it to be real, and fabulous. Reinforcing their trust was Kurniawan's backstory about his purchase of the Nicolas cellar. They desired to own a piece of it. In the end, the fat bankroll was thrust into Kurniawan's hands.

✣

Two candid photos place Kurniawan in his peak days as Dr. Conti. In one that is undated, he's seen with Wilf Jaeger, already a world-class collector when Kurniawan was still a toddler. Jaeger is tall, topped by a mop of blond hair. Kurniawan is on the short side, his sleeked hair a lustrous black. A tall beer mug in Jaeger's left hand bears the logo of Schwelmer Weizen, a German wheat beer. Into it, Jaeger is pouring from a bottle of 1945 Romanée-Conti. His expression is deadpan, while Kurniawan's impish smile seems to give it away: Whatever is being poured, it is not the mythic 1945 Romanée-Conti.

The second photo shows Kurniawan standing with Aubert de Villaine, coproprietor of DRC and Burgundy's most venerated living winemaker. It was snapped in April 2007 at Per Se, scene of a three-day tasting of seventy-four vintages of Romanée-Conti going back to 1870. De Villaine was the guest of honor. The event was captained by Doug Barzelay, who would be the first to warn Laurent Ponsot, one year later, about the faux Ponsots Acker was trying to sell. Barzelay spent years assembling Romanée-Conti vintages ranging from mediocre to glorious from multiple collectors. In the photo, both men are dark-jacketed and looking solemn. Here, at age thirty-one, Kurniawan appears to be awestruck at the company he is keeping.

Kurniawan provided bottles from several vintages to the Romanée-Conti tasting, including the beyond-rare 1945. Barzelay had searched for that same wine for years but failed to find a single bottle. For many of the tasters, it was supreme. If any more bottles survived from among the 608 made that year, nobody knew where to find them. Acknowledging that this was the last vintage to be made from vines that had survived the devastation caused by the root-devouring insect phylloxera in the nineteenth century, de Villaine called the 1945 Romanée-Conti "the lost voice of Burgundy."

❧

Kurniawan morphed quickly from wine neophyte to rare wine dealer trusted by corporate titans. At just twenty-six, he was cultivating Brian Devine, then CEO and chairman of the giant Petco pet supply chain with 1,500 stores in the United States, Mexico, and Puerto Rico. In an email dated September 16, 2003, under the heading "Florida Cellar," he wrote, using an alias:

Brian,

Here's the shortened list of the most incredible offering from the 20 million dollar cellar. (I deleted those that aren't rare or great.) They are priced reasonably low (20-25% below auction) as the family [Kurniawan has referred elsewhere to a private Florida cellar that he purchased] would like to liquidate asap. Please keep in mind that the list is offered to major brokers and collectors as well. . . . This may be the only chance to get some of the rarest btls that still exist in the world, and prices are extremely fair and low. The provenance are definitely great w/o any doubt and authentic.

Please kindly advise asap.

Cheers,

Leny

ps. You might be the largest collector in the country with all the rare wines you have.

Devine, who Kurniawan may have met through BurgWhores, was being conned. "Leny" is a variant of the name of Kurniawan's non-English-speaking mother, Lenywati Tan. Leny's email address, hzw@hotmail.com, is actually Kurniawan's. Its first three letters correspond to the initials of Kurniawan's Chinese name. The so-called "20 million dollar cellar" invoked by Kurniawan/Leny may be an early version of the so-called "Magic Cellar" or, as John Kapon called it, "THE Cellar." Its source, Kurniawan claimed, was the legendary stocks of French retailer Nicolas.

Four days after receiving the "most incredible offering," Devine promised to send "Leny" a check for $638,183 and added, "P.S. I have spent $1.5 million in 3 months. Glad I haven't known you for years, or my wife would have shot me."

But Devine did "know" Leny for two more years. By July 2005, he had written thirty-four checks to Leny totaling $5,320,602.50. At no time did he meet his dealer, or suspect that he was actually Kurniawan. "All of my purchases were done through internet communications," Devine wrote in an affidavit in June 2014.

In 2005, Devine attempted to sell a large trove of his wine, most of it purchased from "Leny," through New York auctioneer Zachys. The consignment was rejected. Along with a return to owner (RTO) list from Jeff Smith of Carte du Vin, a wine management firm, Devine received a letter stating that Zachys "took a very hard line on anything and everything from Leny Tan. . . . [S]adly, this represents most of the juiciest stuff in the parcel."

Juicy but also, as bottle-by-bottle inspection showed, amateurishly fabricated. Some bottles bearing the names of prestigious wineries were sealed with corks that were too short or blank rather than being branded with the names of the properties and the vintage. Other corks showed signs of the original vintage having been sanded off and replaced with a more desirable vintage. The cork of a magnum labeled as Château Cheval Blanc 1947 was branded on one side with that classic vintage, but the other side still carried the year 1985—a vintage far less collectible than 1947.

When Zachys asked where it should return the wine, "Leny" responded with a postal box number at a Mailboxes Etc. location. He was informed that Mailboxes Etc. was not a warehouse and could not accept dozens of cases of wine.

Why did Kurniawan claim to be Leny rather than himself when selling to Devine? At this early stage of his career (he was twenty-seven), Kurniawan may have thought it wiser not to present himself as a dealer with a deep inventory of historic bottles. After Devine's parcel of wine was rejected by Zachys, the collector asked Kurniawan where to find Leny, according to a law enforcement source. Kurniawan responded that he had no idea where to find Leny. Devine refused several requests to speak about his dealings with Leny/Rudy. And not only to me. So determined was Devine not to be served with a subpoena relating to Kurniawan that, in order to elude the process server, he once had himself driven away from home while hidden in the trunk of his car.

Devine's ability to purchase expensive wine in 2003 outran his expertise in vetting it. That wasn't true of Wilfred Jaeger, who had sought out rarest wines well before Kurniawan came on the scene. In March 2002, he hosted what guest of honor Michael Broadbent called an "unprecedented" tasting of Romanée-Conti in San Francisco, going back to the 1865 vintage. "My first experience with Rudy was very interesting," Jaeger says. "A friend, also a collector, had made me aware that Rudy had purchased a large cellar in France. He had bought extensively from this collection. I gave Rudy a call. I vividly remember that he was quite resistant. It took me several attempts to get him to send me a list of what he had."

Did Kurniawan fear selling his wine to a highly seasoned taster?

Jaeger adds: "He did eventually send it, and I purchased a fair number of bottles for several hundred thousand dollars—a case of 1945 Mouton, some Pétrus and Lafleur from the 1940s, quite a lot of DRC, some Vogüé Musigny and old Roumier. Everything that comes in I let settle for a few weeks. And then I'll taste it, so I know what I'm getting."

Jaeger identified a problematic theme that ran through Kurniawan's wines. Too many of them had a "uniform oxidative quality," which makes the wine sherry-like. As oxidation advances, it ambers a white wine and dulls the color of a red wine. "Virtually every one of them had this, even if it was only a penumbra of oxidation," Jaeger says. "I am very sensitive to oxidation. It's not something I like to drink. I remember finding that quality in a bottle of the 1945 Mouton, so I tasted a second bottle, and a third. They all had it. So I ended up returning almost all the wines to Kurniawan. After some inaction, he was good enough to give me back some money or young wines as replacements."

Jaeger's assumption was that the wines "were not well-stored examples." He also knew that old wines from Nicolas, which the labeling indicated some of them to be, had been recorked and reconditioned by the firm. Oxidation could have crept in during their handling. But it would turn out that neither storage nor actions by Nicolas was the problem. A decade would pass before Jaeger would learn the real reason why so many of Kurniawan's wines were oxidized.

Kurniawan failed to penetrate the defenses of Don Cornwell, another expert collector whom he met early on. Cornwell is a successful commercial lawyer with a well-honed appreciation for the wines of Burgundy—so long as they are real. Cornwell had long collected fine French wine. An early work experience had exposed him to the practice of upping the value of a bottle through fakery. It happened in the basement of a Los Angeles retailer where Cornwell was working part-time. There, as he tells it, the proprietor routinely changed undesirable 1983 bordeaux bottles into sought-after 1982s. New 1982 labels were printed locally. On the pinewood cases, the last digit of "1983" was sanded off and replaced by a "2." Cornwell notified the local district attorney and assisted him in looking into the scam. He may as well not have bothered—the proprietor escaped prosecution, but fired his young employee.

Cornwell says that John Kapon introduced him to Kurniawan at an Acker pre-auction tasting in Los Angeles in 2001. Kurniawan told Cornwell what he had told others then but would be less forthcoming about in later years: that he was the son of a wealthy family that, among other businesses, imported Heineken into Indonesia, and that his only real job was to care for his mother, who lived with him in Arcadia. His monthly stipend allowed him to buy not only expensive wines at auction but entire wine cellars in the United States and Europe.

Kurniawan queried Cornwell about his favorite burgundy producers. Along with Romanée-Conti, Cornwell named Domaine Georges Roumier. Kurniawan asked which was the oldest Roumier vintage that he had tasted. Cornwell named the 1969 Bonnes-Mares. "Rudy then proceeded to tell me that within the last year he had tasted the 1945, 1949, 1955, and 1962 Roumier Bonnes-Mares as well as various vintages of old Roumier Musigny." Taking the measure of this young wine warrior who had been a child when Cornwell himself had first tasted Roumier, Cornwell felt he had just met a show-off, possibly a faker.

Kurniawan also came up cold against John Tilson, editor of *The Underground Wineletter* and a taster with decades of experience. In 2006 in Los Angeles, Tilson was at a multi-vintage survey of La Romanée, a grand cru burgundy, when he "observed a young man scurrying around pouring wine from a big bottle. I did not know the person and it was very curious since we had not budgeted or planned on serving any wine from a big bottle at the event." The event organizer, a physicist named Bipin Desai, informed Tilson that the pourer was Kurniawan—"a wealthy collector from Indonesia who had shown up in Los Angeles recently and had a phenomenal collection of old wines." The wines, he was told, were "mostly a lot of old Pomerols in big bottles" as well as old burgundy. "When names like Lafleur, Pétrus and Romanée-Conti began to get tossed around," says Tilson, "my BS meter went into overdrive."

Maureen Downey, an independent wine authenticator, first met Kurniawan in New York in 2002. She told *Wine Spectator*'s Esther Mobley that she remembers Kurniawan as "then having a penchant for merlot—good merlot, like fifty-dollar merlot." Seven months later, when Downey was working as a wine specialist for Zachys, she again met Kurniawan in New York. This time, she "barely recognized him. He had gone from being this totally geeky kid to being this cool dude with a posse."

Kurniawan now wanted to consign a batch of rare wines to a Zachys auction. Downey instructed him to first send her a list of the proposed sale wines. Kurniawan shipped her the actual bottles instead. All were labeled as vintages from the 1940s and 1950s and carried the name of a Belgian wine firm called Vandermeulen. Active in the 1950s, Vandermeulen catered to the Belgian taste for Pomerol. It imported fine French wine by the barrel and for bottling in its own cellars. Downey knew it was rare for old Vandermeulen bottlings to find their way to the United States. Before accepting Kurniawan's offerings, Downey needed information about their provenance. How had he acquired these wines? Did he have receipts, or a bank wire entry, a credit card record, or some other paper trail proving the purchase? Even an email exchange between him and his supplier would be helpful. But Kurniawan could produce nothing except a "fax of a fax in Chinese." That wasn't enough to convince Downey. She rejected the wines.

Kurniawan boosted his profile at summer's end in 2003 by inviting top collectors to a dinner at wine-friendly Mélisse in Santa Monica. There, he opened twelve magnums of pre-1970 Château Pétrus. Thanks largely to rave reviews by Robert Parker, Pétrus was the highest-priced wine not only in Pomerol but in all Bordeaux. The oldest vintage poured at Mélisse was 1921, from that era when Pétrus was still an obscure small farm, far removed from the realm of elite châteaus in the Médoc. Parker, who partook of a 1921 Pétrus magnum at a tasting marathon hosted by accused German fraudster Hardy Rodenstock in 1995, awarded the wine a perfect one-hundred-point score. It was, "to state it mildly, out of this universe!"

Magnums of 1921 Pétrus, as it would turn out, may well have been from some other universe. Paperwork from that era no longer exists at the château, but the Moueix family, owners of Pétrus, are doubtful that magnums were produced at their property in that year. That is what billionaire collector Bill Koch's emissary was told when he had the magnum of the 1921 vintage brought to the château to be inspected (it was found to be fake). That view is backed up by John Tilson. In 2012, six years after meeting Kurniawan, he wrote in the *The Underground Wineletter*, "I had never seen or heard of the existence of any large format bottles of Pétrus from the pre-World War II period." Never say never! Michael Broadbent claims that he did come across one—a 1934 imperiale (which holds eight regular bottles). It was provided, however, by Hardy Rodenstock who, like Kurniawan, plied important tasters with real as well as fake wines— Pétrus first and foremost. "Where Hardy Rodenstock finds these wines I know not," wrote Broadbent. "There are simply no records of production, of stock, or of sales prior to 1945." In December 2016, Zachys auctioned off a jeroboam, equal to six regular bottles, of 1924 Pétrus from a reputable source: the cellar of Nath. Johnston & Fils, a centuries-old Bordeaux négociant firm. The jeroboam had apparently lain there for ages. It sold for $46,550. No reliably provenanced prewar magnums of Pétrus, however, have surfaced.

The guest of honor at Kurniawan's Mélisse event was Edouard Moueix, grandson of Pétrus co-owner Jean-Pierre Moueix. If Moueix doubted the authenticity of the 1921 magnum, he was polite enough not to express his concern. One attendee who was not confident about another legendary vintage of Pétrus opened at the dinner, the 1947, was Kurniawan's mentor, Paul Wasserman. In a tasting note, he wrote: "If there's one bottle I have serious doubts about tonight, this is it."

Oversized bottles were not easy for châteaus to acquire immediately after the war. The British wine critic Harry Waugh described the dearth in Bordeaux in 1947, when he found "many of the 1944s still in cask at a number of châteaus and this was on account of the shortage of bottles and corks. At one property, at least, they had to put a vintage into burgundy bottles!"

The postwar bottle famine observed by Waugh may not have impacted the mighty first growths of the Médoc. It would have been another story for châteaus in the then "backwoods" of Pomerol. Even Pétrus could well have had difficulty accessing the "big glass" required to bottle their 1945 vintages in magnum or larger. Yet Kurniawan had no problem supplying one of his clients, New

York–based real estate titan Michael Fascitelli, with six regular bottles of 1945 Pétrus and one each in magnum and double magnum. The price per bottle, in ascending order of size, was $6,500, $15,000, and $35,000. All bore Nicolas stickers, according to the offering sheet.

Nicolas holiday catalogs did sometimes offer Pétrus. The earliest listing I found was for a regular bottle of the 1906 vintage in Nicolas' 1933 catalog. It sold for eighty francs (then less than four dollars). The 1960 catalog offered the 1948 (an off vintage) Pétrus in regular bottle. Only the 1966 catalog offered Pétrus in Kurniawan's beloved magnum format: the 1953 vintage. In 2011, at Nicolas headquarters near Orly Airport south of Paris, I thumbed through an almost complete set of the firm's old holiday catalogs. None of those offered 1945 Pétrus.

Below the thin air at the wine summit, where illusion and reality were difficult to separate, Kurniawan's offerings of fine, rather than trophy, French wine could be authentic and splendid. "In 2006, I pleaded with Rudy to get me a really good 1955 bordeaux as a gift to Thomas Keller for his birthday—that was his birth year," says Paul Wasserman. The celebrated chef and restaurateur had just opened Bouchon Bakery in the Time Warner Center in New York, steps from his East Coast flagship restaurant, Per Se. "After much pushing, Rudy got me three bottles of 1955 Vieux Château Certan." Until the rise of Pétrus, Vieux Château Certan was considered to be Pomerol's finest wine.

"The labels on these bottles were falling off, so they must have been stored in a super-humid cellar," says Wasserman. "They weren't very expensive—maybe three or four hundred dollars each. Not bad for impeccable old wine. One was delivered to Thomas for his birthday."

Wasserman eventually put the remaining two bottles of Vieux Château Certan on the shelf at the Wine Hotel, a wine shop that he and Kurniawan had opened together in downtown Los Angeles.

"A Chinese guy came in and asked what I had that was interesting. I showed him these two bottles. He said, 'Let's pop one open. If it's good, I'll pay for it and buy the other one.' The wine was a stunner." And undeniably the real thing.

Stunning, too, were the real wines Kurniawan used to cast his spell on the leading American burgundy critic, Allen Meadows. Meadows often partook at Kurniawan's dinner tastings. The catalog for Acker's Cellar I auction in January 2006 included an introduction by Meadows:

> I have known this collector for several years now and been fortunate enough to drink and discuss great wines with him on dozens of occasions; his passion, like my own, is Burgundy. . . . I have had some of the most extraordinary wine experiences of my life due to both his unparalleled generosity and the sheer breadth of his collection. He has the nose of a bloodhound and the tenacious persistence required to track down the rarest of the rare. He is one of the most knowledgeable collectors that I have ever met and is absolutely obsessed with the underlying details of provenance, condition, and label minutiae and of course impeccable storage for his wines.

Later events would deflate certain elements of Meadows' praise along with that of numerous other fans of Kurniawan. Yet he was accurate in stating that Kurniawan did seek out real great bottles. At the British dealer Southwick Court Fine Wines, for example, Kurniawan bought pallet loads of wine including top champagne and such rarities as half bottles of the superlative 1961 Château Palmer in case lots. They were sourced from the Bordeaux négociant Mähler-Besse, part owner of Palmer. Over four months in 2007, Kurniawan's orders at Southwick totaled a quarter of a million dollars before airfreight fees. "I can assure you that everything was one hundred percent genuine," George Rhys, the firm's proprietor, tells me. "I have no worries whatsoever."

But Kurniawan also purchased old burgundy from Southwick that was of commercial rather than collectible quality. It was bottled by Seguin Manuel, a négociant in Beaune that was long in the second tier. Kurniawan was not known to sell Seguin Manuel wines, which would not have fetched attractive prices. Years would pass before it would become clear what his purpose in buying the wine was.

Unlike some collectors who reject bottles that do not appear pristine, Kurniawan didn't mind bedraggled bottles so long as the wine within held the promise of giving pleasure. Matthew Hayes, a British-born wine merchant and blogger living in France, once offered for sale a problematic cache of bottles and magnums of 1978 Jaboulet Hermitage La Chapelle, a prestigious Rhône Valley wine from a classic vintage. The drawback was that the bottles had spent twenty-five years in a damp English cellar, leaving their labels in a "parlous state." Jaboulet had promised to relabel the bottles but reneged. Few collectors would have wanted these besmirched bottles. But Kurniawan did.

On his lively blog, *Legless in Burgundy*, Hayes (a biking accident left him wheelchair bound) writes: "Rudy, Dr. Conti and Counterfeiter *extraordinaire* stepped up and paid me relatively top dollar for these *bona-fide* bottles. . . . So, if back in 2006 you bought a cache of La Chapelle '78 from Dr. C, even if the labels looked suspiciously new, I can guarantee that the wine was genuine. Let that be a relief!"

Hayes wasn't the only one to note Kurniawan's fearlessness in the face of a dirty label. A Los Angeles collector named Michael Zitterman tells of bumping into Kurniawan at a wine-storage facility where they both had lockers. Zitterman mentioned that he knew a woman who owned a single bottle of 1945 Mouton Rothschild. It had been given to her mother by her late father and now the daughter wanted to sell it on one condition: The purchaser was duty-bound to return the empty bottle to her to keep for its sentimental value.

Another complication was the appearance of the bottle. Years earlier, the home garage where the wine was stored had been hit by a flash flood. Many bottles had been soaked and caked in mud. "The Mouton was horrible-looking," says Zitterman. Kurniawan bought it anyway, for $3,000.

"I don't drink the label," he told Zitterman, who calls Kurniawan "a very unpretentious, very gentle little guy."

Most likely, that bottle of Mouton 1945 was real. So was its sentimental value to a mother and daughter. But what if it had been fake? Paul Hayes Tucker, a renowned expert on the paintings of the impressionist Claude Monet, has had to break the bad news to "hundreds" of owners who believed their work was created by the master's brush. "I tell them, very gently, that if they have gotten pleasure out of the picture for years, they should go right on with it." In the same way, anyone who has savored—as many of Kurniawan's clients did—wine that they did not realize was counterfeit, and even believed that it was the stuff of which mythic bottles are made, might well keep their pleasurable memories, even salute the skill of the one who made the wine—and resolve to more carefully check the provenance of the next big-ticket purchase.

Like Brian Devine, another corporate titan who put full trust in Kurniawan was billionaire David Doyle, cofounder of Quest Software. A global seeker of the best in food and drink, Doyle purchased epic amounts of wine from Kurniawan. Just three months after the gigantic Romanée-Conti tasting, Doyle received an offer from Kurniawan to purchase six bottles of 1945 Romanée-Conti. The price was $13,000 each. They were in a parcel whose total price was more than $3 million. Doyle, apparently startled to be offered this treasure, received an explanation in an error-littered email dated June 14, 2007, here quoted verbatim:

The 45 rc is not a mistake. I bought 19 btls 5 yrs ago from the cellar [i.e., "THE Cellar"] and drank 7 already including the tasting with Aubert and Allen meadows rated 100 pts. All same batch, there are btl variation based on what I've drank but none less than 97pts on the scale. (I sold 1 to Wilf before.) I am keeping 5 myself. I can send you Pics if you like . . . but as far as authenticity, I guarantee the. I would not sell any of these gem if I am not strap for cash, plus I know that you like and respect these wines as much, if not more, than I do . . . so, they will be in good hands!! :)

The next day, Kurniawan's Wells Fargo account received a wire deposit from Doyle for $3,227,000.

For months after alarm bells rang at the "faux Ponsot" auction, Doyle was still trusting. Twenty days after that auction, he wired $3.9 million to Kurniawan. Three months later, he remitted an additional $1.5 million. His total purchases from Kurniawan mounted to more than $15 million. All payments were wire transfers except for one: a 2004 Aston Martin Vanquish V12 sports car with just 850 miles on the odometer. Doyle valued the car at $200,000.

Another trusting customer was Michael Fascitelli, the former CEO of Vornado Realty Trust and, before that, head of real estate at Goldman Sachs. Fascitelli is a legendary deal maker, but when it came to wine, he was no match for Kurniawan. In autumn 2006, Kurniawan convinced Fascitelli to purchase 914 bottles of ultra-rare wine. Fascitelli wired payment of $5.5 million. Delivery was promised for the end of December. By the following spring, just 812 bottles had arrived. Robert Bohr was hired by Fascitelli as his wine consultant— but too late for him to head off the deal with Kurniawan.

"We were in his living room and his wife was in the kitchen when he showed me the spreadsheet of what he'd bought," Bohr tells me. "I said, 'Mike, there is no way.' People really wanted to believe. They really thought that one individual was special enough to have a full case of 1959 Roumier Musigny. At Cru, we had one of the biggest allocations of Roumier in the country. But we got only two bottles of his Musigny."

It took eight months for most but not all of Fascitelli's wines to arrive at a Mamaroneck, New York, warehouse. Instead of being in original containers, they were in "liquor boxes and Acker cartons." Bohr, his business partner David Beckwith, and a third expert inspected each bottle. "We all came to the same conclusion," says Bohr. "If these wines had been stored in a hermetically sealed vault in Switzerland, they would not have looked this good. Still, we had no proof."

Fascitelli heeded Bohr's suggestion that he hire an independent expert to inspect the wine. They selected Michael Egan, a respected Bordeaux-based consultant. His judgment, after spending three days in the warehouse, was that 691 of the 812 bottles (85 percent) were fakes.

Kurniawan had one more deal for Fascitelli, which he proposed in early April 2008. This one dwarfed the earlier transaction. Its cascade of heroic labels and vintages of bordeaux and burgundy filled eight closely spaced pages. Kurniawan estimated the value of this trove at $53.5 million. But he was willing to sell it all to Fascitelli for the bargain price of just $30 million. Buried in this offering was an astonishing cache of 220 bottles of Ponsot Clos Saint-Denis in vintages 1929 to 1971.

For Kurniawan, the timing of his offering could not have been worse. Barely one week after Fascitelli received the spreadsheet, Laurent Ponsot declared that Clos Saint-Denis from those vintages never existed.

Even without that thunderbolt, the grandiose offer to Fascitelli suggests that Kurniawan was flying off the rails. In that spring of 2008, he was mired in debt to Acker and a covey of its clients. Loans by auctioneers to important clients are nothing new. Like every other auctioneer, Acker must offer special monetary inducements if it wants to snag a big consignment away from the competition. For a time, few collectors carried more weight, or dangled the prospect of bigger commissions, than Kurniawan. His outstanding loans, nineteen in all between January and October 2007, totaled more than $8 million. The loans were to be repaid out of future auction proceeds, but the triumphs of his Cellar I and II sales would not be repeated.

One hard-knuckled loan agreement dated three months before the Cellar II auction states that Acker had already lent Kurniawan $6.75 million. Acker expected him to deliver $12 million worth of wine to its warehouse prior to that auction. Kurniawan also agreed to ship at his own expense $4.5 million in artworks to a New York warehouse as loan collateral. The works were to be put in Acker's name. Once the wine and art were received, Kurniawan would be loaned an additional $2.5 million. Each time he delivered additional wine worth $1.25 million to Acker, the auctioneer "will use its reasonable efforts to lend or arrange for a loan to Rudy in the amount of one million dollars."

The agreement acknowledges that Acker "intends to borrow the advance" to Kurniawan. Therefore, if he doesn't repay the loan on time, "there will be additional damages" that he must pay for. Acker's direct loans to Kurniawan were supplemented by additional loans from a bank and from certain Acker clients. Among them were Michael Fascitelli, hedge fund kingpin Robert Bishop, Edward Milstein, Robert Rosania (of the Twelve Angry Men), and Roy Welland, owner of Cru.

Many of the loans were direct wires. Another type of loan came as a special privilege during Acker auctions: Kurniawan was permitted to buy wines at the confidential reserve price when other bidders opted out. Auctioneers do not like to have to "pass" a wine lot, and Kurniawan was there to prevent that. Unlike other bidders, however, he did not have to pay promptly for the wine. The purchase price took the form of a loan. It was to be paid back, like the direct loans, from his future sales.

The catalogs for the Cellar I and II auctions trumpeted an unusually liberal return policy. It was spelled out under the header "Special Conditions of Sale for THE Cellar": "There will be a money-back guarantee for any unopened bottles purchased at this sale UNTIL 90 DAYS AFTER THE SALE." This was a departure from standard auction house conditions of sale, which permit no returns unless the lot as delivered is misrepresented in the catalog description. While Kurniawan stood behind the guarantee for the Cellar auctions, it was Acker that had to pay up once wine was returned. The returns from just two heavy bidders at Cellar II, Don Stott and Ed Milstein, totaled $1.09 million. It was up to Acker to recoup the money from Kurniawan. Acker's accounting to Kurniawan early in 2007 shows that, after all loan repayments and reimbursements to customers who returned wine were subtracted from the $25.5 million proceeds from the Cellar II sale, Kurniawan ended up *owing* Acker $15,500.

All that year, Kurniawan kept borrowing from Acker and its clients—at least fourteen times. Based on his frenetic wine-buying, it appears that he was intent on replenishing his legitimate cellar after the big depletions the year before. On a single day (April 23, 2007), he purchased wines for $11,000 from Magnum Wines in Chicago, $36,000 from Wally's Wine in Los Angeles, $1,900 from Brentwood Wine Company in Oregon, and, in six separate transactions, $136,000 from New York Wine Warehouse. The next day, he purchased wines for $32,000 from New York Wine Warehouse and $14,000 from Hart Davis Hart in Chicago. He also reached out to a pair of London firms, spending $27,000 at Elliston Fine Wines and $69,000 at Southwick Court Fine Wines. That day, too, he paid $22,000 to Connoisseur International Distribution, a British shipping service that specializes in airfreighting wine.

While Kurniawan's black American Express card was getting an almost daily workout, his financial situation was hurting. Late in 2007, he applied for a $3 million loan from Fine Art Capital, an arm of Emigrant Savings Bank specializing in loans secured by works of art. The bank is owned by the Milstein family, one of whose members is Edward Milstein, who bought wine from Kurniawan privately as well as through Acker. The two men were also occasional drinking companions. According to FAC loan officer Barbara Chu, tasked with checking out Kurniawan's loan application, Milstein told her that Kurniawan was "one of the world's top-five wine collectors" and had sold more than $30 million of wine over the previous two years through Acker.

The applicant claimed overseas family wealth, but, Chu noted, "As is typical of such families, the details and distribution of family holdings is not widely known, even by family members." Kurniawan's income, Chu concluded, was "nominal." His primary assets were two personal residences worth $11.2 million, a $15 million wine collection, and art worth $8.7 million. His debts, consisting of mortgages and tax liability, were $7.75 million. Chu pegged his net worth as $33.9 million, cautioning that his assets were "almost entirely illiquid."

Kurniawan's loan application omitted the fact that he owed millions of dollars to Acker and certain of its customers. Despite his sketchy financials, the loan was approved—although not before Kurniawan pledged twenty-five artworks as collateral. All were by big-name artists, including Andy Warhol, Ed Ruscha, Robert Indiana, Damien Hirst, Richard Prince, and Donald Judd. There were also works by Qiu Zhijie and the avant-gardist Gu Wenda, some of whose pieces incorporated semen, placentae, and sanitary napkins solicited from women from sixty countries.

Barbara Chu twice called Kurniawan in December 2007 to try to get a better handle on his financial situation. What were his annual expenses excluding mortgage payments? He estimated them at $150,000. That was way low. That month, he spent $10,000 on air charter services. On January 9, 2008, as he awaited loan approval, he charged $121,585 at Hermès and $2,600 for dinner at Eleven

Madison Park, one of New York's priciest restaurants. The next day he was back at Hermès, charging $68,000 and, the day after that, an additional $18,661. There were also visits to the Louis Vuitton and YSL boutiques. It had taken him just two days to charge his way through the annual personal expense estimate submitted to Chu.

Additional millions of dollars passed through his personal checking account at Wells Fargo Bank. The deeper Kurniawan plunged into debt, the more he spent.

Chu approved the loan, but the terms were tough. Besides the ample cushion of art collateral, a $60,000 origination fee and a $50,000 "due diligence" fee were subtracted from the $3 million loan. Kurniawan's real interest rate was nearly 13 percent. On January 18, the day he got the loan, he contributed $64,000 to Project Angel Food, which provides meals to homebound people with AIDS and other illnesses. The next week, he contributed $100,000 to City-meals on Wheels.

He might have gotten half a leg up and over his wall of debt if Laurent Ponsot had not blocked the Acker auction that fateful spring and if he could have succeeded in sealing the $30 million sale to Michael Fascitelli, or even a portion of it. Instead, with his reputation tarnished and his credit card spending unabated, he was stumbling. Added to his personal spending were continuing purchases of wine from European and American dealers, which he planned to resell at Acker auctions. But that was not to be.

One week after the faux Ponsot auction, Acker moved to protect its overdue loans to its former star client. Kurniawan was forced to sign a security agreement that blocked him from selling any and all wine in his possession or held at a warehouse used by Acker. He also agreed to pledge eighteen artworks as collateral against the unpaid loans. He failed to tell Acker that those same works were among the twenty-five already pledged to FAC.

Seven months later, both FAC and Acker discovered the double-pledging scheme. Rather than declare Kurniawan's loan to be in default, FAC secured his agreement to auction off the pledged artworks. Most went on the block at Christie's in spring 2009. Despite the recent Wall Street meltdown, they sold well: $722,500 for a Zhang Xiaogang, $880,000 for an Ed Ruscha, and $626,500 for Damien Hirst's *Acetylnucleic Acid (Spot Painting)*. In all, the proceeds exceeded $3 million. That was more than sufficient to cover FAC's loan exposure. The surplus of $551,000 went to Acker as partial pay down on its loans to Kurniawan.

Three weeks after FAC closed down the loan, Kurniawan was dealt another blow. This was when Acker compelled him to file the sworn "confession of judgment" in a New York court admitting that he owed Acker and its clients an astonishing $10.4 million. That sum included principal and interest on overdue loans, unpaid wine purchases, and legal costs. Attached to the confession was a list of fourteen loans extended to him in 2007. Apparently, Barbara Chu at FAC knew nothing about those loans.

Along with his financial struggle, Kurniawan was faced with the shredding of his reputation as a dealer boasting a wizard-like knack for offering rarest wines. Most sensational was the Ponsot debacle, but one year earlier, he had suffered a far less public hit at the Christie's auction in Los Angeles where the catalog cover featured six magnums of 1982 Château Le Pin, the micro-jewel of Pomerol. Le Pin produced only 250 cases in 1982. A bare handful were in magnums. Robert Parker called 1982 Le Pin "as thrilling a wine as I have ever tasted." The price shot up accordingly. Proprietor Jacques Thienpont had released the 1982 at $11 per bottle. By 2006, it had sold at auction for more than $5,000 per bottle. At the Los Angeles sale, the six magnums were estimated to sell for as much as $100,000 plus a buyer's premium of 18.5 percent. The catalog listed no provenance for the six magnums other than to identify them as the "property of a fine wine connoisseur." That was code for Kurniawan.

Thienpont and his wife, Fiona Morrison (she holds the British credential master of wine), were alerted to the Christie's sale by a rival auction house, said to be Sotheby's. Viewing the catalog photos of the magnums, they noted a small detail on the labels, known only to them, that was incorrect for the 1982 vintage. Duly warned, Christie's was forced to call in an independent specialist. The capsules were cut from the necks of the magnums to reveal the corks. According to a person who was on hand, one of the corks was blank. Le Pin does not have blank corks, ever. Christie's quietly withdrew its banner lot from the sale.

The withdrawal of his sale-leading Le Pin magnums was a defeat for Kurniawan. But he could celebrate the successful sale of the trio of magnums on the catalog's back cover. They were labeled as Georges Roumier 1962 Bonnes-Mares. These magnums, like the Le Pins, were listed as the "property of a fine wine connoisseur." Followers of Acker auctions would recall that Kurniawan had many times offered 1962 and other old vintages of Roumier Bonnes-Mares. At this sale, the three magnums sold for $66,175.

This catalog was sprinkled with other high-priced lots that should have begotten suspicion. Why did the labels of several DRC lots—a case of 1962 La Tâche, a case of six magnums of the same wine, a magnum of 1959 Romanée-Conti, three magnums and a full case of 1971 Romanée-Conti—all have the same anomaly: an accent mark over the *e* in *propriétaire*? With one exception, that accent did not appear on authentic DRC labels until 1978. (The exception was a small number of 1971s released later than normal to DRC's new American importer, Wilson Daniels. However, that importer's sticker is absent from the three magnums of 1971 Romanée-Conti in the catalog photos, making it unlikely that they are late releases.)

The DRC lots listed above, carrying that errant accent, were estimated to fetch as much as half a million dollars. All found buyers. The most glamorous lot in the sale was a case of 1945 Mouton Rothschild, a contender for the greatest Bordeaux red wine made in the twentieth century. It was estimated to sell for up to $150,000. But those bottles, like the DRCs, had an anomaly: The serial number on the label of each bottle was stamped on a slant in baby-blue ink. The normal color of Mouton's serial numbers is black and they are not slanted. Time would tell that the baby-blue stamping originated with the unnamed "fine wine connoisseur." The lot did not sell.

The year ended for Kurniawan with new trouble, this time with Andrew Gordon, a Goldman Sachs partner. Gordon had paid Kurniawan $2.2 million for old and rare wines, but not before asking about their provenance. Kurniawan responded that the wines were sourced from auctions, private sales, and the Nicolas cellar he claimed to have purchased, although he provided no paper trail. But Gordon did require him to sign a legal agreement that he would "repurchase the wines at fair market value if [Gordon] was unable to sell the wines 'due to lack of traceable provenance,'" according to an FBI sealed complaint filed in 2012.

Some months after his purchase, Gordon threw a dinner party at which wine specialists from an unnamed auction house were hired to handle the wine. As described later in the FBI complaint, "During the course of the evening, [Gordon] was informed by the Wine Professionals that they had tasted the wine being offered that night and that two of the bottles were, in their judgment, counterfeit. Both bottles were from Kurniawan."

When Gordon brought up these concerns, a cocksure Kurniawan responded, according to the sealed complaint, that "sometimes the experts do not even know what they are drinking." He wasn't wrong about that.

The next year, Gordon invited an unnamed auction house to inspect five hundred bottles that he wanted to sell. All were rejected owing to "too many discrepancies with the bottles and labels." Most, perhaps all, of the bottles were from Kurniawan. Gordon now wanted all his money back. Kurniawan agreed, but failed to follow through. In spring 2009, the $2.2 million debt was converted into a "note and security agreement" obligating Kurniawan to sell at least

$2.5 million worth of wine during the coming autumn at Christie's New York. Gordon was to be repaid out of the proceeds. One month after the security agreement was inked, it was reinforced by a new one warranting that Kurniawan had "good and marketable title" to all the wines slated to be auctioned.

In that agreement, Kurniawan also warranted that he had gotten "approval of all appropriate persons to grant the security interest" in the collateralized wine. He also agreed to notify Christie's that Gordon had a "first priority security interest" in the consigned wines. Gordon must have thought that he had buttoned down his payback. But he didn't yet know that Kurniawan had already signed a similar agreement with John Kapon one year earlier. That agreement called for Kurniawan to keep his wines "free and clear of all liens and claims whatsoever."

Kurniawan had already double-collateralized his art. Now he had done it with his wine. For his Christie's sale of Gordon's wines, the auctioneer required the wines to be sold "free and clear of all liens, claims and encumbrances." Kurniawan agreed to do that without revealing his security agreements with Gordon and Acker. He instructed that payment of his proceeds from the sale be made only to himself.

Gordon soon found out about Kurniawan's directive to be sole beneficiary of the upcoming Christie's sale. On August 20, a new consignment agreement was signed by Kurniawan, this one stating, "Seller has since informed Christie's that Gordon holds liens on the Property. Seller now represents and warrants that there are no liens on the Property other than the ones held by Gordon."

That was false because Acker still had claim on *all* Kurniawan's wines.

Barely a day before the Christie's September 2009 auction, Acker also discovered the unpermitted sale. Once again, Christie's had to change the consignment agreement. Now it stated: "Acker also holds liens on the property." Kapon was furious. Hours before the auction, he wrote to Kurniawan: "You have some freaking nerve. The ONLY reason we are in this position is because you put us all here, trying to sneak around our security agreement hoping we wouldn't notice. Are you kidding me? You have known full well you couldn't sell ANY of your wines without our written consent—but you did it anyway."

Kurniawan's garbled response: "I have not done anything behind, this wines [sic] belonged to Gordon, not me."

Geoffrey Troy was as upset as Kapon over the impending Christie's auction, but for a different reason. As required by state law, Christie's needed a retail partner, and for years it had been Troy's firm. On catalog covers, its name came first: "NYWinesChristie's." Troy's own name was listed on the inside front cover along with the listings of Christie's staff. Troy had sounded an early alarm about the faux Ponsot wines. More than a year later, Kurniawan had yet to reveal their source to Ponsot or Kapon. His reputation among collectors was badly compromised. When Kurniawan was flying high, Troy had sold him more than $4 million worth of wine—"*Real* wine," says Troy.

Yet here was Christie's about to offer 56 Kurniawan lots at a September 2009 auction and 139 more in October. In neither catalog was the consignor identified beyond being described as "a long time friend to Christie's." (Given that Kurniawan was just turning thirty-three, that characterization was a bit of a stretch.)

Bluntly put, both catalogs were studded with photos of certain bottles that appeared to be hugely expensive counterfeits, each carrying tiny but telling anomalies that were the marks of Christie's "long time friend." There was a four-bottle lot of 1959 Romanée-Conti (sold for $28,800) and a five-bottle lot of 1962 Romanée-Conti (sold for $48,000). Two magnums of 1962 La Tâche ("an ultra rare treasure") sold for $42,000. Clearly visible in the full-page photos of most of these bottles, on the main labels, were the errant *accents aigus* over *propriétaire* that did not appear on authentic bottles until years later.

Elsewhere, in photos of other bottles, bumpy, dull red wax capsules similarly betrayed Kurniawan's handiwork.

Troy felt it was wrong—dishonest, even—to offer Kurniawan's dicey wines to unsuspecting bidders. Christie's, after all, had already been stung by the debacle of the six magnums of Le Pin it had been forced to withdraw in 2007. Troy put his protest in a letter to the auctioneer, and also wrote a spate of emails opposing the sale. Additionally, he complained to Charles Curtis, the recently appointed head wine specialist for Christie's in North America. Deep into the night prior to the September 12 auction, according to Troy, Christie's lawyers and wine specialists pondered what to do. Christie's London-based head of wine, David Elswood, joined in the deliberations. In the end, the assembled experts and lawyers opted to go forward with selling the wine.

Proceeds from the September sales totaled $698,326. That sum was split by Andrew Gordon and Acker to partially satisfy their liens on Kurniawan's wines. The October sales brought in another $508,050 to satisfy Acker's lien.

Troy soon separated from Christie's as its retail partner. Curtis, a master of wine, was promoted to head of wine sales for North America, then took over as head of wine for Christie's Asia.

By that autumn of 2009, Kurniawan's finances and reputation as a dealer (he had yet to reveal the source of the faux Ponsots) were in total tatters. Worse yet, he would soon feel the wrath of the billionaire from Kansas who was on a scorched-earth, cost-be-damned crusade against wine counterfeiting and the auctioneers and dealers who did not do enough to combat it.

CHAPTER 6

The Sheriff

What could bring sudden tears to the eyes of a gruff industrial titan, an admirer of the Wild West and its six-shooter justice, as he was being interviewed on a 2014 segment of ABC'S investigative TV show *20/20*?

The answer lay in Bill Koch's two wine cellars, one in his Palm Beach home, just up South Ocean Boulevard from Donald Trump's Mar-a-Lago, the other at his Cape Cod summer place. Belatedly, he learned that both cellars had been infiltrated by counterfeit wine. He put the number of fakes, as identified by experts who prowled his cellars and tested bottles in overseas laboratories, at no more than four hundred. That wasn't a lot in a collection exceeding forty thousand bottles. But these were among the most expensive wines he owned. They cost him $4 million.

Those bottles were hateful to him, and his anger at discovering the truth about what he thought were genuinely rare wines was inflamed by much more than monetary loss. "A great wine, like a great painting, has been made with an artist's love," he told me. "You share it with friends and together you appreciate its beauty. To find out that it's fake is like you've celebrated a Black Mass."

And then Koch switches imagery, his delft-blue eyes taking on an icy hue: "I abide by the rules of the Old West. If you cheat me, I'm coming after you."

And so he did. In a decade-long hunt, Koch saddled up and chased auction houses, retail merchants, and individuals whom he believed had sold him false goods in a bottle. His chosen weapons were not blazing six-guns, of course, although he owns a vast collection of historically important firearms, including General Custer's rifle and Jesse James' gun and even the gun used to fatally shoot the infamous bandit. Instead, Koch mobilized an international strike force of lawyers, scientists, and private investigators against the shadowy foe. Retired agents of the FBI and CIA as well as Britain's Scotland Yard and Military Intelligence Section 6 (MI6) went on Koch's payroll to comb the United States, Europe, and Asia to uncover facts about the fakes and fakers. One investigation would feed into another, and Kurniawan himself would end up in Koch's crosshairs. In two meetings with Kurniawan at Los Angeles eateries, Koch's investigators probed for information about fakes in his cellar. Koch even sent investigators to Singapore, China, and Indonesia to collect facts about Kurniawan, his family, and its purported wealth. In Jakarta, Koch hired a former CIA station chief to do the snooping.

Opening a scientific front, Koch sent a gamma ray detector to the University of Bordeaux, where physicist Philippe Hubert tested suspect very old bottles for traces of the radioactive isotope cesium-137. Before the first nuclear bomb test in July 1945, cesium-137 had been absent from the atmosphere—and from wine. All vintages thereafter had a trace of the isotope. The first gamma ray detector sent by Koch was too small to hold magnum bottles, so he sent a second, larger device. When Hubert refused to accept payment for his services, Koch donated both machines to the physicist's laboratory.

Labeling on questionable bottles was another avenue for investigation. Koch invited Eric Soulat, a Bordelais printer, to Palm Beach. Soulat's family firm had designed and printed labels for château bottlings for generations. He arrived with his wife and a satchel packed with archival labels, including early vintages of Pétrus. He spent two weeks examining labels in Koch's cellar. On this, their first US visit, Koch lent the couple his beach house in Palm Beach. The Soulats then flew to Koch's Cape Cod home (also waterfront), where Soulat examined labels in Koch's summer cellar. Over three weeks, he identified more than one hundred fake labels.

The bill for Koch's legal and investigative efforts would eventually surpass $20 million. In spring 2016, when Koch sold twenty thousand bottles—slightly less than half his wine—his chosen auctioneer, Sotheby's, estimated that the sale would fetch between $11.5 and $15 million. When the final lot was hammered down, the total had reached $21.9 million. "No matter how much the wine sells for," Koch had said on the eve of the sale, "it will not make up for what I've spent to fight the fakers." That was a fact, not a lament.

❧

Growing up wealthy but unspoiled in Wichita, Kansas, Koch was one of four sons of a brilliant oil refinery engineer and a handsome, socialite mother whom he feels did not give him enough love. He was schooled early in fraternal combat. He and his twin brother, David, fought regularly with words and fists. In *Sons of Wichita*, a biography of the Koch clan, Daniel Schulman recounts how, when tempers flared, a family property manager loaded the tall and rangy twins into a pickup truck and drove them to a desolate spot. He laced up their boxing gloves and stood back while the boys flailed away their anger.

The twins both attended Massachusetts Institute of Technology, their dad's alma mater. Athletic as well as academically gifted, they played on the basketball team. David was the better player. "My brother was the team's center, and he still holds an MIT scoring record," Bill says. "I mostly sat on the bench." Bill earned three MIT degrees, including a ScD, all in chemical engineering. "We'd have parties once a month to break up the pressure of hard work," he says. "I got hepatitis and couldn't drink for a number of years, which was great. Saved me from being an alcoholic." Koch discovered that, while he couldn't drink the hard stuff, he could drink wine, and that it was "the best-tasting form of alcohol out there."

Despite an attack of sciatica that left him pale with pain, David Koch attended a grand dinner, awash in great wines, cohosted by his twin in Sotheby's Manhattan boardroom in May 2016. It was the eve of the three-day, record-breaking auction of just half of Bill's collection. The walls of the boardroom were ornamented with great art (including an early cubist Picasso in my sightline). The wines to be poured with dinner—samples of lots to be offered at the auction—were massed in a side room. No matter whether you favored Bordeaux, Burgundy, or Rhône wines, there would be superlative examples in your glass.

Koch, long and lanky in a dark blue, gold-buttoned suit, pink window-paned shirt, and nautical-themed tie and socks, rose to greet the guests. He was in high spirits despite having to bid adieu to so much expensive wine that would be drunk instead of bid on. And determined, it seemed, not to let the proceedings get too solemn, even if that meant making light of himself. Acknowledging his brother, Koch said, "He's the real Koch brother. I'm the black sheep." At MIT, "he got the girls. I got the textbooks." Recalling his introduction to wine in those days, Koch said, "I started with Château Twist-Off. Then I drank Lancers, because it had a cork in it. I got to the point where I bought a $100,000 bottle, but it was fake."

While Bill was building his cellar, he was also battling David and their older brother, Charles. The two of them could be as cool as he was impulsive. The legal firefights between the brothers lasted nearly twenty years. At issue were sore points centered on stock valuation of Koch Industries, the vast energy enterprise built by their father. For many of those years, the twins did not speak to each other except through lawyers. Eventually, Bill separated from the family business, taking with him an abundant fortune. Only in their sixties did the twins make up. At Bill's 2002 wedding to Bridget Rooney (her family founded the Pittsburgh Steelers), David was his best man.

Back at the Sotheby's dinner, Koch recalled a late night escapade at his Cape Cod compound where he and Netscape cofounder James Clark, burgundy lovers both, drank "three bottles *each*." Now that they were fully fueled, Clark proposed that they launch Koch's mahogany-hulled Chris-Craft for a post-midnight spin on Nantucket Sound. In the dark, the boat suddenly halted. Its propeller had become ensnared in a buoy's sturdy mooring rope. "Being a macho guy, I pulled out my Swiss Army knife." Here, Bill pulled that very knife out of his jacket pocket. He had tried to cut through the rope, but to no avail. They were stuck for the rest of the night. Koch, lightly dressed and no longer warmed by good burgundy, felt cold, and Clark lay on top of him to keep him warm. "He snored and farted all night long," Koch said. At dawn, they were rescued, "and by about 6 AM, they were in the hot tub."

"I think that's enough, Bill," David called out from the far end of the room. But the other guests were happy to hear more, and Bill, as generous with his anecdotes as with his wine, needed no encouragement. Not every billionaire can make light of himself, but Koch had no problem doing that. As the evening wound down, the old sailor delivered a farewell toast: "There are good ships and wood ships that sail the seas, but the best ships are friendships, and may they always be." The exception would be any ship cargoed with counterfeit wine. Koch would do his best to send that vessel to the bottom of the briny deep.

The last word went to Koch's cohost, Sotheby's wine head Jamie Ritchie, a gentle-mannered Englishman, as reserved as Koch was freewheeling. Turning to his cohost, he said, "Many enjoy wine. Few pour it so freely." Indeed. The evening had begun with 1985 Krug champagne in magnums and concluded with 1959 Château Latour. It was a selection worthy of Kurniawan in his glory days.

Koch got serious about collecting wine in the 1980s. "My wife calls me a hoarder," he says. And not only a hoarder of wine. As a serial collector, he has chased after diverse artistic and historic objects that spill out onto the lawns of his Palm Beach home. Once a visitor is cleared to pass through the high-walled front gate, his penchant for big sculpture comes into view. At the top of the lawn is *The River*, a strong female figure by Aristide Maillol. It reclines at the edge of a flowing pool created for it. Flanking the left side of the entrance portico is a bulbous, five-figure family (mother, father, child, dog, and cat) sculpted by the Colombian Fernando Botero. On the right, a second Botero cat, this one gigantic, glares hungrily at the family. On the even more generous back lawn are diverse works: a blue Robert Indiana *LOVE* resting on a travertine marble base, a batch more of Boteros, and, at one end of the swimming pool, a double water slide with gangly arms. It was commissioned from Tom Otterness, known to New Yorkers for his mischievous sculptures in several West Side subway stations and in the parks of Battery Park City. Like the Koch brothers, Otterness is Wichita-born.

The house is designed in easygoing Mediterranean style. The front doors open to a sitting room. On the right hangs a nearly abstract Monet water lily painting. Opposite it is a reclining Modigliani nude, painted in 1916. A similar nude by the same artist sold for $170 million at Christie's New York in 2015. The model's arms are cast back behind her head and one knee is thrust up. Her skin glows in warm tones of orange and brown. The painting is so loved by Koch that it goes with him between homes (as do the Botero sculptures). Standing in front of it one Sunday afternoon in 2014, Koch asked me, "Do you think she just had sex and is satisfied, or had it and is ready for more?"

Koch uttered his most public sexual remark upon his startling victory in the 1992 America's Cup race. He called the triumph of his yacht, *America3*, over the Italian yacht *Il Moro* "better than ten thousand orgasms." The racing establishment had sneered at this son of a landlocked state who had never raced for high stakes and who compared the wind blowing at sea to "waves of wheat." The scorn of others only incited him to be innovative in designing a winning racing yacht. Reportedly, Koch also sent divers down to secretly inspect the hulls of rival craft. He also insisted on being a skipper of the winning crew, even though he had been counseled that all hands should be experienced competitive sailors.

A significant swath of underground space at Koch's home is dedicated to a fleet of precisely rendered, dramatically lit models of each and every defender and challenger that competed in the America's Cup yacht since the debut race in 1851. That display room adjoins Koch's wine cellar. The bottles are stored in a splendid march of arched chambers built from antique, buff-toned brick laid in herringbone pattern. Key sightlines are ornamented with ancient mosaics. The sixteenth-century stone floor was imported from Austria. European artisans were brought in to construct this palace of wine, so generous in proportion and rich in appointment that windows would only be an intrusion.

Koch divides the inventory into wines for collecting and wines for drinking. Those he won't pull the cork on include the consecutive vintages of his beloved quartet of the crème de la crème of bordeaux wines. There's plenty left for drinking. On that Sunday afternoon in 2014, Koch called for his hefty cellar book and asked me what I'd like to drink with lunch. No respectful guest would have dared to pick the wines that Koch proposed, least of all 1961 Château Pétrus. The previous evening, two magnums of that wine sold at auction in New York for $79,625.

At the rear of Koch's wine cellar is a nook enclosed by heavy wrought-iron bars. Its inmates are four bulbous, darkly tinted bottles that Koch once believed were his collection's most precious holdings. They are the infamous Jefferson bottles: Château Branne Mouton 1787 and 1784, and Château Lafite 1787 and 1784. The letters "Th. J." etched into the bottles are the reason that Koch paid $400,000 for them. If authentic, these bottles would likely have been owned by a founding father who was a wine collector as avid as Koch.

In 1985, a single Jefferson bottle had been auctioned off at Christie's London, generating intense excitement. The sale was a coup for Michael Broadbent, who as head of the firm's wine department had probably tasted more historic wines than anyone else on earth. In an insert to the auction's catalog, Broadbent had written in detail about various theories supporting the authenticity of both the bottle and the etching. He did add that those theories were "impossible to substantiate either way," but added that "we are confident that we have in this sale more than a little bit of history." The winning bidder was Christopher Forbes, whose father, Malcolm, was as obsessive a collector of historic objects as Bill Koch. The price paid by young Forbes, $157,000, is still one of the most expensive single bottles of wine ever sold at auction. The consignor of the bottle had been none other than Hardy Rodenstock, purveyor of many a suspect bottle of very old Pétrus and other rarities.

Unsurprisingly, Rodenstock was soon discovering more Jefferson bottles. Koch's interests in rare wine and American history converged in these artifacts. After Forbes' record purchase of a single bottle, Koch purchased a single bottle of his own from Chicago Wine Company, then three more from Farr Vintners, a leading London retailer. These squat bottles, smaller than a modern bottle and so dark that the liquid within couldn't be seen, were for a brief time the pride of

Koch's wine collection. Quite the opposite is true now, but Koch still takes perverse pleasure in showing them off to guests.

He might have lived happily ever after with his Jefferson bottles and all his other fakes had not the Museum of Fine Arts (MFA) in Boston mounted a giant exhibition of diverse art and objects from his collection in 2005. Called *Things I Love: The Many Collections of William I. Koch*, it included the installation of two yachts on the museum's front lawn. Set at rakish angles, as if the wind were freshening their sails, they were *America3*, his victorious America's Cup yacht, and the vanquished *Il Moro*, which Koch purchased after the race. Koch says the museum also wanted to show his Jefferson bottles. MFA curators routinely asked for information about provenance. Koch had nothing specific to provide. He had relied on the assurances of Michael Broadbent, who had written in the 1985 Christie's catalog insert that "there is an immense amount of circumstantial evidence supporting [Jefferson's] ordering of this wine and its identification, but, of course, no proof." The "circumstantial evidence" wasn't good enough for the curators. They wanted to see a paper trail, or other explicit evidence, that the bottles had belonged to Jefferson.

Koch's team of investigators was directed by Brad Goldstein, his in-house troubleshooter. A feisty ex-journalist, standing only shoulder-high to Koch, Goldstein worked out of an office next to his boss's in West Palm Beach. Tasked with finding evidence about the Jefferson bottles, Goldstein contacted the Thomas Jefferson Foundation at Monticello, keeper of Jefferson's voluminous archive. A researcher there responded, "Jefferson's daily account book, virtually all of his letters, his banker's statements, and miscellaneous internal French customs forms survive for this period and mention no 1787 vintages."

In fact, the provenance of the Jefferson bottles was always alarm-bell sketchy. The tale told by their purveyor, Hardy Rodenstock, was that the bottles were discovered sealed away behind a wall in the cellar of an ancient house in Paris that was being demolished. Rodenstock waved away the two obvious questions: Who had sold him the bottles and what was the location of the house? The French are loath to pay taxes, he explained, and therefore the seller wanted neither his identity revealed nor the spot where the bottles had supposedly slumbered for centuries.

That explanation looked empty in the light of the Jefferson Foundation's doubts. It now dawned on Koch that his Jefferson bottles might more accurately be called the Rodenstock bottles. The controversy ignited a debate over the most reliable way to judge whether a wine of uncertain provenance is true or false. Should a tasting by experts be the decisive factor? Broadbent had done the taste test by opening one of the Jefferson bottles, a 1787 Branne Mouton. He pronounced it "sensationally good," adding, "If anyone had any lingering doubts about the authenticity of this extraordinary old wine, they were completely removed."

Broadbent's catalog prose had halted a well-honed knife edge away from actually pronouncing that the bottles once belonged to Jefferson. "Admittedly, there is no written evidence that these particular bottles had been in the possession of Jefferson, but I am now firmly convinced that this indeed was the wine that Jefferson ordered."

James Elroy, a retired FBI agent hired by Koch, hand-carried his four Jefferson bottles and two other supposed eighteenth-century bottles to France to be tested for the presence of cesium-137. This was before Koch's donation of gamma ray machines to the University of Bordeaux, so the bottles were tested in a lead-lined chamber deep under a mountain in the Alps. To Elroy's extreme disappointment, the liquid within was free of the isotope. Whatever its age, it predated 1945. Broadbent's claim that not only the Jefferson bottles but the wine within was from Jefferson's time had not been disproved.

Elroy's suspicion was confirmed by an expert at the Corning Glass Museum in upstate New York. The markings were judged to have been etched by an electric dental drill or possibly even a

Dremel tool, available at any good hardware store. Years later, a team of investigative journalists from the German magazine *Stern*, working in conjunction with Koch, would track down the two engravers. They lived in the same town in the Black Forest where Rodenstock had resided. In a videotaped interview, the engravers admitted that an unidentified person paid them to etch Jefferson's initials into the antique bottles.

Having nailed down the incriminating facts, Koch sued Rodenstock in a New York federal court in 2006, claiming that he had orchestrated the fraud. Finding that the court had no jurisdiction over the defendant, a judge tossed out the lawsuit. Koch amended his complaint, and in 2008 got a default judgment against Rodenstock, who had refused to appear in New York.

The Jefferson bottle investigation led Koch to focus on the provenance of the rest of his collection. So he began to "pull back the curtain on Oz," as he later put it. Behind it, he first found Eric Greenberg, a northern California Internet mogul turned rare wine dealer. Koch had purchased nineteen supposedly ultra-rare bottles of bordeaux at two Zachys wine auctions in 2004. They were among hundreds of Koch's bottles that were eventually identified as fakes by a parade of experts who examined the contents of his cellar.

The consignor had been Greenberg. Koch claimed that this seller knew, or should have known, that the wines he sold through Zachys were fake. Koch also sued Zachys on the grounds that its experts, too, should have identified the fakes and refused to sell them. Zachys eventually settled. The next year, Koch sued Chicago Wine Company for selling him fifteen fake bottles, including a Jefferson bottle. He also sued Julienne Importing Company, also of Chicago, accusing it of being the source of wines he purchased from Chicago Wine Company. And he sued Royal Wine, a New York retailer, accusing it of hawking fake wines that the firm sourced from Rodenstock.

Koch next took aim at Acker Merrall & Condit, claiming in a lawsuit that he had paid $77,895 for four bottles that he learned were counterfeit: a 1949 Lafleur, a 1947 Pétrus, and two bottles of 1934 Romanée-Conti. Kapon's public response was conciliatory. "We go to extreme lengths to try and make sure that every bottle of wine that we sell is as described. . . . If a few fraudulent bottles out of hundreds purchased went undetected, then we stand ready to refund Mr. Koch's, or any purchaser's, money."

Koch's lawsuit against Acker, dated April 23, 2008, does not name Kurniawan as the source of the fake bottles. Koch did, however, suspect that it was Kurniawan, but he says that "Kapon refused to corroborate." Two days after the filing, Kapon was forced to withdraw the faux Ponsots. All suspicious eyes now focused on Kurniawan. The next year, Koch directly sued Kurniawan for selling him those bottles. The lawsuit, filed in a California court, charged fraud and asked for damages to be determined at trial.

The following year, Koch sued Christie's, charging that it and Hardy Rodenstock were "involved in a continuing scheme to sell counterfeit wines." Since he had purchased one of his Jefferson bottles in Chicago, the three others in London, and none from Christie's, that aspect of the lawsuit was a stretch. But, Koch argued, he never would have purchased the bottles if Christie's had not lent its prestige to the Jefferson bottle tale. "The reason I bought the Jefferson wines is because Michael Broadbent authenticated them," Koch told *Wine Spectator*. And he also charged that a bottle of 1870 Château Lafite that he bought from Christie's was a fake, as he suspected it would be even before he bid on it. The bottle cost him $4,200.

Koch had this bottle, too, tested for cesium-137. The test was positive, proving that the wine in the purported 1870 bottle was modern.

"To me, the simple, straightforward solution to this problem was for Christie's to recognize that its wine department was acting as an independent, rogue division, admit it, and clean it up immediately," Koch told *Wine Spectator* at the time he sued the auctioneer. "That would have resulted in an easy settlement with me and greatly enhanced Christie's reputation in the collectors' world as an auction house that will not tolerate selling fakes of any kind."

"We have great respect for Mr. Koch," a Christie's spokesman responded. "We believe the allegations in this complaint are incorrect." From the other side of the Atlantic, Broadbent called Koch "an absolute bully."

Federal judge Barbara Jones ruled against Koch, pointing out that by buying a wine that he already suspected was fake, he was no longer playing the part of a reasonable consumer: "He was acting as an investigator who chose to pay $4,200 despite knowledge that the wine was worth far less." Koch appealed Jones' decision, but to no avail. In 2012, an appellate panel ruled that Koch had delayed too long in bringing suit. After all, doubts about the Jefferson bottles had surfaced as early as 2000. "For wine, timing is critical," wrote district judge John Koeltl for the three-judge panel. "The same is true for causes of action."

At this point, the costs of Koch's lawsuits were hefty. Now, with the approach of his first trial, they were about to become outlandish. In the spring of 2013, after four years of skirmishing, Koch began a civil fraud proceeding in Manhattan against Eric Greenberg. Koch accused Greenberg of consigning at least two dozen counterfeit bottles to Zachys. Koch had bought them for $355,000 at an auction at which he spent a total of $3.7 million. Among his purchases were the once impossible to find but now commonly offered magnums of 1947, 1949, and 1950 Château Lafleur. Koch even picked up a few nineteenth-century first growths, including a bottle of 1864 Château Latour. None of the contested bottles had been sourced from Kurniawan (most could be traced back to Hardy Rodenstock, whose conduit to American collectors was Manhattan retailer Royal Wine Company), but this trial would open a window on Kurniawan's early days as a wine dealer as well as showcase the breadth of Koch's investigations.

In *Koch v. Greenberg*, the opponents differed starkly in background, although they had in common an entrepreneurial spirit. Greenberg, born in Brooklyn, grew up in Las Vegas. His father was a Clairol salesman who barely scraped by, his mother a casino worker. In early years, Greenberg worked as a shoe salesman. Greenberg founded two consulting firms in the 1990s, while Koch built an industrial empire of his own after separating from the family business. When the dot-com bubble popped in 2000, much of Greenberg's wealth evaporated. By then, the wine cellar under his home held seventy thousand bottles—dwarfing Koch's forty-thousand-bottle assemblage. The value of Greenberg's wine held up reasonably well in the downturn. And so he became a wine dealer.

Rather than go to trial, Greenberg had earlier tried to placate Koch by sending him a check for the full amount of the questionable bottles plus interest. Greenberg also proposed that the wines in question be tasted by a panel of experts in a public event with the proceeds going to a children's charity.

Koch returned the check. He wanted justice, not money.

With millions of dollars already spent on preliminary legal fees and more millions yet to be billed, Arthur Shartsis, the fatherly head of Greenberg's legal team, labeled the case "the stupidest trial in America." Koch, naturally, saw it differently. By teaching this single adversary an expensive lesson, he was putting the entire high-end wine trade on notice that it better clean itself up.

As the trial began, almost twenty lawyers and paralegals crowded the "well" in front of trial judge J. Paul Oetken. Newly appointed to the federal bench, Oetken seemed agog at the seething legal mass before him. He announced that he needed to find a bigger courtroom.

For his own overflow legal forces, Koch rented a suite of offices in a building across from the courthouse and converted it to a war room. His litigation team was headed by John Hueston, a short, compact, laser-focused Californian who gained legal fame in 2006 as a coprosecutor of top Enron executives. Hueston's three-day cross-examination of the imploded energy company's former chairman, Kenneth Lay, shattered that smooth-talking defendant's confidence and foreshadowed his conviction.

Unlike the Enron criminal case, set off by the largest bankruptcy ever, Koch's civil action against Greenberg involving twenty-four bottles of wine was flyswatter-sized. Yet Hueston cross-examined Greenberg as intensely and as coldly as he had Lay. At one point, Greenberg blurted out that this was "the most horrible experience of my life."

The trial would reveal that both Sotheby's and Christie's had inspected Greenberg's cellar months apart and informed him that it was infected with fakes. Therefore, Koch's lawyers argued, Greenberg knew, or should have known, that the bottles at issue were fake.

Normally, both Greenberg and Zachys could have taken refuge behind the small print in the rear of the catalog under "Conditions of Sale." It stated that all goods are sold "as is." But that clause could be nullified if the sellers had "peculiar knowledge," unavailable to bidders, that the merchandise was problematic. So the pivotal question at trial was not whether the wines were fake but whether Greenberg knew they were fake when he consigned them to Zachys.

Irate emails gathered through the discovery process revealed Greenberg's own anger at buying possible fakes from Kurniawan. As early as 2002, just two years after his Opus One epiphany at Fisherman's Wharf, Kurniawan was already hawking iconic rarities. Greenberg complained to Internet auctioneer WineBid that he believed Kurniawan to be the source of dozens of fakes Greenberg had bought. Greenberg angrily emailed WineBid CFO Steve Griffin: "My goal is to bury the consignor's reputation in the wine world; we have too much faking going on. . . . Further I want to know where he got the bottles as well. . . . These are so fake you have no idea. . . . Ignorant kids cannot make bad buys and think they are going to pawn their mistakes off on unsuspecting others."

But Greenberg soon reversed course and made temporary peace with the "ignorant kid." "I just had lengthy conversation with Rudy Kurniawan," he now wrote to Griffin. "I am convinced that he did not know what he was selling was not right. I will send back the bottles and take full refund."

In May 2004, Greenberg bought a batch of rare wines at an Acker auction, some with their lead neck capsules previously cut to reveal the branding on the cork. He recognized the way it was done as a bond with Kurniawan: "You and I are the only people that cut our capsules the same way, so I am positively sure that [these wines were] yours," he wrote to his fellow dealer. Five months later, Greenberg purchased an additional trove of wines directly from Kurniawan. They included 1947 Lafleur and 1961 Pétrus, both in regular bottle and magnum, and 1929 Romanée-Conti. It was a covey of rarities that, quite possibly, no other dealer on earth could have delivered. Yet here was a twenty-eight-year-old conduit, new to the wine game, who did just that.

On an October afternoon, Kurniawan personally delivered the wines to Greenberg's home in Ross, a wealthy enclave in the hills of Marin County north of San Francisco. In appreciation for Kurniawan's five-hundred-mile road trip from Arcadia, Greenberg uncorked a star of the small but great 1961 vintage, a magnum of Château Latour à Pomerol. A decade later, Greenberg testified at his trial that he and his cellar master, Thierry Lovato, found the Latour à Pomerol to be "magnificent." But his guest "didn't think it tasted right. And Thierry and I were looking at each other, because we had this wine many times, and it tasted great to us. And so he was saying, 'Well, I don't know if it's right.' And I'm like, you know what, you're full of shit, Rudy."

Soon after Kurniawan's visit to Ross, Greenberg offered a list of extra-rare bordeaux magnums to John Kapon at Acker. Greenberg wanted these wines to be sold at Acker's December 2004 auction along with other wines that he had earlier consigned. Included were magnums of 1945, 1947, 1950, and 1961 Latour à Pomerol. Those were identical to vintages that Kurniawan had delivered to him. Kapon gave estimates for the wines, sight unseen, which satisfied Greenberg. Once he received and inspected the magnums, however, Kapon had second thoughts and sent Greenberg unwelcome news: He had found bottles with photocopied labels, corks that were improperly branded, and wine whose color appeared too youthful for its purported age.

Especially glaring—damning even—was the branding on corks of five magnums of Lafleur, none younger than 1950. All the branding was vertical. But, as Kapon knew, that was incorrect. Whoever had done the branding had neglected to notice an arcane detail about old Lafleur corks: The branding was horizontal—that is, the name of the château encircled the cork. Vertical branding did not come into use at Lafleur until 1966. The reason for the change may have been that vertical branding made it easier to read the name of the château on the cork when the bottle was lying down, as it typically would be in a cellar.

As for a single magnum of 1961 Hermitage La Chapelle, a legendary Rhône wine offered by Greenberg, Kapon wrote: "Clearly fake to me. I could not sell it." Acker returned all the rejected magnums to Greenberg.

In spring 2005, Greenberg and Kurniawan were again doing business together. In an email to the wine buyer for the Wynn Resorts hotel group in Las Vegas, Greenberg trumpeted a million-dollar offering from "the same Nicolas collection that went berserk at auction with Acker this past weekend." This was a reference to lots consigned by Kurniawan to the Acker auction held in New York that April. "I own about 1.5M from this collection," Greenberg wrote. "My partner bought $8 million worth. . . . [H]e has more that he will part with, and I am getting more for me and some others. I want to show you this first, for obvious reasons. . . . I am ordering a bunch more, and can get whatever you want immediately."

Greenberg did not identify his "partner," but it could only be Kurniawan. His offering to Wynn included 1947 Lafleur in bottle and magnum, 1961 Pétrus in bottle and magnum, and 1929 Romanée-Conti—all wines that Kurniawan had delivered to Greenberg the prior fall. Although these wines ranged from ultra-rare to effectively extinct, Greenberg also said he could get "a bunch more."

Really, a bunch more? Veteran British wine writer Stephen Brook, in his book *The Complete Bordeaux*, writes that he has never tasted a Lafleur earlier than 1948. Neither does he mention ever sampling 1961 Pétrus. As for 1929 Romanée-Conti, Michael Broadbent, in two volumes comprising thousands of tasting notes spanning more than half a century, has just one note on this rarity—a bottle from the cellar of a ninety-year-old British painter with whom he shared it at a private dinner in 1968.

In the fall of 2005, a year after Kapon had returned rather than sell his Pomerol magnums and other rarities, Greenberg felt validated when Zachys agreed to sell seventeen thousand bottles from the embattled cellar under his house. Quite possibly, some of those rejected magnums were included. "I trusted Zachys more than I trusted Rudy Kurniawan, and it was at this stage that I realized that this guy had a problem," Greenberg would testify.

⚜

Each day of the trial, the twenty-four bottles were toted into the courtroom from a secure storage space in the courthouse, specially fitted out with a wine refrigerator—tender treatment for wines that even Greenberg's team acknowledged were not fit to be sold. On the witness stand, Koch admitted that until the day he discovered that his Jefferson bottles were a scam, he had never bothered to check out the provenance of his multimillion-dollar wine purchases. "I was bloody naive," Koch testified. "In hindsight, I was stupid."

Hearing that, defense lawyer Arthur Shartsis raised an eyebrow. "Mr. Koch, you own a four-billion-dollar company. How naive are you?" he asked.

"When it comes to my hobbies, my biggest fault is that I'm too trusting," Koch said.

Shartsis pressed on: Hadn't Koch spent a hundred million dollars on collecting?

"I have spent a ton of money, but I don't want to know [how much], and I don't want my wife to know." That response echoed Brian Devine's 2003 email to Kurniawan, a.k.a. "Leny": "Glad I haven't known you for years, or my wife would have shot me."

As the trial dragged on, the ranks of opposing lawyers nattered and squabbled over minutiae. A refreshing moment of showmanship occurred during the testimony of James Martin, a materials analysis expert hired by Koch. Martin's job was to put a time frame on the Greenberg bottles by analyzing and dating the paper and printing of their labels. Rising from the witness chair late in the afternoon of the seventh day of the trial, Martin was permitted to approach the jury box. He handed a bottle labeled 1928 Château Latour, one of Koch's purchases from Greenberg, to a female juror.

"Let's do a little show-and-tell," Martin said.

Giving an ultraviolet flashlight to the juror, he instructed her to shine it on the label of the bottle. Instantly, the pale ivory label fluoresced bright blue.

"Now, shine it on my white shirt," Martin said.

It, too, fluoresced bright blue. This was happening, Martin explained, because both the label paper and the detergent residue in his shirt contained optical brightening agents that were not used until the 1950s. The ink on the label and the glue used to affix it to the bottle were also unavailable at the time the wine would have been bottled. Martin told the jury that these "anachronistic markers" were as strikingly wrong as if a photo showed President John F. Kennedy using an iPhone.

The trial lasted for three weeks. At the left flank of his lawyers sat the defendant, dark-suited, stony-faced, and tense. On the right flank of his lawyers sat Koch, sporting a blue blazer and slacks on most days, a tousle of white hair above his cheerful face. His global energy business was deprived of its leader for the duration of the trial, but Koch showed no sign of wishing he were back in his office.

Greenberg's primary defense against Koch's accusation of fraud was to shift blame to Zachys. Had its specialists been suspicious of the twenty-four bottles at issue, they could have and should have been removed from the sale. But culpability bounced back to Greenberg when Jeff Zacharia, president of Zachys, testified that Greenberg never informed him that several experts had already turned thumbs down on those wines prior to their consignment to Zachys.

Koch had sued Zachys along with Greenberg but then reached a settlement with the autioneer. The settlement's terms, Koch says, were threefold: He received compensation, information, and Zacharia's agreement to be Koch's witness, pointing his finger at Greenberg from the witness chair.

The jury took less than two hours to convict Greenberg of wine fraud. It awarded Koch compensatory damages of $379,811 to cover the cost of the twenty-four wines he purchased at Zachys plus a penalty of $1,000 per bottle as allowed under New York consumer protection law. The following day, the jury awarded Koch an eye-popping $12 million in punitive damages.

After the verdict, Koch and lead lawyer John Hueston posed for photographers on the courthouse steps. Gleeful and coatless in the chilly April air, Koch brandished a fake magnum of 1921 Château Pétrus—the same one that he was holding in the photograph on the cover of *Wine Spectator*'s "Crusade Against Counterfeit" issue five years earlier. That magnum had been consigned to Zachys by Greenberg and purchased by Koch for $29,500. Greenberg had offered to refund the purchase price plus costs. Koch rejected that offer. He wanted blood, not money, and now, legally speaking, he had got it. "What Greenberg did," Koch told the press, "was treat me and Zachys the way you treat mushrooms—kept in the dark and fed manure."

One juror, Mary Forbes, stepped up to Koch and shook his hand, saying, "I'm glad it all worked out so well." Another juror, Wally Williams, a retired member of the British Army's Royal Electrical and Mechanical Engineers, who had seemed to doze at times during the proceedings, said that he agreed with Koch's claim that Greenberg, having discovered fakes in his cellar, decided to resell them anyway: "I think because somebody did it to him he decided to do it to somebody else."

The image of Koch, magnum in hand, with his much shorter lawyer on the courthouse steps was bannered on the front page of the next morning's *New York Post*, the city's favorite tabloid.

Judge Oetken slashed Koch's punitive damage award to a mere $768,000. He also rejected Koch's request that Greenberg cover his legal bill of $7,865,872 for the three-week trial. "This was a litigation of choice and principle rather than of necessity or monetary recompense," Oetken wrote. Looking back on the proceedings, he noted that the "legal teams in this case have aggressively fought a battle royale for six years, incurring millions of dollars of fees on each side." The docket listed 36 attorneys and 507 entries. Yet the compensatory damages ultimately sought and awarded were a pittance. That hardly mattered to Koch. His satisfaction was to have dealt a costly blow to his adversary and to once again put auctioneers on notice that they needed to be more vigilant against counterfeits.

As soon as the jury was dismissed following summations at the end of the trial, a posse of reporters and lawyers led by Bill Koch (who was taller than any of them) dashed out of the side door of the classical Thurgood Marshall Courthouse. Crossing Pearl Street, they entered the modern Daniel Patrick Moynihan Courthouse.

There, in a thirteenth-floor courtroom, a slight man now dressed in baggy prison khakis instead of custom Hermès stood before Judge Richard Berman as a date was set for his criminal trial. He looked too young to purchase a bottle of wine.

CHAPTER 7

The Takedown

As a fledgling attorney by day and a wine lover by night, Jason Hernandez worked for a large Washington, DC–based law firm. One spring day in 2007, passing time on a business flight to he doesn't remember where, Hernandez read a *New Yorker* article called "The Jefferson Bottles" by Patrick Radden Keefe. It focused on Bill Koch's costly inquest into those four bottles of wine, which he had purchased for princely sums.

Hernandez noted that Koch had hired an ex–FBI agent to build a dossier that could be turned over to the Justice Department. His goal was to persuade the department to prosecute the purveyor of the Jefferson bottles, Hardy Rodenstock.

"I knew I'd soon be applying for a job as an assistant US attorney, and I daydreamed that one day I could work on this wine case," Hernandez says. "But so many things had to fall in place, starting with how hard it is to be selected for the job. I wanted to apply in New York, but for all I knew, the Rodenstock case could have been brought in Florida, where Koch lived. I had control over none of these things. I was like the kid who dreams of playing center field at Yankee Stadium. Fat chance!"

His Cuban grandparents had migrated to Miami in the 1960s. His parents, although native Spanish speakers, spoke in English at home. At the University of Michigan in the late 1990s, Hernandez was an ace debater, ranking eighth nationally. At the end of Christmas break in 1999, after a series of debates in California, his coach suggested that they spend a few days visiting tasting rooms in the Napa Valley. "He explained that my return ticket to Michigan was already paid for, and the tastings were basically free, so the only cost would be three days of hotels."

Hernandez best remembers a bottle of Williams Selyem pinot noir from the Allen Vineyard in the Russian River Valley. "That was the first wine that I'd ever had that changed over the course of dinner. It started out tight, then gradually opened, picking up nuances. That was my epiphany wine. Back in Ann Arbor, I had the rare good bottle at the Earle, a spot which was known for its good wine list."

In late 2008, Hernandez was sitting at his desk in Washington when he got the call that he was hoping for. It was the Justice Department offering him a job as an assistant US attorney in the Southern District of New York—the busiest judicial district in the nation. "It's very hard to get a job with the SDNY," Hernandez says. "Everyone knows that there is no office anywhere in the country quite like that one. So my law firm understood why I was leaving." With his wife, Dana, he found a small apartment in Hell's Kitchen on Manhattan's far West Side. "We got a good deal on a two-year lease because 2008 was the year of the financial meltdown, and everyone was thinking the world is going to end." He had already started to collect wine— "mostly California pinot noir from Calera, Williams Selyem, stuff like that. I didn't start to branch out from my California comfort zone for another year or so."

The first case he prosecuted was standard fare for a newbie—an accusation that a woman had lied about her income in order to get a federally subsidized apartment. Then came the prosecution of the head of a New York post office branch who had pitched bushels of undelivered first-class mail ("Social Security checks, Netflix DVDs, letters from soldiers overseas") into big green bins. There was also a child pornography case that "was the most disturbing thing I've ever done. It was something I will never erase from my mind."

Slender, fine-featured, and soft-spoken, immaculately groomed and suited, Hernandez was always well prepared in front of a jury. He gave no quarter to the defense yet was never belligerent. His superiors did not delay in moving him up to bigger cases. In 2011, he coprosecuted a trio of lawyers and accountants who were convicted of perpetrating a $7 billion tax shelter fraud—the largest case of its kind. In an art fraud case featured on the front page of *The New York Times* in 2013, his team obtained a guilty plea from a fraudster who sold fake paintings to the prestigious gallery Knoedler & Co. The paintings, attributed to such modernist icons as Robert Motherwell, Mark Rothko, and Jackson Pollock, were resold to clients to the tune of about $80 million.

Knoedler soon closed down. People who should have known better, both sellers and buyers of the art fakes, had convinced themselves that the goods were rare and precious. As with the Jefferson bottles, they did not pinpoint the true identity of the source of these works, purportedly an anonymous collector from Switzerland. Had these buyers who had more cash than caution done thorough spadework, they would have realized that they were being fed a fantasy. But Knoedler's president and gallery director, Ann Freedman, had sent them a letter stating that the trophy paintings she was offering had "been viewed" by eleven experts. So the fact that their provenance remained mostly a blank page could be ignored.

Knoedler's peddling of fakes bears similarities to Acker's. The supplier of the unimaginably rare paintings, Glafira Rosales, was not a known dealer any more than Kurniawan had been before he leaped into the spotlight. Her source, "Mr. X," was a European phantom, just as the "Magic Cellar" was. And Ann Freedman ended up playing a role similar to the one John Kapon had played. Both seem to have convinced themselves that the fake goods they were hawking were authentic. But one difference between Freedman and Kapon was that she was selling fakes for millions of dollars while he was selling them for thousands. Freedman and Knoedler were sued in a New York federal court by Domenico and Eleanore De Sole, a couple who had purchased a purported abstract expressionist work by Mark Rothko for $8.3 million. Their case against Freedman went to trial but was settled just before she was to testify. Knoedler, also sued by the couple, settled with them days later. "Among the mysteries of the case," according to a *New York Times* report on the settlement, "has been how readily the art market embraced works that had no documented provenance." The same could be said for the collectors duped by Kurniawan.

Like those collectors, and given his presumed level of sophistication, Domenico De Sole was an unlikely dupe: He is a Harvard-trained lawyer and chairman of Sotheby's.

Four years before handling the Knoedler matter, Hernandez had been assigned to his first art fraud case. It centered on two enormous paintings bearing the signature of American abstractionist Frank Stella. Normally, the works would have been held at the FBI art fraud facility in Queens, but, too large to fit in the freight elevator there, they were being stored in a commercial facility in Brooklyn. That is where Hernandez traveled from his Lower Manhattan office to view the works and to meet with the agent who was handling the case.

Stella was also there to eyeball the paintings and weigh in as to whether they were from his own hand. He brought with him a coffee-table art book that had reproductions of the paintings in question. Stella was clear: The colors on the canvas were off in the same way they were off on the pages in the book. Whoever had duplicated the paintings had faithfully followed the incorrect color palette on the pages. Another tip-off: Notations he would have made on the back of the canvas were missing.

Returning to Manhattan, Hernandez and the agent got stuck in traffic. "Still in the back of my mind was the Jefferson bottle case. I was wondering who in the FBI had last worked on it. Once I realized this agent's specialty was the collectible area, I figured maybe he knew who got the case. If not, maybe he could look up this information in some kind of internal database."

But that would not be necessary.

"That's *my* case," said Special Agent James Wynne.

Hernandez was astonished. "Of thousands of FBI agents in the country, I was sitting next to the one guy who knew all about the Jefferson bottles. And I learned from him that the case file was sitting right in my own office. But it wasn't moving forward."

Four prosecutors had taken on the case, only to drop it. That wasn't abnormal. "We all got cases where you run into a roadblock, and you conclude that you need to put it on the shelf," says Hernandez. "Getting rid of a case can be like manna from heaven if it's one less case on your docket. And it ends up like millions of other cases that you've never heard of. So when a young whippersnapper like me asks for a file, the response from the supervisor is, sure, let him have it."

Bronx-born and an accountant by training, Wynne first worked for a bank and "hated it." In 1983, at age twenty-nine, he shifted over to the FBI. He soon specialized in theft and fraud involving art, antiques, and collectibles. That would be his calling for the rest of his thirty-year career. "Jim enjoys an occasional glass of wine, but he is no expert," says Hernandez. "I'm a different breed."

When it came to art, Wynne was the different breed. His eye is as sharp as is Hernandez's palate, as he made clear on his first visit to Bill Koch's mansion in Palm Beach. Near a staircase leading to the second floor hangs a cluster of nautical paintings on the wall. Two are iconic watercolors by Winslow Homer. They are the ones that the eyes of most visitors are drawn to. Four other works are finely rendered paintings of sailing ships. Wynne threw them a glance as he passed by.

"Buttersworth," he said.

The reference was to London-born James E. Buttersworth (1817–1894) a leading maritime painter whose work fetches high prices at auction. Brad Goldstein, Koch's troubleshooter who was escorting the agent, was startled. "You're the first visitor here to identify the artist," he said. "How did you know that?"

"I had a case," said Wynne. It involved Ken Perenyi, a notorious forger of artworks across the ages. In his autobiography, *Caveat Emptor*, Perenyi calls Wynne "the country's top art cop."

Wynne felt no need to be a wine expert in order to pursue a wine-fraud case. "The Jefferson bottles weren't like wine that you buy in a liquor store, they were a collectible," he tells me. "Whether a collectible at issue is art or antiques or wine, I ask one question more than any other: What is the provenance? My mother's pearl necklace will not fetch as much at auction as one that belonged to Jackie Kennedy. The difference is provenance. This wine case also rested on provenance. So back when this retired agent, Jim Elroy, called me on behalf of Koch to ask if the Bureau would be interested in this case, I said, 'You're in the right place.'"

"I learned that Jim Wynne never gives up on anything," Hernandez says. "So he was thrilled, really thrilled, that somebody was affirmatively interested in this back-burner case and would pursue it."

The earliest information in the file was about Hardy Rodenstock and the Jefferson bottles. Much of that was on the wrong side of the statute of limitations.

But Hernandez also found "quite a bit" of more recent information about Rudy Kurniawan. "Jim and I chose to focus on him because this was going to be the most provable case."

Most provable thanks to the previous year's faux Ponsot auction. "Before that auction, Rudy had quite a few defenders," says Hernandez. "But that dramatically changed when he failed to identify the source of the Ponsot bottles and collectors were suddenly having trouble reselling his wines."

In May 2011, Hernandez was nearing the end of his eleven-week tax shelter scam trial. Whiling away time at the government table during jury deliberations, he says he read the *Wine Spectator* article featuring Bill Koch on the cover, holding the fake magnum of 1921 Pétrus with the warning, "I plan to put people in jail." Doubters in the wine world still dismissed Koch's words as bluster. Fake wine at the top level was undoubtedly being made, but nobody yet had been put in jail for doing it. There were higher priorities, such as the tax evaders Hernandez had just prosecuted. For Hernandez, the article "was helpful as a road map for getting started on the Kurniawan case."

The giant tax shelter scam resulted in a guilty verdict. Hernandez went home to Florida for a week's vacation before returning to start working with Jim Wynne. "It's a big misconception that the prosecutor sits in his office and waits for the agent to bring in the evidence," he says. "In the real world, we talk back and forth about which witnesses to interview, which subpoenas to send out. We analyze the documents together. It's a real partnership. Not that we do everything together. Certain things, only agents do. In a drug case, an assistant US attorney doesn't sit in an unmarked car staking out a stash house. On the other hand, in fraud cases, he is probably the one who works the most with the documents."

Not that Wynne, being a trained accountant, was a slouch when it came to picking through financial documents.

"We investigated this wine-fraud case like any other financial-fraud case, using traditional tools—bank records and credit card purchases. You start by obtaining a lot of stuff using subpoenas issued in the name of a grand jury. That could compel production of documents such as Kurniawan's bank records including wire transfers. For that, no search warrant is required. But at the next level, you can't go to Microsoft and just say, 'Give us all Rudy's emails from his Hotmail account.' You first have to go to a magistrate judge and convince her that there is probable cause in the totality of circumstances that his emails are likely to contain evidence of a crime or fruits of a crime. For each email address searched, you need a separate search warrant. Rudy used three email accounts."

Three years earlier, Laurent Ponsot had been puzzling over whether Kurniawan was victim or villain. As Hernandez and Wynne began their investigation, they asked the same question: Had Kurniawan been duped into selling fakes that he had unknowingly purchased from one or more of the many domestic and European dealers from whom he was buying vast quantities of wine? Or did he have a direct and knowing hand in sourcing them?

The answer took shape only after long hours of combing through thousands of emails sent and received via Kurniawan's most used of three accounts, rh8@hotmail.com. "You go through line by line," Hernandez says. "Probably one reason no previous prosecutor had done it is because it's incredibly time-consuming."

Kurniawan had charged massively on his Centurion American Express credit card—the "black card." His brothers Darmawan ("Dar") and Teddy also had cards linked to his account, and they were also free spenders. Their bills were paid by Rudy. On a not untypical bill dated February 28, 2007, Rudy's domestic charges for the month were $1,554,833. Dar's Hong Kong charges were $90,359, and Teddy's Indonesian charges were $78,443. The total for that month of $1,723,636, as usual, was paid by Rudy from his Wells Fargo checking account.

By mid-2008, Kurniawan's Membership Miles (one for each dollar spent) exceeded twenty-six million. That was way more miles than the ultimate frequent flyer, Ryan Bingham, played by George Clooney, achieved in *Up in the Air*. (Bingham was congratulated by an American Airlines captain during the flight when he achieved a paltry ten million miles.) In theory, Kurniawan could have traveled freely in first class anywhere in the world. But that was out of the question. Had he flown out of the United States, he would not have been allowed back in on his expired student visa. Yet when Kurniawan was asked at a wine dinner if he liked to travel, he smiled brightly, as if summoning up memories of faraway places, and said, "I love to travel . . . I love to travel . . . I *love* to travel."

Scattered among Kurniawan's massive wine purchases, boutique forays, and restaurant tabs on his monthly credit card bills, the investigators found what Hernandez calls "the occasional gems."

"A Lamborghini-driving guy can be buying office supplies and paper towels from Staples like the rest of us," Hernandez says, "but why the heck did he buy thirteen packages of warm white Ingres paper, ink pads in various colors, and large amounts of French wax? Why was he asking for empty bottles to be shipped home after expensive meals? That seemed to be telling us something."

Particularly intriguing were Kurniawan's dealings with Letter-Seals and Atelier Gargoyle, two domestic sources for specialty wax. In its molten state, sealing wax has been used for centuries to be imprinted with a heraldic or personal seal on letters and official papers. Or to seal wine bottles, especially magnums or larger, in lieu of lead (no longer used) or other foil capsules. In more recent times, some wineries, including Sine Qua Non, have used wax to seal their wines with a flourish.

Anyone who has chipped open a wax-sealed bottle knows the wax makes a mess when it is shattered. In a 2006 query to LetterSeals, Kurniawan asked, "Are the faux wax brittle, like a traditional French seal wax? I am looking for a brittle wax sealer." Kurniawan spent more than $7,000 on wax at the two companies. After one of his orders, Atelier Gargoyle told him, "You've been such a good customer, we're throwing in shipping."

And where was Kurniawan acquiring the bottles that he was topping with wax? One source was the New York restaurant Cru, scene of those deep-into-the-night bacchanals where he often picked up the entire check. Koch's earlier investigation had turned up the information that seventeen shipments of empty bottles from those dinners had been FedExed to Kurniawan's home. When two bottles arrived broken in one shipment, Kurniawan wrote to Cru's wine director, Robert Bohr, that he was "extremely bothered by it since this is the second time it happened. ESP the 23 Roumier BM [Bonnes-Mares] bottle that I wanted to keep."

"My scarlet letter was sending those bottles back," Bohr told me years later. But he rejects any allegation that he was complicit with a bottle-refilling scheme. "Do these people know that guests come in and they buy a bottle from the year of their wedding, or a birth year of a parent or child? That vintage has some meaning to them. They spend some significant or insignificant amount of money on that bottle. Before they leave, they may ask to take it home. You know what I say? 'Let me wrap it up for you carefully in plastic.' The logical extension is that when a guy who is buying twelve bottles for six figures and who is wearing a seventy-five-thousand-dollar watch asks for the same courtesy, the answer is, 'Don't schlep them home. I'll FedEx them.' I did it with pride. The one time I delegated the packing to an assistant sommelier, he put the bottles in a regular box without Styrofoam and wrapping. A couple of bottles arrived broken. I was angry that we hadn't lived up to our side of the agreement and apologized to Rudy."

The investigators also learned that Kurniawan had insisted on the return of at least two hundred empty bottles and their corks from dinners he hosted at Mélisse in Santa Monica. He had taken over the restaurant to throw a sixtieth-birthday party for his mother. His personal high point was when the actor Jackie Chan jumped up on a chair brandishing an empty magnum of Château Pétrus and announced, "Rudy, you are the greatest."

Yet more empty bottles were FedExed to Arcadia from the extraordinary three-day tasting of seventy-four vintages of Romanée-Conti organized by Doug Barzelay at New York restaurant Per Se in April 2007. Kurniawan contributed a number of vintages to that event, then pestered Barzelay until the empty bottles arrived.

No matter how many empties Kurniawan wangled for home delivery from restaurants, he wanted more. And they couldn't be just any bottles. It wouldn't do to use a modern, machine-molded bottle for, say, a 1911 Romanée-Conti or a 1900 Château Margaux. An authentic bottle from an earlier era would likely have been handblown and heavier than modern models—as were the "faux Ponsot" bottles. And the punt—the conical sediment catcher extending up from the base of the bottle—had to be deep.

Where did Kurniawan find an additional supply of old bottles? Emails from 2007 and 2008 detailed his purchases of hundreds of old red and white burgundy wines from Caveau de la Tour, a dealer in the village of Meursault. These commercial-grade wines were mostly made by Patriarche Père et Fils, a long-established firm whose wines were not meant for long cellaring or the auction market. In a May 31, 2007, email from Anders Naumann, a specialist at Caveau de la Tour, under the subject "Old Patriarche," Kurniawan is offered hundreds of bottles of old burgundies, probably long forgotten in the depths of the négociant's cellar. The oldest was 1904 Beaune. At €1,060 per bottle, the price seems high for a wine that was not bottled for long keeping.

Kurniawan wrote back, "Will take all if they are all correct period bottles."

Naumann responded: "Will confirm that all are original bottles with deep punts."

The next month, Caveau de la Tour was back with a new offering, this one a stash of Patriache's Meursault Charmes 1971. The vintage was a good one, although probably over the hill, or even undrinkable. At first, Kurniawan believed that he was being offered twenty bottles of Charmes. Then Anders corrected him. The number was actually 120 bottles at sixty euros each.

"I'll take them all," Kurniawan responded.

In total, Kurniawan bought 908 bottles of old commercial red and white burgundy from Caveau de la Tour. Were they to be infused,

Viagra-like, with youthful California fruit bombs, those tired old Patriarche commercial red wines could be primed for their new role as treasures worthy of the wealthiest collectors. As for the Meursault Charmes, it could—and almost certainly would—resurface as white burgundy boasting domaine labels far more expensive than humble Patriarche.

Kurniawan's emails, incriminating as they were, left a key question dangling: Was he the craftsman—or were others doctoring the bottles under his direction? Hernandez and Wynne closed in on the answer when they learned of Kurniawan's June 2006 purchase of seven authentic bottles of 1962 Romanée-Conti. They were sold to him by two West Coast companies owned by David Parker, a former tech executive turned wine merchant. The wines, acquired from a private collection, were in bad shape. Due to corks that were past their prime, all seven bottles had suffered significant evaporation, or *ullage*—the vertical distance from the bottom of the cork to the top level of the wine. Their condition may have been poor, but Parker, knowing their provenance, was confident that they were real.

When he bought the seven bottles, Parker had recorded the serial numbers of each one with its corresponding ullage. The range was between 2-1/8 and 2-5/8 inches. That put the integrity of the wine at risk and sharply discounted its value. At auction, bottles with such a low fill level would have drawn sneers from collectors. Still, Kurniawan purchased all seven bottles for just over $6,000 each.

But why?

Dave Parker discovered the answer to that question when he saw photos of several of the same bottles in Acker's catalog for Cellar I. He knew they were the same because he could see the serial numbers that he had recorded before he sold them to Kurniawan. But something had mysteriously changed: The ullage in each bottle had been reduced by at least one inch. The new levels were now acceptable to a collector who paid $50,000 for the six bottles of rejuvenated wine.

"Wine levels can go down over time. They cannot go up," says Hernandez.

So what happened here? The most plausible explanation is that Kurniawan had pulled the corks from the bottles and used a donor bottle to bring up the fill level of the six bottles to an acceptable level. Then he had recorked and refoiled the bottles. Most likely, the seventh bottle had been the donor bottle. "Rudy probably drank whatever was left over," Hernandez says.

By early 2012, Hernandez and Wynne had built a potent case against Kurniawan. But they still made no move to arrest him. Enter lawyer and amateur bottle detective Don Cornwell. He speaks not a word of French. But he does read it with precision when the words are on the label of a bottle of French wine, especially if it is burgundy. With his 10X jeweler's magnifier in hand, he can spot tiny variations in the labels, capsules, corks, and even the tint of glass of old bordeaux and burgundy bottles that could be indicators of fakery. Cornwell keeps orderly files of authentic labels, amassed over thirty years of collecting and drinking burgundy.

In late January 2012, Cornwell's eyes fell on the pages of the catalog for a wine auction to be held in London on February 8. It was being mounted by California-based Spectrum Wine Auctions and its British partner, a self-described "luxury drinks" specialist called Vanquish. London was a new venue for Spectrum. The plan was to "make a proverbial splash 'crossing the pond,'" according to the sleek black catalog's introduction, jointly signed by Jason Boland, Spectrum's president, and Richard Brierley, head wine specialist for Vanquish.

Paging through the catalog, Cornwell was struck by certain offerings that were wildly rare—none more so than a single bottle of 1945 Comte de Vogüé Musigny Blanc and five bottles of the 1962 vintage of the same wine, estimated to sell for $12,000. De Vogüé is by far the largest owner of vineyards in the grand cru of Musigny. Almost all of its production is red wine meant for long aging. The production of Musigny Blanc, a chardonnay, was always minuscule—less than two hundred cases per vintage. No other Musigny can claim to be white. This unicorn was said to exist only because the late Comtesse de Vogüé asked her husband to create a white wine for her personal pleasure. (Buy Musigny Blanc, Robert Parker once advised, and you are "paying for prestige and rarity rather than profoundness.") Almost as rare were offerings of Domaine de la Romanée-Conti's 1966 Montrachet and a whole swath of DRC reds going back to the 1930s.

It was unusual—or should have been—for an auctioneer to offer such relics retrieved from the mists of wine time without at least a hint about their provenance. Where had they been all these decades? The catalog offered potential bidders scant information. They had to trust the assurances of Boland and Brierley that their "team of experts spent many long days and nights . . . scrutinizing every fine detail of each consignment."

Their scrutiny was not so sharp as Cornwell's. Peering at the catalog photos, he saw signs of a familiar hand. Here were images of DRC bottles whose labels bore errors identical to those on bottles that Kurniawan had previously sold. The most glaring one, first noticed by Geoffrey Troy and his wife, Jane, several years earlier, was the errant accent aigu in *propriétaire* on the upper portion of the main label. This accent, with a minor exception, did not appear on the labels of authentic DRC bottles until 1978.

Cornwell's eye was also caught by the serial number on a jeroboam of 1971 Romanée-Conti, one of a trio estimated to sell for $100,000. He knew that the number, 018, had appeared on a jeroboam of the same wine sold at Acker's Cellar II auction in New York in 2006. Yet a third jeroboam numbered 018 had been sold at the faux Ponsot sale two years later. Deepening the mystery, Troy, who had inspected one of the big bottles in a New York storage facility, reported that it was still in the possession of his client.

Cornwell posted these fractious facts, and more, on Wine Berserkers, an Internet chat board for impassioned wine folk. His first post began: "In the last 48 hours I have confirmed from multiple sources that Rudy Kurniawan is once again offering millions of dollars worth of wine for auction—this time at an auction to be held in London."

And then Cornwell dropped an additional bombshell: While the catalog was silent on the identity of the consignor of the rarest lots, Cornwell had learned that the wines were being "officially consigned through an agent—one Antonio Castanos—who is known to have acted on Mr. Kurniawan's behalf in selling wines to third parties since the infamous Acker Merrall auction held on April 25, 2008, in New York." Castanos is a Los Angeles restaurateur who also held a wine dealer's license. Cornwell did not reveal how he knew about the Castanos connection. But he did report on a conversation he had just had with Spectrum's consignment director, unnamed in the post, whom he told of his certitude that Castanos was "acting as agent for Rudy Kurniawan."

Instead of stonewalling, the consignment director, disturbed by the situation, unloaded on Cornwell. Yes, he admitted, Spectrum was "well aware that the wines belonged to Rudy." He had "vigorously opposed Spectrum having anything to do with Rudy or his wines." But management had overruled him.

Cornwell, a wee-hours worker and not early to rise, was awakened by a phone call from Jason Boland at eight o'clock the next morning. The auctioneer had just arrived in London for the upcoming sale and knew he had to deal with Cornwell's alarums. He insisted that Kurniawan was not a consignor to the auction. That may have been technically true, Cornwell responded, but Castanos was the consignor "on behalf of Rudy." Boland did not deny that, but did insist that the information was privileged. Five minutes after that call, the consignment director called Cornwell to say that he was retracting his statements of the previous evening.

After speaking with Cornwell, Boland posted for the first and only time on Wine Berserkers: "Just to reiterate the facts from my conversation with Don. Rudy is not a consignor in this auction and has not been a consignor with Spectrum since we have started. . . . All the wine in this auction went through an elevated inspection process by our experts before being placed into the sale."

In the remaining days leading up to the auction, Wine Berserkers was a beehive—make that a wasps' nest—of activity. Opinions, insults, and quips flew at the rate of dozens per hour. Cornwell contributed none of them. After two long posts revealing Kurniawan's stealth entry into the auction catalog and detailing issues with numerous bottles, Cornwell had gone silent. But his impact was being felt in London. In a move unprecedented in its 280 years of doing business, Corney & Barrow, exclusive UK distributor for Domaine de la Romanée-Conti, announced that it had a "responsibility to make public its concerns about Mr. Cornwell's comprehensive critique of a significant number of Domaine de la Romanée Conti lots in this forthcoming auction."

Corney & Barrow stopped short of demanding withdrawal of the lots targeted by Cornwell. But the damage to Spectrum-Vanquish was done. It announced that "out of an abundance of caution" it was withdrawing thirteen lots of Romanée-Conti wines worth a quarter-million dollars. So much for Jason Boland's claim of an "elevated inspection process."

By the time Richard Brierley stepped up to the podium at the Mandarin Oriental Hotel in Hyde Park, more beyond-rare lots had been withdrawn: a magnum of 1961 Château Latour à Pomerol carrying the circular red Nicolas stamp and the five bottles of 1962 Comte de Vogüé Musigny Blanc. "These lots have been withdrawn on very good authority," Brierley told the audience. Bidding was scant on some lots, spirited on others. A jeroboam of 1990 Romanée-Conti sold for $63,676 against an estimate of $47,460.

The single bottle of 1945 Romanée-Conti, ultimate rarity in this or any sale, fetched $45,482.

Moments after the auction ended, Boland, responding to a *Wine Spectator* query about the withdrawn lots, told me, "We were up until three and four AM, doing everything we possibly could, debating what to do. We pulled them because the domaines questioned them. They have the best experience to tell us what is right or wrong."

Certainly, that was true. Yet Boland's response was befuddling. His own wine specialists, in combination with Brierley, formerly Christie's wine director for the Americas, had "carefully inspected and vetted" the bottles being offered. How did they fail to notice the multiple red flags that Don Cornwell pinpointed solely from catalog images? Another question: How did Antonio Castanos, whose wine dealings were not known to include treasures of bygone days, become a secret consignor of mythic bottles to this auction in London? Was he, as Cornwell claimed, merely a straw man for Rudy Kurniawan?

Troubling questions, those.

Hernandez and Wynn had already constructed a detailed case against Kurniawan. Now an additional avenue of investigation opened. In West Los Angeles, local FBI agents visited Antonio Castanos at his traditional Italian restaurant, Guido's. Castanos said that he had known Kurniawan for ten years, after first striking up a conversation with him in a wine shop. Kurniawan called him "Dad" and his wife "Mom." Castanos had occasionally sold wines for Kurniawan beginning around 2006. He admitted that Kurniawan had personally delivered to his home 429 bottles to be sold in London. A Spectrum truck took them away. In return, he was to receive a commission of 5 percent of the reserve price on all lots that sold. His son, too, acted as a consignor.

On March 5, 2012, less than a month after the London auction, the government filed a lengthy sealed complaint against Kurniawan in the Southern District of New York. Two of the five counts charged him with defrauding Fine Art Capital by giving false information about his financial situation and by double-pledging artworks as security for a $3 million loan. The third count charged him with arranging for an "International Auction House" (Christie's) to sell wines that had a prior lien on them by a "New York Auction House" (Acker). The proceeds from the sale had also been promised to "a California wine collector" (Andrew Gordon). Count four charged Kurniawan with trying to sell "rare and expensive" Ponsot wines that he knew were counterfeit. Count five charged him with attempting to sell Domaine de la Romanée-Conti wines that he also knew were counterfeit at the Spectrum-Vanquish auction.

Though not easily ruffled, Hernandez is irritated at the suggestion that Don Cornwell's warnings about the Spectrum auction were the reason that the complaint was filed when it was. "Some complaints are two pages long," says Hernandez. "This one was fifty pages." Highly detailed complaints of that length do not get composed overnight, so Hernandez's point is that this one was already prepared, except for the Spectrum count.

A warrant to arrest Rudy Kurniawan was issued the next day in New York.

✿

Kurniawan did not hesitate to open his front door when a person identifying himself as a neighbor knocked at eight thirty on the evening of March 7. The stranger said that he was searching for a lost pet. Kurniawan had no way of knowing that the "neighbor" was FBI agent Olivier Farache. Rather than pet-hunting, Farache wanted to confirm that Kurniawan was at home.

Before dawn the next morning, Wynne assembled eleven FBI agents in the parking lot of a strip mall near Kurniawan's home. Hernandez was on alert in a hotel room in Marina del Rey. Wynne's team donned bulletproof vests before driving to the unremarkable, stucco-walled, four-bedroom home with a Lamborghini in the garage and a Mercedes and Land Rover in the driveway.

The agents took up their positions as Wynne watched from the periphery. At precisely 6:00 AM, an agent carrying an arrest warrant (but not a search warrant) stepped up to the door to "knock and announce."

"FBI. Open the door."

No answer. The agent pounded louder. When it seemed certain that no one in the house could still be asleep, the agent said, "Get the ram." Wynne winced. ("Once the door goes down, I'd need to post an agent there all day to preserve the evidence inside," he explains.)

Just then, Kurniawan, pajama-clad, opened the door. He was ordered to step out to the narrow side lawn to be handcuffed. Who else was in the house? Only his mother, he answered. She joined him but was not handcuffed. Several agents entered the house to make a "protective sweep"—standard procedure to ensure that no person lurked within who might harm the agents. For that, they did not need to have a search warrant.

A jumble of wine cartons and crates were stacked almost to the ceiling on the right side of the foyer. Agent Farache, the first to enter, noticed that one of the crates was branded "Louis Jadot." He recognized the name as that of a Burgundian négociant. He moved farther into the house, past the dining room and kitchen, down one hall, then another. Toward the rear, he came upon a locked room.

Out on the lawn, agents asked Kurniawan for the key. It was in his pocket.

The agents unlocked the room. Eleven feet square, it was lined on four sides with wine racks. In one corner were three file cabinets. As Farache recounted later that day in his belated application for a search warrant, the agents discovered "bags containing wine labels, bags of wine corks, wax used to seal corks, rubber stamps used to stamp the year of a wine vintage, empty bottles of wine (including large format bottles), wooden wine crates, bottles submerged in water to aid removing the labels, computer equipment (including printers), and stacks of pre-printed wine labels printed on high quality paper."

In-progress counterfeiting operations were also evident in the kitchen, living room, and family room. Bottles were soaking in the kitchen sink to remove their labels prior to being transformed into other wines. Unlabeled bottles rested sideways on the belt of a treadmill in the kitchen. Numerous bottles in wine racks had no capsules. Four bottles of 1985 Henri Jayer Richebourg were lined up on a shelf. Already top collectibles, Jayer wines were even more avidly sought after the winemaker's death in 2006 and were a prime candidate for Rudy to counterfeit. Less than six hours before his arrest, Kurniawan had offered these Richebourgs to a Swedish dealer named Kristoffer Meier-Axel: "I have six bottles originally for auction but I think it is better to sell private. Even [if the price is] lower now. . . . Here's pic. Let me know."

Items that Hernandez and Wynne previously knew only from Kurniawan's emails now became real: the tablets and sticks of French wax from Atelier Gargoyle and LetterSeal and stainless-steel cups coated with melted wax; a large assortment of glues and papers; four dusty magnums of Patriarche grand cru burgundies—two each of 1943 Corton and 1955 Richebourg—on a shelf. These were among the 908 bottles ordered by Kurniawan from the Burgundian dealer Caveau de la Tour. Myriad other bottles, old and young, French and Californian, full, empty, and half full, were tucked into wine racks or scattered on the floor. Small bottles were filled with wine under reclosable stoppers. Some bottles had notes scrawled on them: "use for '30's–'40's DRC," "use for 1950s Pomerol."

And so Kurniawan's method of creating counterfeits of classic French wines began to clarify. First, he soaked the labels off very old commercial-grade wines in the kitchen sink. The Patriarche Corton and Richebourg bottles appeared to be poised for that. The bottles would then be uncorked and a portion poured out. An equal portion of premium or mundane California wines would be poured in. For that, Kurniawan's shelves were stocked with worthy transfusion stand-ins. For burgundies, they included the highly rated 2008 Marcassin and 2008 Aubert pinot noir. For bordeaux, there were the renowned 1974 Heitz Martha's Vineyard cabernet sauvignon and obscure 2003 Blankiet Estate merlot. Thanks to his tasting acumen, Kurniawan could then fine-tune a custom blend to mimic the wine he was planning to sell. If he got it right, a purchaser, even one familiar with the authentic wine, would swirl, sniff, taste, and . . . marvel at the result: authentic funk of decades-old burgundy or autumnal essence of long-ago bordeaux yet, miraculously, still holding on to a streak of vibrantly youthful fruit!

Had Kurniawan chosen to recraft those old Patriarche bottles into, say, 1949 Armand Rousseau Chambertin (a producer and vintage sure to set collectors' hearts to thumping), he only had to dip into his inventory of labels for the appropriate one. And then he could add cachet in the form of a circular Berry Bros. & Rudd label applied to the bottle's shoulder: "By Appointment to H.M. the Queen, Wine & Spirit Merchants." The bottles would be sealed with old corks from Kurniawan's collection, or possibly a reused Rousseau cork or a rebranded new cork. Finally, the corks themselves would be coated with molten, burgundy-tinted wax—less tricky than fitting on a metal capsule.

At Acker's April 2008 sale, Kurniawan sold one case and one jeroboam of 1949 Rousseau Chambertin adorned with the BB&R sticker and sealed with wax. As earlier noted, BB&R wine director

Alun Griffiths had been unable to locate any record that this wine had been entered into either the handwritten inventory book used by his firm in the 1950s or the current electronic log. Griffiths pronounced the BB&R sticker to be a modern version not used in the 1950s, when the wine would have been released.

But Griffiths had backed off after Charles Rousseau, then the domaine's octogenarian proprietor, was shown photos of the lots in the Acker catalog. The old man declared that the bottles were authentic and that he even remembered affixing the BB&R labels himself! Hearing about that claim, Laurent Ponsot was not persuaded, declaring that he would not trust his own father's memory at the same age.

Now the question was resolved in Ponsot's favor. Among eighteen thousand labels in Kurniawan's operations center, the agents discovered both Rousseau Chambertin examples and BB&R shoulder stickers identical to those in the Acker catalog photos. High bidders paid $60,000 by the case and $42,000 for the jeroboam for the 1949s, plus commission of 21 percent.

The revelation of Kurniawan's wine-concocting method solved another mystery that had puzzled Wilfred Jaeger. He wondered why so many of the old wines purchased from Kurniawan uniformly had a slight "oxidative quality," giving a sherry-like taste. Jaeger had assumed that the wines "were not well stored." But that was off the mark. The correct answer, Jaeger now believes, was that "Rudy neglected to do one thing which is done in the winery. They always put a bit of anhydrous sulfur in the bottle before inserting the cork so that the wine stays reduced." (Reduction, in wine, is the opposite of oxidation.)

An instinctive judgment made by critic Allen Meadows at a dinner at a Los Angeles restaurant also now appeared to be confirmed. At the table were French winemakers Erwan Faiveley and Bernard Hervet, former general manager of Domaine Faiveley. Also on hand was Kurniawan's original mentor and partner in the Wine Hotel, Paul Wasserman. "Rudy finally showed up," says Meadows.

"He'd brought a bottle of Dujac. And then he casually puts down another bottle: a '99 Romanée-Conti"—not 1999, but 1899. Meadows' view is that it would be beyond disrespectful to plop down a more-than-century-old bottle of what is commonly considered to be the world's greatest wine. It is an "event wine," to be offered with ceremony.

But only if it is real.

"That was a defining moment for me," Meadows tells me. The days of his praise for Kurniawan were over. Among the labels now found neatly banded in the house on Naomi Avenue were ones for 1899 Romanée-Conti.

The discovery of the elaborate wine-counterfeiting shop in Kurniawan's house was what Wynne called "a jaw-dropper." Although counterfeiting materials had been mailed to Kurniawan's home address, logic dictated that the workshop would have been located elsewhere, possibly in a commercial wine warehouse where Kurniawan stored his wine in a space custom-built for him.

Hernandez, in his room at the Marriott Hotel in Marina del Ray, thirty-five miles from Arcadia, was also startled when Wynne called him with the news of what the agents had found. To anyone who wonders why he was not closer to the action, Hernandez responds: "I get up when the agents get up. But I do not carry a gun, I do not operate handcuffs. I do not get in the way of the arrest. My job was to be at my laptop so that I could type up the papers for the magistrate."

Kurniawan was considerate of his wine: The home thermostat was set at a chilly sixty-two degrees. Both he and his mother slept in bedrooms furnished with space heaters. The agents found numerous boxes of luxury goods scattered around the house, many unopened.

Done with their protective sweep (Kurniawan's lawyers always insisted that it was much more than that), the agents escorted Kurniawan and his mother back into the house. At the dining room table, the prisoner was asked if he would answer questions. "He said several times that he wanted to cooperate, but was undecided whether to go ahead and do so immediately," according to the arrest report. He was allowed to confer with his mother in Mandarin. An agent who spoke the language monitored their conversation: "Kurniawan told his mother he wanted to help the investigation, that he did not know what to do, and that he was afraid. [He] asked his mother whether he should cooperate. [She] did not ask him what he had done, and advised him that they did not know the customs or law, so he should speak with a lawyer."

The agents fetched clothing for the prisoner and took him away. His mother, who was upstairs, heard him call out, "Mom," as they led him out the front door. To avoid the possibility that his mother might destroy evidence, the agents advised her to leave the house for the day. She refused. She did answer questions posed by Wynne via the Mandarin-speaking agent. From Wynne's notes, here is the exchange, scrawled that morning in real time:

Q: Why washing bottles in the sink?
A: She doesn't know and doesn't meddle.

Q: Why so many bottles?
A: He drinks a lot.

Q: Did he drink the bottles on treadmill?
A: Day and night he opens bottles.

Q: Room near garage with wine racks?
A: He does not want her to go inside. He does not want her to mess up wine. She has broken bottles in past.

Q: Why does he have wax containers?
A: She does not know what wax is. Does not touch his stuff.

Q: Do people come to the house?

A: She does not know any of his friends. Relatives come—
her sisters who live in Indonesia.

Q: Who is Darmawan?
A: Her son. He is in real estate business in Indonesia.

Q: Who is Teddy Tan?
A: Her son. In real estate—some together, some different.

Q: Does Dar send $$ to RK?
A: I don't know. I think he helps RK.

Q: Does Dar own Heineken distributorship?
A: She does not know what Heineken is.

Q: RK have girlfriend?
A: No, single now, but had girlfriends in past in Indonesia.

Q: What is RK's business?
A: I think he is in wine selling business because of all the
wine he brings in, but I don't know.

Q: Why was RK arrested?
A: She doesn't know. Was going to ask.

Q: Tell her: RK arrested for selling wine that is fake.
A: That's not possible.

Kurniawan appeared at a bail hearing that afternoon. "A mag-
istrate wants to know if the person is a danger to commit another
crime or a flight risk," Hernandez says. "If so, he can be remanded
rather than be bailed. In Kurniawan's case, we had somebody with
no legal status in this country. He's got plenty of money and he's a

citizen of Indonesia, with whom we have no extradition agreement. This is a powerful case for detention. So here I am in Los Angeles for the first time ever, asking my colleagues in the local US Attorney's Office if the judge will follow our strong recommendation against bail. Their response was that absolutely, no question, Rudy would be locked up."

So Hernandez was stunned when the magistrate, over his protest, set bail at a modest $150,000. Kurniawan could and often did spend more than that buying wine online in an hour's time. The magistrate ordered Kurniawan to be confined to home detention with "electronic monitoring." Urgently, Hernandez requested that the defendant be detained behind bars for one more day pending appeal. Back in his hotel room that evening, Hernandez wrote the appeal. As an indicator of how seriously the government viewed Kurniawan as a flight risk, Hernandez noted that a wine merchant had recently asked Kurniawan if he was worried that the FBI might arrest him. "If I thought they were going to arrest me, I'd be on the next flight to Hong Kong," Kurniawan said. His response was the same to the urgent call from his friend Jefery Levy. The agents had also interviewed Paul Wasserman, Kurniawan's operating partner at the Wine Hotel. "Jim Wynne asked me, 'What assets of Rudy's can we seize?'" says Wasserman. He, too, warned Kurniawan that the FBI was closing in.

Did the agents fear that Rudy, once tipped off, might disappear? "Not really," says Hernandez. "If he fled the country he could not have gotten back in because of the deportation order. His whole life was here, including his mother."

Kurniawan was not the only one avoiding a reality check this late in the game. So was Wasserman. "I believed that these agents had this conspiracy of not very nice people going up against this very nice guy," he says. "I had sat in the FBI office and told them they got the wrong guy. They were trying to convince me that Rudy was a con man. Never once did they come up with an argument that was convincing."

In his hotel room, Hernandez worked late into the night after the arrest writing an appeal of the bail decision. The next day, a different magistrate agreed to deny Kurniawan's bail.

Two months after his arrest, a New York federal grand jury indicted Kurniawan on four counts of mail and wire fraud—selling counterfeit wine, defrauding Fine Art Capital, double-pledging collateral, and scheming to defraud a California collector (Andrew Gordon) and a New York auction house (Acker Merrall & Condit). A superseding indictment would reduce the charges to just two counts: one scheme to sell counterfeit wine and another to defraud a finance company.

The defendant was flown to New York by the US Marshals Service. He took up involuntary residence in Brooklyn's Metropolitan Detention Center.

The case was assigned to Judge Richard Berman in New York's Southern District. He would preside over the first criminal case in the federal courts involving fake wine. (Two years later, Berman would preside over the first civil case involving the air pressure in a football, dubbed "Deflategate.") Appointed to the federal bench in 1998 by President Bill Clinton, Berman is a calm and methodical judge. Based on his queries during Kurniawan's trial, Berman seemed to know little about wine, and nothing at all about ultra-rare wine—real or counterfeit. He was entering new territory.

CHAPTER 8

Before a Jury
of His Peers

Kurniawan's lawyers at his bail hearing in Los Angeles were civil specialists. They were replaced by Michael Proctor, Yale-trained and with broad experience in criminal defense cases, including a five-year stint as a Los Angeles public defender.

Proctor's best shot at crippling the government's case was to take aim at the warrantless search of his client's home on the morning of his arrest. That seemed to be a violation of his Fourth Amendment right against illegal search. "Over the years, the Supreme Court has found many exceptions to the requirement for a search warrant, such as when evidence is in plain view," Proctor said. But he asserted that no evidence was in plain view that morning. True, the first FBI agents to enter saw cases of wine stacked high and haphazardly in the hallway just inside the front door. But was that evidence?

"It's one thing if you search a person or a car, but a person's home is sacrosanct. If our motion is granted, and evidence is suppressed, it's a whole different case."

Proctor scorned the prosecution's claim that the agents had entered the locked room in the rear of the house in order to ensure that nobody was lurking within. "To reach that room," Proctor noted in his suppression brief, "agents had to walk through the foyer, through the front entryway, make a left turn, proceed down a corridor, pass the staircase leading to the second floor and the wine refrigerator, make another left turn, and proceed down yet another corridor. Using the key they had retrieved from Mr. Kurniawan's pocket, the agent unlocked the door. Because the room is small . . . and has wine racks mounted on all four walls, it would have been immediately apparent that there was nobody inside the room. Nevertheless, during their supposed cursory inspection for dangerous people, the agents observed all of the following in the storage room."

Here, Proctor listed the full contents of the wine-counterfeiting workshop inventoried by the agents, right down to minute details: "While they were supposedly looking for a human threat, the agents stopped to observe the writing on small rubber stamps . . . and scrutinized spreadsheets."

Hernandez defended the warrantless search for three reasons. First: The "protective sweep" of the entire house was required to ensure that nobody was lurking within who might put the agents in danger. Second: The premises had to be secured pending the agents' return with a search warrant. Third: The agents had to make sure that "no one would destroy evidence in the house." In a footnote to his brief, Hernandez noted that Kurniawan's mother refused to leave the house after his arrest. The agents wanted her gone because she "also could have destroyed evidence out of fear for her own potential criminal liability." Could Lenywati Tan have been living in the midst of an elaborate, multiyear counterfeiting operation without figuring out what was going on? She couldn't use the kitchen sink because wine bottles were soaking in it, nor the dish drainer, which had a double-lever recorker draped across it. And she had to navigate around wine bottles of all sizes that littered the floor. After her son was taken away, the Mandarin-speaking agent remained in the house with her until others returned to execute the search warrant.

The prosecution did not go so far as to insist that the FBI search that morning was free of blemish. It acknowledged that "of all the facts underlying the sweep, the agents' entry into the locked room had the greatest likelihood of causing the Magistrate to reject" the search warrant affidavit. If the agent requesting the search warrant had "not been acting in good faith, if he was trying to dupe the Magistrate, he would simply have omitted from the affidavit any reference to the locked room."

But even if the magistrate had tossed out the massive evidence discovered in the home search, Hernandez argued, there was sufficient reason to issue the search warrant. The emails and bank records he and Wynne had legally examined pointed to criminal activity occurring on the premises. And then there were ample fake bottles sold by Kurniawan that had been gathered from his victims.

In a ruling nearly a year after Kurniawan's arrest, Judge Berman denied the defense motion to exclude the evidence found during the home search: "The long and the short of my ruling is that, based on the totality of the circumstances, in my judgment the search warrant was clearly based on probable cause." That ruling was a knockout blow to the defense. If Berman had blocked the fruits of that initial search from being submitted to the jury, Kurniawan might still have had a sliver of hope that he would be acquitted.

Sitting in the front row of the courtroom between two burly US marshals, Kurniawan looked small in his jailbird uniform of mismatched, too-large khaki pants, shirt, and black sneakers. All that remained from his days of sartorial splendor were his black-framed designer eyeglasses. He showed no emotion at Berman's decision. A trial date, the first of many that would be postponed, was set for early June 2013.

Hernandez could impress the jury by showing it dozens of counterfeit bottles sold by the defendant. The same for stacks of packets of carefully crafted counterfeit labels awaiting their bottles. But bottles were only bottles and labels were only labels. Another level of impact, this one with a human face, would come from testimony by Kurniawan's victims. Most obvious were the wealthy collectors whose multimillion-dollar purchases were now worthless. But only Bill Koch was ready and willing to come forward personally. "Koch was a great resource," says Wynne. "He had been defrauded and had no problem saying, 'I'm the victim.' But did you see the other five biggest victims testify? These were hot, hot businessmen. They had been defrauded by a guy who never traveled anywhere except Los Angeles, New York, and Las Vegas. They looked like fools."

Less direct victims of Kurniawan's fraud, albeit harmed in ways deeper than monetary, were the vignerons whose wines he scammed. Laurent Ponsot, the French counterpart to Koch in his willingness to spend his own money to investigate Kurniawan, was ready to appear at trial. But Hernandez also wanted winemakers from two other prestigious Burgundian domaines: Christophe Roumier of Domaine Roumier and Aubert de Villaine of Domaine de la Romanée-Conti. How to persuade them to travel to a New York courtroom and face the daunting prospect of legal proceedings in English?

"These people are not accustomed to being interviewed by American prosecutors," says Hernandez. "But as French citizens, they could not be compelled to testify at trial. We needed them to agree voluntarily. This is far more likely to happen if they meet you and see your demeanor. Once again, this is where the importance of Laurent Ponsot never gets fully captured. He was our ambassador in Burgundy. He had the bona fides to make the introductions and clear the way."

The mission would have failed, Hernandez believes, without the help of the man from Morey Saint-Denis. Ponsot referred to himself as the head of the "French FBI: Fake Bottle Investigations."

So in summer 2012, ahead of the wrangling over the defense's motion to bar the evidence found in Kurniawan's home upon his arrest, Hernandez and Wynne flew to Burgundy. Over four days, they visited key domaines, their retinue grown to include two French police investigators based in Dijon, one of whom was a wine buff from the Jura, a region with a strong wine culture. Also on hand was the FBI attaché to the American Embassy in Paris. The entourage also visited Caveau de la Tour in Meursault, Kurniawan's largest supplier of older wines unsuitable for resale but useful for conversion to "Magic Cellar" icons.

"We took along two suitcases full of evidence from Rudy's workshop to show to the winemakers," Hernandez says. "That really allowed them to see the magnitude of the problem. At DRC, they were floored. They saw stacks of Les Gaudichots labels from 1929—a wine they hadn't seen for many years." (Les Gaudichots was subsumed into adjacent La Tâche in 1933 when DRC purchased the portion it did not already own.) In 2004, a cache of 1929 Les Gaudichots was sold by Christie's direct from the Doris Duke cellar at her New Jersey estate, where it had lain undisturbed since the 1930s. A single bottle sold for $8,813, a case for $88,125. Kurniawan's presence there as a buyer was a reminder that far from every uber-rare bottle he handled was fake.

The downside of the trip to Burgundy, weighing heavier on Hernandez than on Wynne, was that at each domaine they visited, they had to turn down invitations to taste. "We had to say, 'No, we can't.' When you represent the government, you can't accept anything from potential witnesses. You can't investigate a fraud at Disney World and accept free passes and eat a turkey leg. The wines we were being offered were worth hundreds of dollars. The only one we did taste was a 2010 Corton-Charlemagne at Roumier, which was already opened. The rest of the time, when we declined, they sort of understood. Do you know who didn't understand? The two cops from Dijon. We did tell these winemakers that we hoped that one day we would be back. And then we could taste."

Hernandez and Wynne returned to New York with promises secured from Roumier and de Villaine that they would join Ponsot as witnesses for the prosecution. Some wealthy collectors who had been victims of the swindle and who lived only a taxi ride away from the courthouse were unwilling to promise as much. Hernandez and Wynne also came home with, courtesy of the domaines, a reference collection of authentic labels to compare against Kurniawan's copies.

For Hernandez, the burgundy buff, the trip had only one failure: "We had a three-hour window in our schedule where I hoped we could fit in a wine tasting or two," he says, referring to domaines whose winemakers were not connected to the case. "But it never happened."

The ruling by Berman permitting the contested FBI search of Kurniawan's home came in January 2013. That spring, at another pretrial hearing, Hernandez and assistant prosecutor Joseph Facciponti arrived in the courtroom toting plastic shopping bags bulging with items taken from Kurniawan's house. Hernandez scooped out several rubber-banded packets of fake labels and held them up for the judge, Kurniawan, and his lawyer to see. He also displayed the long-handled cork inserter taken from the kitchen dish drainer. The prosecution had such an overflow of physical evidence, Hernandez said, that he was requesting a long table to be placed in front of the jurors' box where it could all be displayed.

That "show-and-tell" had dual aims, Hernandez tells me. "Nobody had ever seen a wine-counterfeiting case. So by showing this unfamiliar evidence, we were educating the judge. We were also giving Rudy the chance to see the instruments of his crime. If you're locked up in the MDC [Metropolitan Detention Center], it's important to remind you of how much evidence, communicated in a visual form, the jury will see and handle. That may lead you to conclude that this will be a very difficult case to win."

The message to the defendant was clear: If conviction is in the cards, then the wise course is to cop a plea. "More than ninety percent of defendants in federal criminal cases plead guilty," says Hernandez. "Of the remainder, an extremely high number are convicted at trial. So the overwhelming number of cases are plea deals."

Why didn't Kurniawan do the math? If he had pleaded guilty, his jail time could have been negotiated down. And his hefty legal fees, including cross-country travel expenses for two lawyers, paid for by his overseas brothers, could have been sharply reduced. The high cost of a trial to taxpayers could also have been eliminated. Both Kurniawan's first trial lawyer, Michael Proctor, and the duo who would succeed him, insisted that there *was* a reason to go to trial: It was the only way Kurniawan could preserve his right to appeal the government's admission of evidence discovered during the initial warrantless search of his house. If an appellate panel were to rule in his favor, a new trial, minus shopping bags full of evidence, might be in the offing. A long and expensive gamble, to be sure, but Kurniawan chose to go for it.

As summer 2013 approached, skirmishes between the two sides slogged on. The trial date was pushed back by three months. The new date, in early September, allowed the three French winemakers to make a quick trip to New York to testify prior to starting their harvests. But owing to an emerging rift between Kurniawan and Proctor, it was not to be. Earlier, all had seemed well at the defense table. The two men leaned close as they conferred in whispers. But by late June, relations appeared to turn cool, even hostile. Few words were exchanged between them. Twice, Berman called the defendant and his lawyer into his chambers for private discussions. And then he announced in open court that Proctor had asked to be released as Kurniawan's defense lawyer. What had caused the split? Possibly, Proctor had advised his client that, once Judge Berman had ruled that the mass of evidence found in the house search could be admitted, there was no point in going forward with a trial that was sure to end in a guilty verdict. If Kurniawan chose not to take that advice, then Proctor would have no reason to litigate into the jaws of defeat. A court-appointed attorney, Dawn Cardi, was standing by to replace Proctor, if necessary. But Kurniawan's new choice to be his cocounsel was a pair of experienced criminal lawyers. In the lead was Los

Angeles–based Jerome Mooney, whose career included sixty-four parachute jumps in the Air National Guard and a stint representing *Penthouse* magazine in the courthouse. He was assisted by Vincent Verdiramo Jr. from nearby Jersey City, New Jersey. The pair was not ready to sign on just yet. First, they had to get, as Mooney put it, "the uncomfortable stuff out of the way." That was a roundabout way of saying that until Kurniawan's family in Asia wired his legal fees in advance, he and Verdiramo would not formally take over the defense.

Berman pointed out that the defendant had been in jail a very long time without justice being done. Hernandez, too, was anxious to keep the trial on track for September 9. The potential delay was "now jeopardizing the date that we can have our three foreign witnesses testify live. If this trial is in December, I am going to lose two of my three witnesses," he warned.

"This trial is *not* going to be in December, I promise you," Berman growled. Not a promise that he could keep, owing to the need of the new defense team to prepare its case.

As the hearing ended, Berman stared grimly at the four defense lawyers now gathered before the bench: Proctor, about to depart, and three potential replacements, Cardi, Mooney, and Verdiramo. "My urgency and insistence [on speeding up the proceedings] is really on behalf of the defendant," Berman said. "There seems to be a lot of extra motion going on here. And I don't mean motion in the technical sense. I am a patient person, but I just want you to understand that I really think it has been unnecessary. I have never had a situation quite like this and I am assuming and hoping that when we get on track, we *will* be on track."

It was Berman's judicial way of saying that he was royally pissed.

Just over a month before the trial was to open, Kurniawan's lawyers provoked a brief firestorm that threatened yet a new delay. They asked Berman for permission to "have forensic psychiatrists conduct an evaluation of our client." The prosecution shot off a letter to the judge the same day warning that if the defense had "decided to establish a defense of insanity," it was too late in the game for that. The rules required prior notice of an insanity defense.

The prosecution need not have worried. The two clinicians who examined Kurniawan found him to be sane. One even called him "charming."

At last, on a brisk morning three weeks before Christmas 2013, Kurniawan faced a jury of his peers in room 1312 of the Daniel Patrick Moynihan United States Courthouse in Lower Manhattan. From the day of his Los Angeles bail hearing, it had taken twenty months, six lawyers, and sixteen pretrial hearings to get to this moment. Wary of yet more delays in the case, Judge Berman warned both sides that he intended to go on a holiday vacation, so the trial had better move along without delay.

The first prosecution witness was Barbara Chu, the loan officer from Fine Art Capital (now called Fine Art Finance), who had processed the $3 million loan to Kurniawan. On his application, Kurniawan had written in the space for "citizenship" that he was a "PR." Puzzled, Chu queried him about the abbreviation. Kurniawan told her that it stood for "permanent resident." That was untrue. In 2003, immigration authorities had ordered Kurniawan, whose application for political asylum had been rejected two years earlier, to leave the country.

Assistant defense attorney Vincent Verdiramo, who was as fiery as Mooney was mellow, drilled Chu about the role of Edward Milstein, whose family owns Emigrant Bank, in granting the loan. Chu held firm to her claim that she had talked just once with Milstein about Kurniawan and that he rated him as "one of the world's top-five wine collectors and confirmed that he sold over thirty million dollars of wine over the last two years [i.e., 2006–2007] through Acker Merrall & Condit, wine auctioneers."

FAC's final loan terms cut Kurniawan no slack and included taking possession of twenty-five artworks as collateral. Chu estimated those to be worth more than double the value of the loan. Typically,

FAC would allow the borrower to continue to enjoy the artworks at home. But Kurniawan, who could show no reliable source of income, or even proof of his claimed family wealth overseas, was apparently deemed too risky for that privilege.

That was prescient. Once the loan was foreclosed, FAC received just over $3 million from the sale of Kurniawan's paintings at Christie's. After repaying itself, FAC had enough left over to send $551,000 to Acker.

"So it's fair to say that as a result of this entire transaction you didn't lose a penny?" Verdiramo asked.

"That's correct," said Chu.

FAC had come out whole, but in the government's view, that did not scrub the slate clean. Kurniawan had lied on the loan application, and that was fraud.

The next witness was Truly Hardy, operations director of Acker Merrall & Condit. His appearance was a sore disappointment to Kurniawan watchers. They hoped that Hardy's boss, John Kapon, would be called to testify. He and Kurniawan had been intimately bound together in public and private ways. Each had nourished the other. What did Kapon know, or suspect, about Kurniawan's fakery of the very wines that Acker had sold for millions of dollars and that had vaulted the firm to the top of the auction world? At the very least, if Kapon chose to be a cooperative witness, he could have pulled back the curtain on his unique business and personal insights into Kurniawan. But both sides knew that was a pipe dream. Kapon was shielded by a tough legal team that had fought tooth and nail even to keep Bill Koch's lawyers from deposing their client. If Kapon was not going to be a cooperative witness, then Hardy was the fallback.

A person familiar with the prosecution's thinking but not wishing to be named explained its strategy to me via email: The prosecution needed a witness from Acker who could confirm some basic facts. "He had to identify a particular Acker catalog, confirm that Rudy was the consignor of lots X, Y, and Z in that catalog, and that a certain victim bought [those]." And he had to testify that certain of Acker's financial records were accurate.

"The two most informed people at Acker were Kapon and Hardy. But Kapon would not and could not have ever been the person to be a prosecution witness because he would have refused to testify to anything—even that an Acker catalog was an Acker catalog. His grounds would have been that testifying would have violated his right against compelled self-incriminating testimony, i.e., the Fifth. Hernandez would have had to grant Kapon immunity to get even that mundane testimony from him. Once a witness is granted immunity, he must testify or face imprisonment for contempt of court.

"If Kapon had been immunized, then Jerry Mooney could have attacked him on the stand for days, trying to persuade the jury that Kapon was complicit in Rudy's scheme. And that could make John seem like a person who is himself avoiding prosecution. Jurors might then start to feel sympathetic toward Rudy, who *was* being prosecuted. And so the prosecution called Truly Hardy."

Hardy testified that he "became aware" of Kurniawan in 2001, "when he was buying a certain amount of wine that increased over time."

"What, if any, other names did you know Mr. Kurniawan by?" asked assistant prosecutor Facciponti.

"The nicknames Dr. Conti and Mr. 47."

"Do those names have any meaning in the wine-collecting community?"

"They do. Dr. Conti is a play on Romanée-Conti . . . and it's probably one of the most famous if not the most famous wine in the world. And Mr. 47 is a play on that very famous vintage in Bordeaux."

Hardy shed light on Kurniawan's close monitoring of auction catalog preparation. Not finding a photo of a prized bottle that he wanted used to illustrate the Cellar II catalog, he emailed Kapon: "I am fuckin fuming right now.........where is the fuckin 61 lafleur shot?? that is such an important key shot for lafleur!!"

Kapon replied: "Dude, relax. Everyone is drooling. Got first bite from your list—guy in Japan got catalog already. Call me later this afternoon."

Hardy was cool in demeanor and precise in his responses as he shed light on the complicated financial arrangements between Acker and its biggest client. Questioned by Facciponti, Hardy explained that Acker directly extended "advances and loans" to Kurniawan. In some cases, Acker "negotiated advances and loans where we act as the guarantor of the loan. We do that when we don't have enough money to necessarily pay for the loan ourselves. And we can negotiate with our clients to cover the advance or loan where we are the guarantor."

The three Burgundian winemakers testified on the third day of the trial—an event unlikely ever to be repeated in an American courtroom. Ponsot, silver-haired and nattily dressed in a gray suit and pink tie, took the stand first. He recalled the moment when he had first gazed at images of the false vintages of his family's wines, sent to him by Douglas Barzelay: "I was sitting at my desk, fortunately, otherwise I would fall down," Ponsot said, eliciting smiles from the jurors.

In a long monologue, to be bested in length only by one of Bill Koch's the following day, Ponsot described the progression of his feelings upon discovering his wine had been counterfeited: "The first idea you have is a bit of glory. You say, wow, somebody is counterfeiting my wines? It means my wines are at a good level. So this is a human being. Everyone that is a winemaker when he has this problem goes through the same feeling. But very quickly I said to myself, yes, but someone one day will open a bottle and he will be disappointed because it's not the wine I made. And this is not good for the reputation of the winery. But on top of it—and this is what my idea was—it's dirtying the spirit of the appellations of Burgundy. What I didn't mention when I showed you the map is in Burgundy, seventy kilometers long, one kilometer wide, you have 1,250 different appellations. I think you know now what an appellation is. It's a type of wine. So 1,250 on a very small surface. This is what we call the terroir. There is no translation in English. *Terroir* means location. . . . This means the location where the vine is growing, where the wine is produced. Due to all of the elements that nature gave us plus the human being that is in the middle as an element of the chain between the roots of the vine and the glass of wine. So, this is very important to say: Through the fake bottles, I think that this spirit, this unique thing on the planet, is dirtied. My idea was to try to wash clean the integrity of the terroir of Burgundy."

Christophe Roumier, the lean, crew-cut, third-generation winemaker of his family's domaine in Chambolle-Musigny, was next to testify. Like Ponsot, he had drawn on arcane family history to smoke out a skillful fake. It was a label for 1923 Domaine Georges Roumier Bonnes-Mares. In smaller letters, beneath the vineyard name, were the words, "Ancien Domaine Belorgey." That was a reference to the previous owner of this portion of Bonnes-Mares.

Hernandez handed several packets of labels for this wine to the witness, and asked him to look closely at the 1923 vintage. "Do you think it is authentic?" he asked.

"I say two things. I say, first, in 1923 my grandfather was not yet established. [Domaine Georges Roumier commenced in 1924]. Second . . . he could not produce *ever* in this time any Belorgey wine because he purchased the vineyard in 1952, not before."

Roumier had been guest of honor at a dinner hosted in January 2007 by mega-collector Don Stott at his New Jersey home. Scott Bryan, then the star chef of Veritas, prepared the seven-course meal. Fourteen vintages labeled as Roumier were served. The oldest was a Bonnes-Mares 1919, apparently harvested five years prior to the domaine's founding. The second oldest was the 1923 Bonnes-Mares Belorgey, featured in a color photo on the menu cover. It was served with a low-key dish meant to give primacy to a wine in its dotage: roasted veal loin, fingerling potatoes, and tarragon.

The prosecutor now asked Roumier's opinion of that 1923 wine.

"The wine was tasting old. It was not a very good wine. That is all I can say."

Prodded by Mooney on cross-examination, Roumier did say more: "I wrote that it was not authentic."

Two months before the Stott dinner, a different bottle of the 1923 Bonnes-Mares Belorgey, among others, had been consumed at a dinner hosted by Kurniawan at Cru. As usual, Kurniawan wanted the empties returned to him in Arcadia. But all did not go well with the shipment. Cru's wine director, Robert Bohr, received an email from Rudy saying, "I received all the wines we drank at cru (some missing) and ALL but 2 are broken....I am extremely bothered since this is the second time it happened. (Esp the 23 roumier BM btl that I want to keep). In any event, we are unable to do the photoshoot we originally planned to record this historic event. What a pity......RK"

The duplicity embedded in this message is stark. As Roumier testified, the bottle could not have been real and the claim of a planned "photoshoot" was a farce. Most likely, Kurniawan was unhappy that he could not replenish the fake and resell it for a handsome sum.

Spoken quietly in cautious but clear English, Roumier's assessment that the '23 Belorgey was "not authentic" was a damning judgment. For winemakers like Roumier, perhaps even more than for consumers, burgundy can be excitingly good or downright disappointing. But it can never be inauthentic. The downside often comes from vintages when the weather has been cruel to the grapes, diluting them with harvest rain or puncturing their skins with hail, which lead to rot. Stark variations in vintage character are a large part of what makes burgundy wines endlessly interesting, while those ups and downs are largely lost in growing regions where the climate rarely springs unwelcome surprises. In blind tastings of burgundy, it can be easier to distinguish between different vintages (say, 2009, with its rich texture, and 2007, with its transparency) than between different appellations (say, wines of the same vintage from

Gevrey-Chambertin and Nuits-Saint-Georges). A little tension in the air is what makes opening a bottle of any wine interesting. That goes double for burgundy.

Earlier, Roumier explored how a particular wine may never "hold still" long enough to pin down its taste. And yet the eventual judgment held: "As I told you, tasting a wine is always a question of a feeling and you can mistake change, the aromatics can be different from one bottle to another, you yourself can have a different attitude to the same wine. So I wasn't sure. I just wrote down . . . that the wine was not authentic. This was my last word on it, anyway, because the wine did not have, if I may say, a taste that was touched by the tannins that we obtain in Burgundy. It had a very big mouth feeling, a feeling of alcohol and richness not typical of our wines." (But typical of California pinot noir.)

Among the wines found on Kurniawan's shelf of blending wines on the morning of his arrest were both obscure and highly praised California pinot noirs (as well as cabernet sauvignons). Blended with the old, commercial-grade red burgundies that Kurniawan had bought in volume, they could amp up the resulting blend exactly as described by Roumier.

On cross-examination, Mooney asked the witness how many wines had been tasted at Stott's table: "About 13 or 14 wines sound about right?"

"Something like that. We don't drink. We taste. So it means you don't swallow the wine."

Berman, untutored in how experts conduct tastings, said, "It would be helpful to explain."

Mooney: "If you drank thirteen bottles, your tasting of those would be pretty blurry by the end?"

"Yes. The process is that you evaluate the wine by, like I said before, the color, the nose—the smell of the wine—and then you take a little bit of the wine in your mouth. You swirl the wine so that you get a feeling of it on your palate and tongue and then you spit.

You have a small bucket and you spit the wine. You don't drink it all, of course."

The judge appeared perplexed. "So that I understand—dinner is served last at a tasting?"

"Yes."

"You eat the food, so to speak, but you don't drink the wine?"

"Yes, yes."

Mooney wanted to know if, besides the 1923 Bonnes-Mares, Roumier had been suspicious of some of the other wines served at Stott's dinner.

"All of those that carried the name Belorgey and were vintages older than 1952 were wrong to me."

In a 2012 blog post, Doug Barzelay gave an accounting of all the wines tasted at Stott's dinner. "Of the bottles sourced from the two 'Cellar' auctions, 3 were clearly authentic—and superb—6 were clearly fraudulent, one was corked, and one was probably but not clearly fraudulent."

Now it was the turn of the third and, at age seventy-four, the most senior of the Burgundian witnesses. As a young man, Aubert de Villaine worked in New York and married an American. He speaks English perfectly well, even eloquently. Yet he was accompanied to the witness box by a court-approved translator. Except for one brief whispered aside, her help was unneeded.

"What do you do for a living, Mr. Villaine?" asked assistant prosecutor Joseph Facciponti.

"I am what you call in France a vigneron—a winemaker," said the lean, aquiline-featured co-owner of what, at least in the hearts of Francophiles, is the most venerated wine domaine on earth. It was as if the pope were to identify himself as a country priest. Happily, de Villaine and his wife, Pamela, are also truly vignerons at their Domaine A. & P. de Villaine, a property in Bouzeron, an off-the-beaten-path village on the Côte Chalonnaise. There, the couple make authentic but not exalted burgundy wines free of the adulation that wreaths Domaine de la Romanée-Conti. The price differential tells the tale: The lowest US price for a bottle of 2013 Romanée-Conti in 2017 was $11,000. A bottle of A. & P. de Villaine's Bouzeron from the same vintage could be had for $32. For that price, the purchaser would get pleasure on the spot, while the Romanée-Conti would require two decades before it began to reveal all the facets of its subtle glory.

De Villaine had just reached the finale of a seven-year effort to have Burgundy's more than 1,250 individual climats named as a UNESCO World Heritage Site. Nominees must fall into either of two categories: natural or cultural. Burgundy would seem to fall into the "natural" category. But when I interviewed de Villaine in the fall of 2012 at DRC's offices, located behind a locked, high iron gate at the side of Vosne-Romanée's modest village church, he insisted Burgundy belonged in the "cultural" category. Not that he would deny that grape-growing is an agricultural effort. But pinot noir and chardonnay, as grown in Burgundy, nestle into human culture as a dog nestles into its human family. That is why de Villaine refers to Burgundy's *climats*, rather than to the more commonly used *terroir*.

"*Terroir* encompasses only the physical aspects of soil and air," de Villaine said as we gazed out his west-facing second-floor office windows, the legendary DRC vineyards sloping gently uphill before us. "*Climat* is different. It is bound up with centuries of human input into and around our vineyards. It has led to a winegrowing landscape that's been divided into parcels and hierarchies almost to excess. It has also generated a diverse, complex human culture that has stubbornly sought excellence in wine. It's been that way at least since the Gallo-Romans of the third century. And one word is key to that history: *climat*. If you say *terroir*, you forget all the culture."

Facciponti asked de Villaine, "What is your personal history with the Domaine de la Romanée-Conti?"

". . . I always understood that the domaine was something extremely precious that the family had to keep at any price. But I wasn't very close to the land. I was born in 1939, and when I was young, Burgundy was still in a state of difficulties. A lot of young people were doing studies of other kinds and not staying in the vineyards. Myself, that was my case. I did completely different studies. But when I was twenty-five, I decided this was what I wanted to do. So I asked my father and his partner if I could be accepted and they agreed. I started from scratch working in the vineyards [and taking enology courses]. . . . I have been comanager of the domaine since 1974."

Facciponti, leading up to queries about the mythic 1945 Romanée-Conti that was a Kurniawan specialty, asked the witness about the nineteenth-century scourge called phylloxera.

"It was a terrible bug that . . . destroyed all the vineyards [of France] whose only defense was injections [of carbon disulfide]," explained de Villaine. "For a while, many vignerons did that, but it was extremely complicated to practice on a large scale. . . . Little by little, vineyards were replanted . . . except for a very few. And the last one left was Romanée-Conti. My family had so much respect for this vineyard that they couldn't bear to tear it out and replant. So they kept the vines alive with injections until the Second World War, when the chemicals could no longer be found. The vines became weaker and weaker. And at the very end, when they were torn out after the vintage in 1945, production was [down to] two barrels—in all, barely six hundred bottles of Romanée-Conti."

While the quantity was minuscule, de Villaine called it "a great vintage."

"So, it's fair to say that any bottle of 1945 Romanée-Conti is rare, hard to find, and very valuable?" asked Facciponti.

"It is extremely rare. I would be surprised if today you still have a bottle existing, although you find some in auction sales, which is always surprising. But if a real bottle is on the market, of course, it would be a very, very high price because nothing is more rare and looked for than a bottle of Romanée-Conti '45."

Facciponti handed the witness three ziplock bags packed with Domaine de la Romanée-Conti labels from long-ago vintages, some going back to the nineteenth century. De Villaine stared at them as if he were seeing specters.

"Do you have labels at the domaine for these vintages anymore?"

"No, we don't have any more."

Facciponti milked the moment: "So is it surprising to you to see a stack of labels, several dozen if not several hundred, for vintages of wine that probably no longer exist?"

"It is extraordinary—like in a movie." De Villaine gingerly riffled through the labels, front and back. "And we never had these self-adhesive labels."

". . . And do you see labels for the 1945 vintage of Romanée-Conti?"

"Yes, and they are quite well copied."

". . . Would you say there's about twenty or thirty 1945 Romanée-Conti labels in your hands?"

"I never had that many in my hands."

De Villaine next examined a label for Les Gaudichots. He explained that after the purchase of this premier cru vineyard in 1933 it was designated as La Tâche: "So this is a label that doesn't exist anymore."

". . . Have you ever before seen a label for 1899 Les Gaudichots?"

"Never. . . . And maybe I should add to my explanation about the vineyards of Romanée-Conti, including this small vineyard of Les Gaudichots . . . that they were maybe three hundred or four hundred years old. . . . When a vine had given fruit for thirty, thirty-five, forty years, you would bury it by first making a little ditch at the bottom of the vine. Then you would bend the vine into the ditch and cover it with dirt. [In the spring it would grow] two or three new shoots to restart the old vines. This is how the vineyards were reconstituted for hundreds of years."

Ending his questioning of de Villaine, Facciponti asked, "Has anyone named Rudy Kurniawan ever been authorized to print labels for the domaine?"

"No, no."

On cross-examination, Mooney showed de Villaine a Romanée-Conti label printed with vintage year 1942 on one side and 1945 on the other. "Do you ever print labels on both sides?" asked Mooney.

"We don't need to save paper *that* much," said de Villaine with a straight face.

The next witness was Susan Twellman, a somber Californian. As manager of David Doyle's estate, she testified that she handled "all his financial affairs, his family office, and managed his wine cellar."

"Do you know someone named Rudy Kurniawan?" asked Hernandez.

"Yes, I do."

"How do you know him?"

"We were friends with Rudy and I know him from wine tastings and from purchasing wine from him."

Hernandez put up on the screens a copy of an email string between Doyle and Kurniawan. On June 12, 2007, Kurniawan had written:

> David,
> how are you? hope all is well. i am running into some cash issues for daily expense and housing. so i am trying to unload some of my wines to cover them. i would not sell these gems if i don't need to, i know i can sell them at auction for higher prices as u know but i need time to get paid and i'd rather sell them directly asap. you are the first true collector that came to my mind and pls advise if you can help and willing to buy all or any of them.

The "gems," according to the accompanying spreadsheet, included the familiar ultra-rare Kurniawan offerings for which Doyle wired Kurniawan the $3.2 million. The next month, Kurniawan was back with a new request:

Hey Dave, I am just really in need of three mill to pay bills immediately. In real deep, deep, s-h-i-t. Can you help while we wait on others? Only if it is not in your way or whatever reasons. I completely understand. Have fun in Thailand. . . . Thanks, Rudy. Please don't get pissed at me. . . .):

Twellman was not asked, and did not say, whether Doyle sent the additional "three mill." But in an affidavit to the court she wrote, "Beyond the loss of Mr. Doyle's $19 million investment, Rudy Kurniawan's actions represent an utter personal betrayal. . . . We spent a great deal of time together and grew to trust him and his friendship. However, it is now apparent that to Mr. Kurniawan his friendship with us was nothing more than a sham, a means to extract millions of dollars from Mr. Doyle using duplicity and deceit. The result has been personally devastating to both Mr. Doyle and me."

Of fourteen witnesses called by the prosecution, just one was cheerful and full of banter. That was Bill Koch. Rangy and tall, his mop of white hair unruly, he headed to the witness stand in long eager strides. Of all the collectors defrauded by Kurniawan, Koch was the only one to have sued him. That lawsuit, filed in California in 2011, alleged that Kurniawan was the source, via Acker, of a small batch of counterfeit bottles costing $75,000. Unlike most of the main prosecution witnesses, Koch was now seeing Kurniawan in the flesh for the first time.

The billionaire's testimony roamed free of inhibitions. Asked by Hernandez about his three academic degrees from MIT, Koch was launched: "I had a professor once who actually taught my father, who went to MIT as well. He said, 'Why in the world do you want to get a doctorate?' I naturally said, 'Well, because I think it's prestigious and I love science.' He said, 'Well, you know what BS is, don't you?' I said, 'Yes, a bachelor of science.' He said, 'No—the real BS.' And then he said to me, 'You know what MS is, don't you?' I said, 'No.' He said, 'It's more of the same. And you *do* know what a PhD is, don't you?' I said, 'No.' He said, 'Piled higher and deeper.' He was trying to discourage me from spending all that time at MIT."

Asked about what he collected, Koch dove in: art, paintings, sculpture, antiquities, and Western items. He called himself a "Western fanatic." (He didn't mention the nineteenth-century frontier town, complete with saloons, general stores, hotels, and brothels, that he had created at his Colorado ranch.)

"How about wine?"

"Unfortunately, I have a lot of wine—a cellar of forty-three thousand bottles. You see why my wife calls me a hoarder. And I try to collect wines that I think are the very best, that I enjoy and love drinking. Then I have four types of wine that I try to collect every year just to satisfy my obsession with collecting. And I've tried to have every year of, say, Château Lafite, of which I believe I have about one hundred fifty vintages or so. I collect Mouton Rothschild, of which I have about one hundred twenty vintages. Latour, about one hundred vintages, and Pétrus, about ninety. Unfortunately, about half of them are fake."

". . . What do you do with the wines you collect?"

"I have wines that are for drinking and then I have collection wines that I just want to brag about. For example, Thomas Jefferson wines. I bought them because they are very historical. Then I found out they were fake. Now I brag and show people the fake Jefferson bottles rather than the real ones. So I have these collection wines, but ninety-nine percent of my cellar is drinking wines. . . . One of the great things for me is that if I can have good friends, good music, beautiful paintings on the wall and great food and great wine, then I can feel the love that the artist had for his paintings, the love the musician had in playing or making music, and you could taste the love in the wine."

". . . Mr. Koch, when you buy wine, does it matter to you whether the wine in the bottle is authentic?"

"Absolutely. I mean, that's like buying a Picasso painting that's fake even though it's in a beautiful frame. No, the whole value is in the authenticity of the wine."

A few minutes later, Hernandez pointed to three bottles on the table in front of the jury: a double magnum of 1947 Château Pétrus and two bottles of 1934 Romanée-Conti. Koch had purchased them all from Acker Merrall & Condit in 2005 and 2006. What did he feel when he learned they were fakes?

"I was disappointed and I was angry. I got conned. Got cheated. Nobody likes to be conned or cheated."

"And did there come a time when you learned who consigned these three bottles to Acker Merrall & Condit?"

"Yes . . . Rudy Kurniawan."

"Have you looked in your cellars to see if you have other potentially fake wines that you have purchased that were consigned by the defendant?" asked Hernandez.

"Just from Burgundy alone, I've found over two hundred nineteen bottles of wine from Rudy that I paid $2.1 million for. I have not gone through all the burgundy or bordeaux that I own, but I estimate it's about another fifty to one hundred bottles that I paid anywhere from half a million to a million for."

"And when you say you have personally gone through the wines, has anyone assisted you?"

"I've had six or eight experts go through them: an expert in glass, an expert in labels, an expert in glue, an expert in corks, and an expert who studies fake wines. I've even taken wines to the châteaus to ask them if they ever made these kind of wines."

Jerry Mooney picked no fights with Koch. Instead, he introduced a subject close to both their hearts: gun-collecting. Ostensibly, it was a way of understanding how old wines, like old guns, usually have "gone through other people's hands first." Such wines once might have been reconditioned at the winery: replenished with a dollop of the same or similar wine and fitted out with new corks and labels.

Mooney seemed to be trying to implant in the jurors' minds the notion that Kurniawan's home workshop was not so much dedicated to counterfeiting wines as to reconditioning them. French wineries making wines meant for the long haul once reconditioned old bottles for their clients. In an age of counterfeiters, the wineries stopped the practice, lest they inadvertently give fake bottles their imprimatur through reconditioning.

Since most old items, Mooney suggested, had "gone through other people's hands first," it would be rare to find them in "pristine form."

"Well, I have pristine items that have been stuck away," Koch said. "I have a case of Winchester rifles that was never opened. . . ."

Mooney: "For every case of Winchester rifles that were never opened, there are tens of thousands of Winchester rifles that are in various stages of repair in the hands of people all over the place, right?"

"I would say hundreds of thousands."

Lawyer and witness delved deeper into the fine points of old guns. Asked about value added or detracted by repairs, Koch said that it all depends: "The Indians would break a rifle stock, and then they'd put some wet rawhide around it or piano wire to fix it. Now, that adds significance to the gun. . . . But if a guy has a broken stock and, say, his father replaced it, I, as a collector, would want to know that, because it changes the value of the gun."

Judge Berman was growing restive. "So, Mr. Mooney, could we move on from guns to wine?"

"Certainly, Your Honor. Maybe if I could give one more gun analysis first?"

Grimly, Berman acceded. And the gun talk flowed on to a question about abrasives used to "bring back up the shine" of an old weapon. "You don't want that, do you?" asked Mooney.

"It happens. But I'll tell you something else since you brought up guns. I have some guns that have been antiqued and are engraved with somebody's name—Chief Ouray, for example," Koch said, after Mooney had turned the subject to modifications sellers make to improve the appearance of antique weapons.

Koch's reference was to a leader of the Ute tribe in Colorado in the mid-nineteenth century. Chief Ouray tried to be peaceful toward white men while upholding the interests of his tribe. "When I took that gun apart—actually, I had a gunsmith do it—I found it had been antiqued," Koch said. "The documentation that went with the gun was all forged. And so someone sold me what I call a fake gun."

Once more, Berman tried but failed to steer back to wine.

"I bought a gun that was given to 'Lonesome' Charley Reynolds, who was General Custer's personal guide," Koch said. "Died at Little Big Horn. And there was a plaque on the gun that said, 'Given to Charley Reynolds by George Custer.' And it was all tarnished. I bought it from a very reputable, fine, antique gun dealer. And he warned me, 'Do not polish that plaque because you'll show it's too new and ruin the value.' So cleaning up a gun, reconditioning it, you know, if the guy's using the gun and he cleans it just to keep it in good working order, that's one thing. But if he cleans it up to sell it, and he takes off all the original antique stuff, that's a different story. That crosses the line."

Berman: "*Let's go.*"

In due time, Mooney brought the subject around to wine, only to veer off to a query about Koch's home decor: "In connection with your passion for wine, you've used the wine motif in some of the decorating in at least one of your houses, haven't you?"

"Yeah, in two bathrooms."

Didn't the bathroom feature "a wall made of wine bottles . . . that are back lit"? And another that was "wallpapered in labels"?

Koch eyed the lawyer coolly. "Boy, you have done some investigation. Been in my house?"

"You never invited me, sir."

Unlike most other Kurniawan victims, Koch never had direct contact with the defendant. So, despite Koch's lengthy stay in the witness box, Kurniawan was spoken of only glancingly. But at the end of his redirect examination, Hernandez did guide the jury's attention back to the epicenter of Kurniawan's crime.

"One final subject. You were asked some questions about reconditioning. You were asked by Mr. Mooney if you bought a 1962 Romanée-Conti, you'd want to recondition it with a '62 Romanée-Conti, correct?"

"Yes."

"My question to you is would you want that reconditioning to be done by DRC exclusively, in other words, no one else?"

"Absolutely right. I would only want it done by the domaine."

"If another collector had done it in their home, say in their kitchen, would that affect your willingness to buy that bottle?"

"Absolutely. I wouldn't buy it because he could have put dishwater in it."

That was a reminder to the jurors of FBI photos taken in Kurniawan's kitchen on the day of his arrest. They showed empty bottles soaking in the kitchen sink—in dishwater.

The three French winemakers had put a human face on the more than one thousand years of Burgundian wine culture. Bill Koch had been the solitary face representing Kurniawan's big-dollar victims. As its last witness, the government called Bordeaux-based Michael Egan, its expert witness and de facto pathologist. In his testimony, aided by a PowerPoint presentation, Egan deconstructed Kurniawan's elaborate label-making process. Typically, he started with an authentic label of an old desirable wine. After scanning it at high resolution, he removed details such as the vintage, the proprietor's name, the number of bottles produced, and the individual bottle number (many DRC vintages included these details). Then Kurniawan built the label back up, one component at a time, until he had a range of vintages to send to the printer. Egan showed, for example, how a scanned label of a real 1943 Romanée-Conti was turned into labels for the 1937, 1939, and mythic 1945 vintages.

For these wines, Rudy even had cork-branding stamps manufactured that carried the words "Romanée-Conti Vigne Originelle Francaise non reconstituée." (The domaine wanted collectors to know that these vintages were made from the "Original French non-reconstituted vines," which were the last in Burgundy, possibly in all of France, that had survived the phylloxera epidemic of the nineteenth century.) Pulling that cork, even a wary collector would likely be lulled into thinking that no counterfeiter would have gone to the trouble of having that cork branded with those words.

Judge Berman had allowed the press to come up to the evidence table during breaks to examine the packets of fake labels, cork stamps, waxes, and other counterfeiting exhibits. Many of the labels were printed in multiples and mounted on peel-off sheets. Only a commercial print shop could have manufactured them in that format. But where had Kurniawan found a printer to do that? An American shop, given such an order, might have become suspicious and notified law enforcement. Egan supplied the answer, discovered on the back of a loose label of 1929 Roumier Bonnes-Mares, one of which was now in his hand:

> "When I held this up to the light . . . it really looked like there is a watermark on the label which reads 'Concord,' like the airplane. And having made some research on this, it is actually a printer based in Indonesia who uses this water-marked paper. And for all the counterfeit labels that I've seen from the defendant's house, this type of paper has been used for disparate producers from Bordeaux and Burgundy— Château Pétrus, La Mission Haut-Brion, and also for all

the Burgundy domaines. I don't think, in reality, that these wines going back to 1929 up to the 1940s would be using an Indonesian company which was established in 1983."

Who was overseeing the print jobs for Kurniawan in Indonesia? That question, peripheral to Kurniawan's innocence or guilt, was not raised at his trial.

✣

Light snow was falling in Manhattan as summations began on the fifth morning of the trial. Assistant prosecutor Facciponti addressed the jury for the government. That was in line with the custom that with a two-person prosecutorial team, one delivers the opening argument, the other the closing argument. Facciponti demolished the notion of a "Magic Cellar" filled with "wines so rare and great that they were the stuff of legend." That Kurniawan sold fake wines was indisputable. But that left open the question: Did he know the wines were counterfeit when he sold them? Or, asked Facciponti rhetorically, was he "just another victim who happened to acquire counterfeit wines"? Facciponti's methodical description of the workshop in the defendant's home left no doubt about who made the wines.

The defendant, he told the jury, "was motivated by undying greed."

Butting up against the government's strong wall of damning evidence would have been folly, so Jerry Mooney, sporting one of his signature picture ties, this one a Monet, was folksy rather than combative as he summed up for the defense. Take those seven bottles of 1962 Romanée-Conti the defendant purchased in 2006. They were authentic but in poor shape; their low fill levels had been recorded by the vendor, David Parker. So Kurniawan had reconditioned them.

"Seven bottles with two-and-a-half-inch fill became six bottles with one-inch fill. That's exactly how Roumier told us it should be done," the lawyer reminded the jury, nimbly turning his client into a follower of a great winemaker.

And then, Mooney reprised gun talk to put a positive spin on what his client had done: "It's kind of in line with [how] Mr. Koch talked about the Remingtons that he collected and other memorabilia and the experiences he would have of people getting something old and trying to fix it up. They would want to make it *better*."

Mooney went on to invoke *Antiques Roadshow*, the long-running PBS show-and-tell program. "You watch somebody dragging in the treasure and putting it in front of [the expert], and the guy looking and saying, 'Well, if you hadn't done this, if you hadn't polished it, if you hadn't cleaned it up, if you hadn't made the repair, this thing would be wonderful, but it's not anymore.'" With treasurable wines, Mooney told the jury, it is different. They are not meant to be framed or displayed. They are "designed to be drunk." So, while reconditioning may compromise nonconsumable trophies, it protects wine until the time comes to pull the cork (even if it is not the original cork).

What about those eighteen thousand labels for iconic wines the FBI recovered from Kurniawan's house? As anyone who has ordered a print job knows, Mooney pointed out, "you print one, you get a lot." If his client felt he needed to replace a dirty, disintegrated label on a few bottles of 1945 Romanée-Conti, it was no surprise that he ended up with dozens of new labels.

Mooney hit harder in attacking count two of the indictment, charging Kurniawan with defrauding Fine Art Capital. He called FAC a "glorified pawnshop." Like a pawnshop, FAC requires collateral worth more than the loan. Pay off the full amount, and you get your property back. Violate the loan provisions, and your property is gone. That was what happened to Kurniawan as soon as FAC discovered that he had double-pledged the twenty-five artworks he was required to deliver to the lender's warehouse.

"So when you look at the Fine Art Capital transaction, the evidence screams that there never was any intent on Rudy's part to defraud anybody, because the only person on earth who ends up losing in that deal is Rudy," Mooney said. He went on, "They sell the art pieces, and they are able to recover all the money to Fine Art Capital and five hundred thousand dollars for Acker Merrall. And that wasn't even all the art."

The prosecution's prerogative is to have the last word by rebutting the defense's summation. For that, Jason Hernandez was back in front of the jury. "If you think that the defendant was just polishing up some authentic bottles and that he wasn't intentionally lying to Fine Art Capital," he said, "then you might think that sometime next week, a man with a white beard is going to come down your chimney and leave you a case of 1945 Romanée-Conti under your tree."

The next morning at 10:55, Judge Berman was handed a note saying that a verdict had been reached. The jurors had deliberated for slightly under two hours. They filed back into the courtroom. Kurniawan, dressed in an ill-fitting gray suit, stood tight-lipped, his hands twined in front of him, as the judge's clerk asked, "With regard to count one, mail fraud, the alleged scheme to create, sell, and attempt to sell counterfeit wine . . . you find the defendant, Rudy Kurniawan:"

"Guilty," said foreperson Patricia Gonzales.

"With regard to count two, wine fraud, the alleged scheme to defraud Fine Art Capital . . . you find the defendant, Rudy Kurniawan:"

"Guilty."

Kurniawan's two lawyers whispered to each other. Their client, once lionized as a prince of winedom, now thirty-seven, still looked too young to legally buy a bottle of wine.

Outside the courtroom, Mooney said, "He really just wanted to be accepted. People were very supportive of him, but the moment he was arrested, everybody ran. My theory: He comes up with some wines that are truly rare. Suddenly people want to be with him. When he couldn't find more, he made it."

Laurent Ponsot also dallied outside the courtroom. He had attended every day of the trial. Asked how he found American legal proceedings, he shrugged. "Same as in France—boring."

Was he happy about the verdict?

"Not happy. Satisfied. It's good justice."

❦

How to punish Kurniawan? In an earlier era, Judge Berman would have had wide latitude in sentencing the only person ever convicted in a federal court of selling counterfeit wine. Since 1984, federal sentencing guidelines have set the parameters for punishment. They are contained in a hefty manual that covers a spectrum of crimes ranging from terrorism to odometer-tampering to selling drugs to a pregnant person. But not a word about wine-counterfeiting.

The guidelines require a sentencing judge to assess both the crime and the history of the criminal. Points are assigned for each component of the crime. The worse the impact, the more points added. In the case of fraud, such as Kurniawan's, higher victim loss tacks on additional points. A bank robbery in which death or injury occurs is assigned more points than one in which nobody is hurt. Past crimes also count. If the bank robber is a recidivist, points are added. Kurniawan had no previous criminal record.

Pre-guidelines, a parole board could recommend release of a prisoner for good behavior long before his full sentence was completed. Not anymore. Parole for federal crimes no longer exists. The best a convict can now hope for is a sentence shortened by 15 percent for good behavior plus an additional smaller reduction for release to a halfway house. Initially, federal judges had to follow the sentence guidelines strictly. Since 2004, they are authorized to stray from the guidelines if the circumstances of a particular case tilt that way (usually, up). But the guidelines are still the norm.

The court's probation department prepares a presentencing report for the judge. Berman showed impatience at the initial lack of thoroughness of the investigation into Kurniawan's background. Why hadn't his mother been interviewed? Probation responded that it hadn't been able to arrange for a Mandarin-speaking interviewer. Yet the FBI, knowing that Lenywati Tan didn't speak English, had managed to bring along a Mandarin speaker at six o'clock in the morning when it arrested Kurniawan. Why couldn't probation find a translator to interview her at a regular hour?

The prosecution struggled to get a fix on the losses incurred by Kurniawan's victims. Working against them was the reticence of many victims to admit to how expensively they had been fleeced. The loss amounts fixed by Berman were topped by David Doyle ($13.1 million), followed by Brian Devine ($5.3 million), Michael Fascitelli ($3.6 million), and Wall Streeter Andrew Hobson ($3.1 million). Bill Koch's loss was $2.1 million, but the judge noted that he had effectively "dropped out of the case" after settling his California lawsuit against Kurniawan for $3 million in the previous month.

Once the losses exceeded $20 million, extra guideline points were added to Kurniawan's total. The prosecution asked the court to "impose a sentence within the advisory guideline range of 135–168 months' imprisonment." That was well below the maximum allowed incarceration of twenty years (240 months) per count of fraud.

The defense—no surprise—had a different view of Kurniawan's crime and fitting punishment. Mooney's presentencing memo portrays young Kurniawan entering a realm where high-end fakes were rife. In his "frenzied buying," he had "unwittingly acquired many fakes." What really bothered Kurniawan, and the impetus for his crime, was not a bottle's false label. It was opening the bottle and finding its contents undrinkable:

(*left*) Rudy Kurniawan asked to be photographed with Burgundy's venerated Aubert de Villaine, coproprietor of Domaine de la Romanée-Conti. The occasion was an extraordinary tasting of seventy-four vintages of Romanée-Conti held over three days in New York in spring 2007.

(*right*) Kurniawan holds up his paddle until he wins a barrel of wine at the Hospice du Rhône auction in 2002. The barrel was donated by Sine Qua Non, a small California winery whose wines are highly sought after.

Good times! Left to right: collector Eric Greenberg, Rudy Kurniawan, Hollywood agent Matthew Lichtenberg, auctioneer John Kapon. Image snapped in 2005.

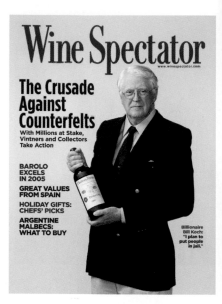

(*left*) Laurent Ponsot, fourth-generation winemaker at his family domaine, when his hair was "Jesus length." Ponsot stopped the sale of his wines purportedly from his domaine at a 2008 auction, leading to Kurniawan's downfall.

(*right*) Billionaire Bill Koch on the cover of a December 2009 issue of *Wine Spectator*. He holds a fake magnum of 1921 Château Pétrus.

Los Angeles lawyer and amateur French wine label detective Don Cornwell examines images of "faux Ponsot" labels in an auction catalog.

RK 0000294

GOVERNMENT EXHIBIT 2-1 11 12 Cr 376 (RMB)

GOVERNMENT EXHIBIT 2-18 11 12 Cr 376 (RMB)

(*left*) The first sight federal agents would have seen when Kurniawan opened his front door: a jumble of wine cartons and crates, stacked almost to the ceiling in the foyer.

(*right*) On a shelf in Kurniawan's house on the day of his arrest, bottles await counterfeiting. Below them are cups of wax used for sealing the bottles.

GOVERNMENT EXHIBIT 2-4 11 12 Cr 376 (RMB)

RK 0000379

Labels were being soaked off bottles in the kitchen sink on the morning of Kurniawan's arrest. A corker and funnel can be seen in the drainer. The window has been covered.

A close-up of the drainer, with the funnel, corker, and cork extractor (used instead of a corkscrew, so as to keep a cork intact).

Kurniawan's Domaine de la Romanée-Conti wax and cork stamps and stencil, to label bottles' wax seals and corks, and to spray-paint the domaine's name onto crates.

A drawer full of wine labels in Kurniawan's home.

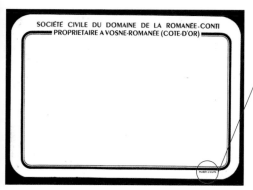

Here, Kurniawan has created a blank frame, the first step in creating a Domaine de la Romanée-Conti label. The name of the domaine's actual printer, Filiber, is at bottom right.

To most eyes, this label would appear to be correct. But over one letter is an accent not used in 1971, giving away the bottle as a Kurniawan counterfeit.

Printing instructions in both English and Indonesian on images of old vintages of Romanée-Conti and La Tâche labels. Purportedly from the cellars of Nicolas, once a source of great burgundies.

Assistant US Attorney Jason Hernandez (far left) and FBI Special Agent James Wynne (rear, reaching back) show fake labels to Christophe Roumier (in white shirt) at Domaine Georges Roumier in Burgundy in summer 2013.

Wine authenticator Maureen Downey uses a jeweler's loupe to examine a suspect bottle labeled as Château Lafite Rothschild.

(*left*) This bottle, vintage 1945, was among purported Domaine Ponsot wines withdrawn from an Acker Merrall & Condit auction on April 25, 2008. But the domaine did not gain access to the grand cru appellation of Clos Saint-Denis until 1982.

(*right*) This methuselah (holding the equal of eight regular bottles) labeled as 1971 Romanée-Conti was purchased by real estate mogul Michael Fascitelli at a January 2006 Acker Merrall & Condit auction in New York. Fascitelli paid $85,000. The wine is counterfeit.

(*left*) Defendant Kurniawan listens as victim Bill Koch is questioned by lead prosecutor Jason Hernandez in a Manhattan federal courtroom on December 13, 2013.

(*right*) Assistant prosecutor Joseph Facciponti presents fake labels to the jury while Judge Berman and Kurniawan look on.

At a Texas recycling facility, thousands of Kurniawan's fake bottles were destroyed in December 2015. The shattered glass was ground up and sold as a decorative gravel in a garden shop.

"Rudy knew he could do better. He knew that he could faithfully reproduce not just the package, i.e., the bottle and all its accoutrements, but the contents—the taste of the wine within. It was a challenge, and he was up for it.

"At first, it was not necessary to recreate the bottle. Bottles from tastings were available. It was not uncommon to keep a fine bottle to remember the experience of the tasting. Rudy had done this. Now, as he looked at the empty bottle, he knew what he needed to reproduce the contents. From his experience, he was able to find just the right mixture of available wines, some with age, some newer, but all adding the flavor that was needed. In this way, what was gone, returned. It was challenging, exciting, compelling and fun—and not a little addictive. More to the point, it was what the in-crowd secretly seemed to want."

Did Kurniawan have assistance in creating counterfeit bottles, as Laurent Ponsot believed he must have had? Mooney insisted that he did not:

"All of the reproduction bottles that Rudy created were carefully created by his own hand in the kitchen of his home in Los Angeles. As shown by the evidence at trial, two or three bottles at a time would be soaked in the sink to remove the old labels. Then the new labels and appropriate stickers were carefully applied. Only after all of this was done and a proper looking bottle created would the bottle be filled with a mixture of other wines that would match, as close as possible, the taste of the vintage that was proclaimed by the label. This was slow, meticulous work."

Mooney linked Kurniawan's growing troubles to his dealings with Acker and John Kapon. The crux of the problem, as Mooney saw it, was the many loans Kurniawan was receiving from the auctioneer and its clients. Amounting to millions of dollars, some of these loans took the form of advances for wines Kurniawan was to deliver for sale at future auctions, while others were booked when he "purchased" lots at auctions at the reserve price without having to immediately pay for the wine. Kurniawan counted on repaying these loans by selling high-priced wines at future Acker auctions, but finally he couldn't. Meanwhile, Kurniawan was also sending millions of dollars to his brothers in Asia. At trial, FBI agent Wynne testified that Kurniawan's Wells Fargo bank statements showed that he wired $12 million to Dar Saputra and $5 million to Teddy Tan. These payments could have been partial payback for the million-dollar-per-month allowance that Kurniawan boasted about in earlier years and that he felt honor-bound to make good on. Karen Strassler, a cultural anthropologist who studies the Chinese subculture in Indonesia, wrote to me: "In general, filial piety is demanded of all sons, and this could mean enormous pressure on all sons not to shame the family and return any money borrowed."

The cost of a trial to both Kurniawan and the government could have been avoided if he had been willing to plea-bargain with the prosecution in return for shortened jail time. But Mooney had stuck with Proctor's strategy of ultimately trying to convince an appeals panel to rule that the search of his home on the morning of his arrest was illegal. That required Kurniawan to stand trial and have the evidence presented, creating a record that would show the court of appeals how important the search had been. The prosecution could have agreed to allow Kurniawan the right of appeal if he pleaded guilty, but it did not do this.

In his client's favor, Mooney pointed out, was that he never denied being a counterfeiter during the trial. Mooney was saying, in effect, that the prosecution should be more lenient with Kurniawan for not fighting back.

Positing lower victim monetary loss figures than the government, and arguing that "actual harm" to Kurniawan's wealthy victims was not disastrous to their lifestyle, Mooney proposed a "guideline range" for his client's sentence of eighteen to thirty-seven months. Given that Kurniawan would do his best to make restitution, and that he had no previous offenses, Mooney proposed a reduced sentence of twenty-seven months—exactly how long Kurniawan had already been deprived of his freedom.

Four months before his sentencing, Kurniawan had broken his silence in a letter to the court:

Dear Judge Berman,

Thank you for your consideration of this letter and for allowing me to express to you my sincere feelings concerning my conduct which had led to me standing before you in this matter. I make no excuses for what I did. What I did was wrong, not only legally, but also morally and socially. I have brought extreme shame and embarrassment to my family. In my culture my conduct has put a stain upon my family's reputation that time and punishment will never wash away. In this Internet age, my name will be linked forever not with great things or great deeds but rather with a crime that soiled the one thing I truly loved and was good at.

Through my family's generosity I was able to experience and participate in a world known only to very few others. I also was graced by God with a talent to taste, describe, and remember the nuances of the wines I was fortunate enough to enjoy. In fine wine I found my passion, a passion that became all-consuming and which ultimately led me here today.

Wine became my life and I lost myself in it. Finding rare wines became an obsession and I relentlessly pursued obtaining them wherever I could find them. What originally started out as buying a few bottles of wine at a local store over the course of years turned into buying millions of dollars worth of wine. I would never buy one or two bottles, I would buy everything. I honestly didn't know the full extent of what I bought but it was thousands and thousands of bottles.

This obsession attracted attention and I admit that I enjoyed it. I met a lot of interesting people who were very successful and intelligent. We shared a common interest in wine and my wines provided me with access to people and experiences I otherwise would not have enjoyed. I thought these people were my friends and I wanted to be accepted into their world. I now realize that all this was false and pretentious and that my priorities were completely out of order. The things I did to maintain this illusion were so foolish. The end was inevitable.

I've come to realize during the past two years that I have been in prison that the things that I thought were so important really weren't important at all. Two years away from my family has taught me life lessons of what truly matters in a man's life. My mother, who is ill, struggles alone every day when I should be there to help her. I have not seen my two remaining brothers in years. They only wanted the best for me and gave me every opportunity to truly succeed in this country. Through my actions all I have to show for their generosity is a criminal record, severe debt, potential judgements in the millions of dollars, and an eventual deportation from the country I have come to love. Additionally, when I am deported my mother will have to decide whether she wants to live in this country alone or travel with me back to Indonesia.

Judge Berman, it is important for me to tell you that I understand that what I did was wrong and that I am genuinely sorry for everything that I have done. I never meant for things to turn out as they did. I never meant to hurt or embarrass anyone. I am not evil or violent. I am truly sorry for the shame and pain I have brought on my family and the embarrassment I have brought on the people I wanted to be my friends. I am willing to make restitution to the people I took advantage of. I have been a model prisoner during my two years in prison. Please allow me to return to my mother. She is 66 years old and in poor health. She needs me.

Respectfully submitted,

Rudy Kurniawan

The things I did . . . Much is left unaddressed by these words. When did the fakery start? Was it only for the money or was Kurniawan also attracted to the challenge of deploying his tasting wizardry to create wines that could fool the experts? And, more damningly, to fool clients who trusted him as a friend? Who else knew what he was doing? Did he have assistance in crafting the false bottles? Label images found on his computer include scribbled instructions in Indonesian and, as Egan discovered, paper used to print the labels, watermarked "Concord," was also Indonesian, so *somebody* was assisting him with label logistics in Indonesia. Kurniawan did not testify, and so could not be asked any of these questions. He remains, as Étienne de Montille nailed it, a "UFO."

Not to be cast aside were the good things that Kurniawan did: Numerous wine lovers are in his debt for the great real bottles that he opened and shared with them. They dined very well on his tab. Of course, Kurniawan went on to extract enormous amounts of wealth from his marks. But he also spread the wealth, when he still had it, to tip-dependent servers, busboys, and dishwashers. In that way, there was a little bit of Robin Hood in Kurniawan. Consider the lunch at Jean-Georges that he hosted on the day after the faux Ponsot auction. It had to be a tense time for Kurniawan, who alone at the table knew he would never be able to truthfully answer

Laurent Ponsot's question about where he had acquired the false wines. Yet his credit card bill shows that he picked up the tab of $8,958.28 and added a hugely generous tip of $2,041.72 for a total of $11,000.

When I first asked Barzelay how the lunch for four had become so expensive, he was puzzled and not a little shocked to learn the amount of the bill. Several months later, he called back with the answer. Looking through old tastings notes, he found one for that lunch. It was for a bottle of 2005 DRC Montrachet, the dearest of all white burgundy. The price for that wine on the Jean-Georges wine list on the day of the lunch is now unavailable. However, dealer Geoffrey Troy reports that in 2008 he sold a six-pack of 2005 DRC Montrachet to another dealer for $4,800 per bottle. Assuming that Jean-Georges paid about the same amount from its supplier, and that the wine was marked up by a relatively modest 50 percent, the price paid by Kurniawan could have easily approached $7,000 per bottle. By springing for this prize wine, perhaps Kurniawan thought that he was buying goodwill from others at the table, notably Ponsot.

As for the fake bottles his wealthy clients bought from him, do these folks not bear some responsibility for not doing their due diligence before throwing silly quantities of money at Kurniawan wine? Absent the guile of a consummate con man, they would have held tight to their money *and* their common sense.

Part and parcel of that guile was Kurniawan's way of seeming incapable of it. "I was surprised when I heard that he was producing fake bottles," Aubert de Villaine wrote to me. "I didn't look at him as capable of doing this. The two times I met him, he gave me the impression of a 'lightweight.'" De Villaine was not entirely taken in, however: "From the first time I met him, I felt I did not want to have anything to do with him, the contrary of an attraction."

Late on a pleasant August morning, Kurniawan rose in Judge Berman's courtroom to be sentenced. The suits that he had been permitted to wear during the trial—Men's Wearhouse, not Hermès—were now replaced by the baggy prison blue and gray sweats familiar from his pretrial hearings. His head was bowed, his hands clasped behind his back. Before passing sentence, Berman said that he had not been swayed by Kurniawan's letter of contrition, in which he "took no specific responsibility for the crimes he had committed." Alluding to the unknown contents of Kurniawan's myriad fake bottles, Berman warned, "We need to know that our food and drink are safe and not some witches' brew."

Eight months earlier, Kurniawan had shown no overt emotion upon hearing the guilty verdict. Now his narrow shoulders slumped. Distress and shame engulfed his face.

The sentence was pronounced: ten years in prison. That was less than the prosecution or the probation department had called for, although almost four times as long as the defense had proposed. There was no realistic chance, his lawyers knew, that Kurniawan would be acquitted. Their goal was to get him the shortest possible sentence. In that, Mooney and Verdiramo admitted, they had failed.

Judge Berman imposed an order that Kurniawan make restitution to his victims of almost $30 million. From payments for prison work, he was expected to pay about $150 monthly into a federal restitution fund. "That'll get them paid back pretty fast," quipped Mooney, a bitter edge in his voice. (Through 2016, Kurniawan was making his monthly payments.) In that summer of Kurniawan's sentencing, Hernandez and Wynne, now both retired from government service, returned to Burgundy for a victory lap. "The first time we visited Burgundy, I told all the winemakers the same thing: 'We can't taste now, but we'll be back,'" Hernandez says. This time, Wynne's wife and sixteen-year-old daughter also came. Laurent Ponsot hosted a welcoming gala picnic for the Americans in the midst of his vineyards. They visited a monastery and a cheese maker. Ponsot also hosted a gala dinner at his winery, high up on the slope of the Côte de Nuits. Other guests were Christophe Roumier and Étienne de Montille.

Hernandez and Wynne gifted Ponsot with a plaque attesting to his role as head of the French branch of the FBI—"Fake Bottle Investigations."

"Laurent asked what other domaines we would like to visit," says Hernandez. His first choice was Coche-Dury, a domaine at the top of the pecking order in Meursault that does not normally welcome visitors. "I could have said that I wanted to see Henri Jayer"—a venerated winemaker who died in 2006—"and Laurent would have exhumed his body." (One thing that Ponsot could not do, apparently, is keep peace with his three sisters, co-owners of the domaine. In March 2017, he walked away from the winery and started a new négociant firm, called simply Ponsot, with his son, Clement.) Aubert de Villaine escorted the Americans on a cellar tour at Domaine de la Romanée-Conti. At the end of their barrel-tasting, de Villaine opened two bottles for his guests as they sat around upright oak barrels turned into tables. One wine was a Bâtard-Montrachet, a hallowed white burgundy, not sold commercially by DRC. "It is the most lush, opulent, effusive white," says Hernandez. "Then Aubert popped open a 1990 La Tâche. It was ethereal—the greatest wine I have ever had."

And surely the best wine that sixteen-year-old Lindsay Wynne ever had.

CHAPTER 9

Aftershocks

Reverberations from Kurniawan's arrest would be felt far and wide. An early impact was on the gargantuan wine list of Rockpool Bar & Grill in Sydney, Australia. The popular restaurant, set among imposing columns in an art deco bank building, was co-owned by David Doyle, Kurniawan's biggest client and now biggest victim. Doyle, retired cofounder of a software company and a billionaire by age forty, had chartered a Boeing 747 to fly a chunk of his California wine holdings to instantly create Australia's greatest cellar at Rockpool (now renamed Eleven Bridge and no longer owned by Doyle).

The restaurant's wine list may have been the only one anywhere then offering the mythic 1945 Romanée-Conti. In a May 2009 report in the *Daily Telegraph*, wine director Sophie Otton proposed a simple dish to match with the wine: wood-fired grilled pigeon with roasted red peppers, grapes, and radicchio salad. It was priced at $34, while the tab for the wine (in US dollars) was $67,125. Doyle had purchased six bottles of 1945 Romanée-Conti from Kurniawan for $13,000 each. Given the typical restaurant markup of at least two times the per-bottle cost, Rockpool was offering a bargain.

Was the Rockpool bottle one of those purchased from Kurniawan, and if so, was it fake? Doyle claimed not. He told a local newspaper that he had also purchased multiple bottles of 1945 Romanée-Conti in Europe years before the purchase from Kurniawan. Still, immediately, precautions were taken at Rockpool. "On the day the story broke," Otton wrote in an email to *Wine Spectator*, "David Doyle called me from the US to let me know what was happening. I went in the restaurant immediately and began going through the list, removing any bottles we acquired through Kurniawan. . . . It was really an alarming situation and we felt it was better to err on the side of caution. As to my own perception, there is absolutely nothing about the wine we held that would cause me to question its provenance, and it was a subject that was discussed in detail."

Word of Kurniawan's arrest disquieted collector friends who had stood by him even after his faux Ponsot stumble four years earlier. One loyalist was Jefery Levy. In 2005, Levy was planning to fly to New York to attend the fiftieth-birthday party of novelist and wine writer Jay McInerney. He wanted to gift McInerney with a rare birth-year wine that had wowed them before: 1955 Leroy Chambertin, a grand cru from one of Burgundy's most revered domaines. In 1980, the late wine critic Robert Finigan reviewed a trio of Leroy wines, calling them "expansively, profoundly lovely wines which remain in one's tasting memory as the best of the best." One was the 1955 Chambertin. Kapon had the same opinion when he tasted the wine at the Deaf, Dumb, and Blind event hosted by Kurniawan in 2003. He called the 1955 Leroy Chambertin "one of the greatest wines I have ever had."

"I was looking for a few bottles of the 1955 Chambertin to bring to Jay, but none were for sale in the world," Levy says. "I did have the wine once with Rudy, so I called him and asked if by chance he had a bottle or two that I could buy from him direct."

"Dude, you are in luck," Kurniawan told Levy. "I have a full sealed OWC [original wooden case]. But I'm not going to sell unless you buy it all." Levy bought the case and brought a few bottles to McInerney's party. They were "amazing." When McInerney visited Levy in Los Angeles, they drank a few more. Levy calls it "a bonding thing."

After learning of Kurniawan's arrest, Levy inspected his remaining six bottles of the 1955 Chambertin. His eye fell on a misspelling of "San Rafael," the location, just across the Golden Gate Bridge from San Francisco, of Domaine Leroy's importer, Martine's Wines. When Levy contacted the owner, Martine Saunier, she concurred there *was* a misspelling on real labels of the 1955 vintage, but it was not in the word *Rafael*. She asked if the corks were branded. They were indeed stamped "Leroy 1955," but *not* "Chambertin," as they should have been. "So this was some lesser 1955 Leroy, which is why Jay and I were fooled," says Levy, "but it was still one of the greatest wines I ever had. Were my feelings hurt that Rudy had sold it to me? Yes, because this was not an auction sale. I bought them from him direct. I was his friend. If I forgave Rudy, it's because with him I also experienced some of the most transcendent wines ever."

Not complete foregiveness. When I mailed Levy to ask if he thought Kurniawan might be a sociopath who lied facilely, he responded, "I think this diagnosis is right on. How else could he have screwed me after we spent so much family time together?"

In May 2013, fourteen months after the FBI raid in Arcadia, Kurniawan's handiwork made an unattributed appearance as lot 1243 in a Christie's catalog for an auction being held at Rockefeller Center. The lot was described as a single magnum of 1962 La Tâche, "cracked wax capsule partially missing, bin soiled label." It was estimated to sell for $16,000 to $24,000 plus buyer's premium of 22 percent.

Even among legendary vintages of La Tâche, 1962 stands out. Though it started out "rather light," according to Michael Broadbent's tasting notes, by age twelve it "filled the entire room with fragrance." Normally, the highest score that Broadbent awards to any wine is five stars, and that only rarely. For 1962 La Tâche, he added a sixth star.

Old and rare wines at auction are most reliably sold not in isolation but as a collection from a single consignor. If there is one such bottle in a cellar, there will likely be more. But this 1962 La Tâche magnum was a one-off. The catalog was mum concerning its provenance. Where *had* it been all these years? Potential bidders would certainly want at least a clue about a wine from a vintage then already so rare that Robert Parker wrote in the 1990 edition of his massive book *Burgundy*: "It has been years since I have seen a 1962, and I have no idea of how they have matured." This from a critic who is welcomed at the domaine and regularly drinks with collectors whose cellars are flush with old DRC. Based on his old notes, Parker estimated that 1962 La Tâche, along with all DRC wines of that vintage, "lived up to their celestial reputation." Before Kurniawan's arrest, an auction house might have slipped a wine like this magnum into its catalog without a word about provenance. But those days were—or should have been—gone.

Don Cornwell, ever alert to rogue bottles, was the first to notice several eyebrow-raising details in the full-page catalog photo of this La Tâche magnum. In a Wine Berserkers blog post, Cornwell noted similarities between this bottle and others withdrawn from the fake-plagued Spectrum-Vanquish auction held in London the previous year. Easiest to spot was the errant circumflex over the *A* in the large word *TÂCHE*, now a familiar Kurniawan marker, which did not appear on labels until the late 1970s. This La Tâche's individual bottle number, 301, stamped at the lower left corner of the main label, was also suspicious. It was printed at an atypical slant and was fainter than domaine versions. And the dull red tint and pocked surface of the wax capsule looked more Kurniawan than Romanée-Conti. In any case, according to the domaine, 1962 La Tâche magnums were released with foil capsules, not wax.

A few days before the auction, I asked Per Holmberg, then Christie's North American wine director, for more information about lot 1243. Who had consigned it? Holmberg responded: "As a matter of practice, we do not identify consignors by name without their express consent. I can tell you, however, that the consignor is a longstanding Christie's collector who has been an active and respected member of the wine community for many years."

But there was more to the story than Holmberg disclosed. At a wine sale in the same sales room on December 10, 2010, when Richard Brierley was head wine specialist, Christie's had sold the same magnum of 1962 La Tâche that was now about to be reoffered. A photo of the earlier lot, number 116, showed that it, too, was stamped with serial number 301. The price, including buyer's premium, had been $22,800.

Looking further into the story for *Wine Spectator*, I learned that the purchaser was an anesthesiologist in Phoenix, Arizona. The magnum had pride of place in his cellar—until, one day, it was spotted by a visiting wine dealer, Josh Wertlieb. No longer in the business, Wertlieb told me that he was then "a broker in high-end stuff." He had dealt with Kurniawan, whom he found to be "always kind, always generous. I was only twenty-three, and he was very inclusive of me."

Eyeballing the 1962 La Tâche at the doctor's home, Wertlieb was startled. "I said, 'Holy crap! That looks familiar.'" Before bidding on other DRC bottles at the 2010 auction, Wertlieb had requested and received photos of the bottles from Christie's. Magnum 301 was among them. At the time, Kurniawan was still more than a year away from being arrested, and the wine community was not yet sharp-eyed enough to spot his mistakes in faking old DRC wines. By the time Wertlieb saw the catalog image of the magnum being resold, the glitches were known. He emailed photos from both the 2010 and 2013 auctions to Don Cornwell, who verified that the magnums were one and the same. They even had the same vertical stain on the right-hand side of the label.

"I told this doctor that he should call Christie's and tell them he wanted to return the magnum," Wertlieb said. "I thought that they would be receptive."

But Christie's was not willing to refund the doctor's money. Not just yet. It proposed instead to resell the magnum. The proceeds would then be used to reimburse the doctor. And so, lot 116 in Christie's December 2010 auction now reappeared as lot 1243 in the May 2013 auction.

The magnum was a source of discomfort to Christie's then retail partner, Geoffrey Troy, who expressed his doubts about it in a letter to Holmberg. Holmberg wrote back, "We sent photos to DRC of the bottle, they told us based on the photos there was nothing that would lead them to believe that there was anything wrong." That would seem to have been the last word. My story for *Wine Spectator*, in which I was trying to establish the Kurniawan connection to the magnum, seemed to be dead-ending. Still, that evening, I emailed a photo of the magnum to Aubert de Villaine to ask if he or anyone at DRC had vouched for its authenticity, as Holmberg claimed, and to ask his opinion of the photo. With my deadline near, I prayed for a prompt reply.

It was in my inbox the next morning. De Villaine said nothing about the domaine having received a query about the magnum from Christie's. As to its authenticity, he wrote, "There is nothing one can conclude from looking at a picture. All I can say is that the capsule or wax (it is impossible to see what it is from the picture) is obviously not original." De Villaine did say that the circumflex and the way the serial number was stamped on the label "doesn't reveal anything." But he concluded, "It is impossible for me to say if the bottle contains authentic La Tâche 1962 wine or not, but faced with doubts, I believe that we would not authenticate it."

Two days before the auction, Holmberg wrote, "The lot in question has been withdrawn from sale to allow additional time for first-hand inspection by additional third-party experts. Christie's has opted to take the additional step of arranging an in-person inspection [of the magnum], given the variations in labeling that often come with older vintages of DRC wines."

After signing a nondisclosure agreement, the doctor received a refund from Christie's. The auctioneer did not reveal what happened to the withdrawn magnum. The Arizona doctor told me that he had a suggestion: "The best thing that they could have done to that bottle was to smash it."

One more tremor from Kurniawan's kitchen handiwork was felt from afar. Hrothgar, an investment firm registered in the British Virgin Islands but operating from Singapore, had purchased 132 bottles of Romanée-Conti for $2.45 million in 2011. The trove included forty-four magnums and one jeroboam, the vintages ranging from 1961 to 1990—all exceptional. Hrothgar was led to believe that the seller was Don Stott, known in collectors' circles as a huge buyer of burgundy wine. In fact, according to a 2016 lawsuit filed by Hrothgar in New York, the seller was a group of dealers in the United States, France, and the UK, fronted by a Manhattan broker, who had sourced the wine from Kurniawan. The wines lay in a storage vault called Wine Cellarage located behind the thick walls of the former American Banknote Building in a downtrodden section of the South Bronx. The renter of the storage space was listed as Dar Saputra—the name of Kurniawan's brother. In an email to an unknown addressee obtained by prosecutors in the criminal case against Kurniawan, Kurniawan referred to the purported DRC wines as "my wines."

At Hrothgar's behest, wine authenticator Maureen Downey inspected all 132 bottles. She declared each and every one to be fake. Hrothgar (the name of a legendary Danish king) sued the quartet of dealers who had a finger in the sale. Kurniawan, already behind bars, is also a defendant.

Still another residual sign of Kurniawan's handiwork appeared in a 2013 issue of a handsomely produced London-based journal called the *World of Fine Wine*. It is a full-page advertisement for Acker Merrall & Condit dominated by a close-up of the label on a bottle of 1945 Mouton Rothschild. The serial number, 20488, is stamped in pale blue ink. The château never used that tint, but Kurniawan did.

⁂

Though shamed and jailed, Kurniawan kept one direct link to the vineyards of Burgundy. It took the form of 250 shares he owned in a partnership created to buy several prestigious vineyards on the Côte d'Or. They included parcels of Beaune premiers crus and Vosne-Romanée Malconsorts, a premier cru adjacent to the grand cru La Tâche. Malconsorts can itself rise to the level of a grand cru. Kurniawan's shares constituted 22.73 percent of a six-person entity, named Étienne & Partners. The shares entitled each holder to dividends in wine from the vineyards. Helming the partnership, and making the wines, is Étienne de Montille, scion of a family long rooted for many generations in the wine-saturated village of Volnay.

The tale of how Kurniawan came to hold those shares begins in 2006. That was when de Montille, who had abandoned a banking career to return to the family winemaking enterprise, was attempting to buy the Thomas-Moillard wine estate—42.5 precious acres of mostly grand cru and premier cru Burgundian vineyards long held by a family that now needed to sell them off owing to inheritance troubles. De Montille was restoring his own family domaine to the size it had been in the mid-nineteenth century, before high-living ancestors in Paris began selling off parcels.

In need of outside investors to swing the $22 million purchase price, de Montille lined up the Seysses family of Domaine Dujac in Morey-Saint-Denis as a partner. The two domaines agreed to divvy up the vineyards, which were purchased by two land companies created for that purpose by de Montille. Shares were then sold to wealthy burgundy lovers. Dujac, for example, brought on British supermarket heir Lord Sainsbury to buy shares entitling him to wine from Bonnes-Mares, while American venture capitalist Wilfred Jaeger gets paid in Romanée-Saint-Vivant.

Kurniawan was introduced to de Montille by Paul Wasserman, then operating the Los Angeles wine shop and storage facility financed by Kurniawan. The occasion was a tasting sponsored by de Montille's local distributor. "Étienne fell under Rudy's charm, just like we all did," says Wasserman.

De Montille doesn't deny the potency of that charm. "It was 2006, and Rudy was the hot guy you wanted to hang out with and share a bottle with," he says. "He was generous, he was a gifted taster, and he was considered in the inner circle of fine wine collectors." De Montille checked with other trusted collectors, who vouched for Kurniawan. Invited to be a partner in the farming company, Kurniawan was late in sending payment. When he did pay, de Montille says, he sent too much money.

Two years later, Kurniawan's standing among collectors took a tumble thanks to Laurent Ponsot. De Montille was disturbed. In 2011, during a visit to Los Angeles, he confronted Kurniawan. "I said, 'There are a lot of rumors and suspicions about you. If they are true, in no way can I be associated with you.'

"He looked me straight in the eyes and said, 'It's all bullshit.' And he said that when you come out of nowhere and build up a great cellar in a short time, as he had, 'people are jealous.' To be honest, when you have no solid proof otherwise, you have to give the person the benefit of the doubt. And yet, I was disturbed, because burgundy is built on confidence. If you buy a Pommard Rugiens [a fine, full red] from Domaine de Montille, there is no scientific proof that it is Rugiens in the bottle. It's all about trust." (De Montille's father,

Hubert, passed away while dining with friends in November 2014. In his hand was a glass of his Pommard Rugiens from the superb 1999 vintage—a final and fitting sensory pleasure.)

When de Montille saw photos of Kurniawan's counterfeiting workshop following his arrest, the winemaker said, "I was more than disappointed. I felt completely betrayed."

Once convicted, Kurniawan had been ordered to forfeit his ill-gotten gains. However, because of restrictions in the French partnership's bylaws, Kurniawan's shares could not be sold at public auction. They had to be sold back to the de Montille family. The US Marshals, charged with getting the highest price for the shares, had no choice but to enter into a private negotiation with de Montille. At the end of 2015, Kurniawan's shares were quietly sold back to the family for $726,000—just a bit more than Kurniawan had paid and, de Montille says, "a little more than I wanted to pay."

Those shares "will never leave us again," he says. As for Kurniawan, he never got to enjoy the dividends of his investment in shares of a Burgundian farming company. "I offered to ship him his wine, but he said, 'Oh, don't worry about it.'"

Too late now.

❦

At the top of Kurniawan's food chain were his counterfeits, beneath which were many thousands of mainstream bottles purchased from legitimate dealers and auctioneers here and in Europe. He had spent $40 million for that wine. Kurniawan's aim was to resell the wines at higher prices, mainly at Acker auctions but also in private sales. In no way could the constant flow of incoming wine fit in his house, already chockablock with bottles in various stages of being transformed. So he rented a gated storage space at Pacific Wine Distributors, a commercial storage facility located a few minutes' drive from home. Antonio Castanos, his friend and occasional front man for selling wine at auction, had never been invited to Kurniawan's house, but he had visited the storage area. He described it at Kurniawan's trial as "huge."

After Kurniawan's arrest, US Marshals took possession of his stored cache of more than six thousand bottles. The wines journeyed in refrigerated trucks fourteen hundred miles to Pflugerville, Texas, an Austin suburb where football scenes in the NBC series *Friday Night Lights* were filmed. There, the wines were deposited in the warehouse of auctioneer Gaston & Sheehan, a vendor of all manner of property confiscated by the government. It wouldn't do for the Marshals to inadvertently sell even a single fake, so before being sold, the wines had to be ruthlessly vetted. "Previously, we'd sold small numbers of forfeited wines—never more than three hundred bottles," I was told by Jason Martinez, the Washington-based marshal in charge of mounting the sale. "Based just on sheer volume, this was the largest authentication job we've ever done."

Kurniawan's inventory included many real wines, but it would prove to also be infested with counterfeits, some of his own making and, probably, others that he had purchased from dealers.

The marshals hired a local appraiser to oversee the inspection. Lacking expertise in rare wines, she retained Arizona-based wine broker Josh Wertlieb to carry out an initial triage. It was Wertlieb who had spotted the Kurniawan-made 1962 La Tâche magnum in the home of the Arizona doctor, which Christie's later attempted to resell. While still a very young bachelor, he had caroused with Kapon, Kurniawan, and a cast of Angry Men at Cru blowouts. An early task for Wertlieb in the wine-inspection process was to order a large rubber stamp that said "COUNTERFEIT." Fake labels would then be stamped in orange indelible ink. Once he had pulled out the obvious counterfeits, Wertlieb handed off the examination of the purportedly most valuable wines to Bordeaux-based Michael Egan. That included all bottles labeled Romanée-Conti.

As the government's authentication expert at both Kurniawan's trial and, before that, at Bill Koch's civil action against Eric Green-berg, Egan was the last line of defense against bad bottles. His challenge, he told me in a December 2015 interview, was to inspect "the more risky bottles with greatest value—the cream of it." In a strange twist of fate, these wines, representing vintages of the rich and arcane wine culture of France tracking back more than a century, had ended up in a featureless concrete warehouse on a drab commercial strip of Texas flatlands.

Egan arrived in Pflugerville in July 2015, armed with his jeweler's loupe and an inventory of real and laptop-based digital samples of labels that were specialties of Kurniawan's workshop. This allowed him to do "exact comparisons" with the labels on the wines now resident in Texas. For five days, Egan took over a borrowed office at the warehouse as pallets of purportedly rarest wines were wheeled in to him for inspection—770 bottles in all.

Certain things struck him at once: "It was odd to see a soiled label on a clean bottle, or vice versa." Other "tells" were indirect, such as missing foil capsules on real bottles of Château Lafleur from "not so good vintages, such as 1992 and 1993." Egan guessed that Kurniawan had carefully removed those capsules. Then he slipped them onto the necks of self-created Lafleurs of legendary vintages such as 1950. "I think Rudy was really good at putting capsules on bottles and rubbing them to make them look older," Egan says. The giveaway to those antiqued capsules came when Egan peeled them back. "You expect to see a bit of oxidation and brown markings on the inside of the capsule if it had great age. But you could see that these were very shiny. There was no patina. "I also saw so many ways that Rudy had experimented with soiling a label—soaking them with just the right amount of dirt in the water. And I found photocopied labels. He was doing that before he got himself organized and got his labels printed professionally." Egan identified 199 fake bottles among the 770 he inspected, including double magnums of Pétrus 1945 and 1961. Each of these "torpedoes," as these big bottles are sometimes called, would have sold at auction for the same money that could have bought a fully equipped Prius. And each would soon come to a violent end.

⚜

Of the real wines to be sold, almost all reflected honorably on France. The exception was three lots symbolizing the shame of France. They were labeled "Hospices de Beaune, 1942, Cuvée Maréchal Pétain." They were meant to be offered for sale at the famed charity auction benefiting the ancient hospital in Beaune held annually on the third Sunday of November. Pétain had been the hero of the Battle of Verdun in 1916. Under the Nazi occupation from 1940 to 1944, however, he had teamed up with the Germans instead of combating them. The white-mustached defender of old French values (God and agriculture, über alles) became leader of the Vichy state. Pétain quickly instituted anti-Jewish laws and soon authorized the arrest of Jews, who were deported to Auschwitz.

In 1941, Pétain was still a hero to most French citizens. That year, the Hospices de Beaune was urged to consecrate a portion of its vineyard holdings to him. A famed premier cru, Beaune Theurons, was chosen. Stonemasons erected a wall around the section. Its gated entrance was emblazoned with the name Clos du Maréchal Pétain.

Thirty bottles from the clos arrived each month at Pétain's headquarters at the Hôtel du Parc in Vichy. More bottles were donated in November 1942 to the Hospices de Beaune auction. They had ornate labels bearing the name of the hospital and the Clos du Maréchal. That same month, the Germans occupied Vichy, cooling the adulation of the French for the head of the Vichy state. As the war wound down, Hitler spirited Pétain to Germany for safekeeping. In 1944, Charles de Gaulle, upon returning to France from wartime exile in England, stripped the old man of his property, including the Clos du Maréchal. The same stonemasons who created the walls of the clos were said to have also torn them down. More than sixty years later, Kurniawan, who had never set foot in France, owned an ornate reminder of the misplaced honor to the leader of Hitler's French partner.

Gaston & Sheehan mainly disposes of seized automobiles, restaurant equipment, and other leftovers from failed businesses. But in November 2015, it morphed into a hotspot of rare wine sales, launching an Internet auction of 4,711 authenticated bottles of "Rudy wines." Because of its size, the sale was broken into two phases, each lasting two weeks. Multiple photos of each of the 905 lots were provided, and all sales were commission-free. Collectors did not run scared from the provenance of the collection. Almost 98 percent was sold for a total of almost $1.5 million. Net proceeds were designated to compensate Kurniawan's victims.

The auction's top lot was also one of the most tattered: three bottles of 1911 Romanée-Conti missing their main labels. Egan had turned thumbs down on other bottles with apparently faultless labels, yet this trio won his confidence. "The capsules remained and looked right for the era and, importantly, their crowns were correctly stamped," Egan told me. He was able to see correct branding on two of the three corks. He traced the provenance of the three bottles to a 2008 sale by highly respected Skinner Auctioneers in Boston. They had long been in a New England family cellar. "We vetted those bottles so that we had confidence in them," recalled Marie Keep, head of wine for Skinner. The color of the wine was "beautiful" and—curiously—the bottles still had their main labels glued on when Skinner sold them for $60,750. So what happened to the labels?

"They're probably still stuck in Rudy's scanner," quipped Egan.

Select California wines drew spirited bidding. Two magnums of 1995 Sine Qua Non Tant Pis reached an astonishing $15,600. And those three lots of the not so honorable Burgundy rarity, 1942 Hospices de Beaune Clos du Maréchal, each sold for between $1,000 and $1,500. The oldest wine offered, an 1838 Bouchard Père & Fils Ermitage, a Rhône wine, got only a single bid, selling for $1,720. Egan tracked its provenance back to a Zachys auction on April 25, 2008. The winning bidder was probably Kurniawan. Hours later, his twenty-two false lots of Ponsot wines were withdrawn from the fateful Acker auction.

One bidder who took special satisfaction from his Texas purchases was Douglas Barzelay, the burgundy collector who had alerted Ponsot to the faux Ponsot lots. Barzelay had bid against Kurniawan at auctions and always lost—the result of Kurniawan's habit of never lowering his paddle. "I bought several things at this sale, wines which I lost out to Rudy at earlier auctions, that had perfect provenance—and I ended up paying less than they would have cost me originally!" One of those purchases, with a few friends including Allen Meadows and Rob Rosania sharing the cost, was the 1911 Romanée-Conti. When they drank a bottle in 2016, it did not disappoint.

✦✦✦

Kurniawan's counterfeit bottles walked their last miles ten days before Christmas 2015. Their execution took place at Texas Disposal Systems, a massive recycling plant in Creedmoor, Texas (population 219). The bottles were unboxed by hand into a twenty-cubic-foot, concrete-bottomed tub and smashed by a three-ton magnet dropped from a crane. A door at the bottom of the tub was opened, allowing the rogue wine to flow onto piled earth. The heady scent infused the dry air. After mixing, the "drunk earth" was carted to a two-hundred-foot-long compost heap kept at a steamy 145 degrees

Fahrenheit by microbial activity. "The sugars and nitrogen in the wine will be a good benefit," I was told by Paul Gregory, director of organics and recycling for Texas Disposal Systems.

Had his firm ever before recycled bottles of wine? "We've done beer, water, and Gatorade," Gregory said. "But people don't usually bring me wine. They drink it."

The bottles were pulverized into tiny nuggets, then sold as decorative glass at the firm's shop, Garden-Ville. Purchasers would never know that the shiny stuff under their shrubs and flowers was once the false glitter of the wine world.

The real wines, the ones made with devotion and which, even in old age, whisper the truth of their home soil, live on. In vino veritas.

Epilogue

ike Jay Gatsby, Kurniawan and his wealth emerged from shadowy origins. Both men shed their birth names. Both were stylish, charming, adept at mixing and mingling, and able to throw a great party. If he hadn't ambushed his own life, Kurniawan would also have become the master of a grand mansion—not waterfront, and not as ample as Gatsby's, but still impressive—at which he could have received his guests instead of having to meet them at restaurants or at their homes. Kurniawan was also kindly, and unknowable. And while he may not have been an accessory to an actual hit-and-run accident, such as the one that led to Gatsby's downfall, Kurniawan did run his wheels over the good faith of his victims.

A distant green light across the water symbolized Gatsby's longing for Daisy Buchanan. If Kurniawan gazed at any such beacon in his mind, it might have symbolized a bottle of wine even more perfect than 1945 Romanée-Conti.

Kurniawan's game remains far from fully explained. The question that first teased FBI agents when they entered his Arcadian home workshop—whether he could have fabricated all those fake bottles by himself—remains open. Whatever the answer is, it pits firm fact against equally firm opinion. The fact is that the FBI found no evidence that any hands other than Kurniawan's directly fabricated his fakes. The opinion of a cohort of Kurniawan's drinking companions is: No way!

"I was with Rudy on dozens of occasions," Rob Rosania tells me. "He was *the* most non-work-ethic-driven person. This is not a guy who could run a light manufacturing setup. For sure, there were other people doing the dirty work." In the documentary film *Sour Grapes*, Rosania's Angry Men colleague Jefery Levy concurs: "Rudy was the last person I'd ever suspect of being able to do any kind of intensive arts and crafts. He doesn't have the attention span. It's a time-consuming, laborious thing to do, and he could never do that. He's ADD. I could not see him doing it and I still don't believe it."

Josh Wertlieb, not an Angry Man but often on hand at Kurniawan events, is succinct: "The guy didn't have the bandwidth." The in-house evidence discovered by the FBI contradicts the naysayers. Whoever was in the house could indeed do light manufacturing, *was* skilled at arts and crafts, and did not have ADD—*if* the task at hand was to recreate old French wine.

⁂

Ponsot, no stranger to bottle production, insists that Kurniawan could not have done it alone. He estimates that to carry out the steps required to fabricate a single bottle of most wines would take one hour—two hours for Romanée-Conti. Maureen Downey begs to differ. Her view of how he worked is similar to how defense attorney Mooney described it in his presentencing memo. His first step, she believes, was to experiment with blends of old and new wines until he came up with one that he felt could mimic the real wine. Bottles would then be filled and corks inserted. Bottles returned from restaurants required no new labeling. For those that did, he affixed fake labels, most of which were delivered incomplete from overseas. Vintage-specific details were then printed onto the labels by his large home printer. Kurniawan also had to keep track of signatures of proprietors as they changed. Old vintages of Château Lafleur, for example, carried the flowing joint signature of "T. et M. Robin." After the death of Thérèse Robin, only the signature of Marie Robin was on the label. The names of the proprietors on labels of DRC wines changed many times during the last century. On labels bearing individual serial numbers, such as Château Mouton Rothschild and all DRC wines, Kurniawan used custom-fabricated stamping devices to stamp the numbers. He also had custom-fabricated wax stamps to imprint the domain seal on the molten wax caps of bottles slated to be DRC.

For the new labels, Kurniawan had ordered specialty papers with antique finishes—this had caught the eye of Hernandez and Wynne in the emails—that could become the base for making labels look old by additional liquid staining, dirt smearing, sanding, and tearing. (Hopefully, he did not prematurely "brown" labels, as Chinese counterfeiters of ancient pottery once did, by dunking them in a sewer!)

"I absolutely believe Rudy could have made ten cases in a day," says Downey, "provided that he had prepared his blend formulas and his materials."

Not that Kurniawan handled every step personally. He employed overseas commercial printers to produce labels superior to what he could make on his own color laser printer. His handwritten instructions in Indonesian on label images indicate the care he took to mimic the details precisely. Packets of labels bearing both Indonesian and Japanese writing were submitted in evidence at trial. But no emails concerning them were found. Who saw to the ordering and paying for the print jobs? How were eighteen thousand labels delivered to Arcadia? Did he get help from his brothers in Asia?

Two weeks before the faux Ponsot auction, Kurniawan queried Kapon: "Can you get dar 100 to 200 cases of cheap 80s bord[eaux]? Like 81 to 88? [$]400 - 700 a cs."

Kapon replied: "will look into it but those prices barely exist anymore." Among the wines "Leny" sold to Brian Devine in 2003 and rejected for resale by Zachys, there was one magnum labeled as the fabled 1947 Cheval Blanc. It was rejected because its cork was stamped 1947 on one side and 1981 on the other. The latter vintage was utterly overshadowed by the glamor of the 1982. Why was Kurniawan looking for a large quantity of old but mediocre vintages of bordeaux for his brother? Was his intent for the wine to be transformed into more desirable vintages? If so, Hong Kong, where collectors are relatively new to the wine game, would have been an excellent place to sell the remade wine.

Another question looming over Kurniawan: What was the true source of the family wealth that he once tapped into to become, as Kapon called him, the "biggest wine buyer on the planet"? His early story of family control over the Heineken franchise in Indonesia did not pan out. Barbara Chu of Fine Art Capital, charged with getting facts about Kurniawan's family wealth, came up cold: According to her internal report approving the loan, "FAC has consulted special investigators who are unable to confirm or refute legitimacy of Borrower's wealth and reputation." Bill Koch's investigation of Kurniawan's family points to a darker and closely shielded reality centered on two family members, each convicted of embezzlement on a gigantic scale from Indonesian government entities. The combined sum approached $1 billion. Little of that money has ever been recovered and may have been hidden in offshore accounts. Some of it may then have found its way into Kurniawan's hands to support a lifestyle for which no other source of funds has ever been found. Brad Goldstein, in charge of Koch's investigation, is "99 percent sure" that the two criminals, Hendra Rahardja and Eddy Tansil, are brothers of Kurniawan's mother, Lenywati Tan. And, therefore, Kurniawan's uncles.

Koch hired a former CIA station chief in Jakarta to look into Kurniawan's family roots. One result was the creation of a maternal family tree. Topmost on the tree is Kurniawan's maternal grandfather,

Harry Tansil (Tan Tek Hoat), a banker who set the tone for the next two generations by fleeing the country with purloined funds in the 1960s. But not before he begot, among other children, the late Hendra Rahardja (Tan Tjoe Hien), Eddy Tansil (Tan Tjoe Hong), and Lenywati Tan (Tan Lee Woen). Another daughter, Tan Lee Chuan, married the owner of a large department store chain in Indonesia. The siblings were all born in Makassar, capital of South Sulawesi, a peninsula pointing south on the large Indonesian island once known as Celebes.

Hendra Rahardja (b. 1943) first prospered by selling Vespa motor scooters and Yamaha motorcycles, then diversified into real estate and banking in Hong Kong and Singapore. He eventually controlled three banks with hundreds of branches throughout Indonesia. Between 1991 and 1996, those banks granted six loans to various property companies controlled by Rahardja's family. Some of that money was used to buy property in Australia. During the Asian financial crisis of 1997–98, the Indonesian government pumped money into teetering banks by creating a liquidity support fund. Rahardja was accused of misappropriating hundreds of millions of dollars of those funds.

Rahardja fled to Australia, where he was arrested. In 2002, an Indonesian court convicted him in absentia to life in prison for having siphoned more than $390 million from the liquidity support fund. In 2003, he died, possibly of cancer, while awaiting extradition to Indonesia. Only a trickle of the purloined funds has been returned to Indonesia from Australia and Hong Kong. The rest, according to news reports, is suspected of having been funneled to offshore entities including Sunshine Worldwide Holdings Ltd. and South East Group Ltd., both registered in the British Virgin Islands.

Rahardja's brother, Eddy Tansil (b. 1954), made his first fortune as an agent for three-wheeled taxis imported from India. He moved on to beer-brewing, first in Indonesia, then in China. Through his Golden Key Group, Tansil got large loans from the national economic development bank to build a petrochemical complex in West Java. The money was diverted to other purposes. Tansil was convicted in 1996 of embezzling $565 million from the national bank and sentenced to twenty years in prison. Shortly after his incarceration, Tansil walked out of the prison to a waiting car, ostensibly to be transported to a medical appointment. He was not seen in Indonesia again and may be at large somewhere in China.

What about the sister of the two embezzlers? Lenywati Tan has been living legally in Arcadia since 2001, at first with two sons. One probably committed suicide; the other went to prison. Her lode of diamonds and Birkin bags suggests that she has access to wealth. One source may be identified in the Offshore Leaks Database compiled by the International Consortium of Investigative Journalists. It shows that a "Lanywati Tan" is a beneficial shareholder in Premium Famous Corporation, an entity incorporated in 2006 and registered in Tortola, British Virgin Islands. The purpose and assets of Premium Famous are hidden from public view. The normal purpose of offshore registration is to hide significant assets. Could Lenywati Tan have gained access to some of the ill-gotten gains of her two brothers? The wealth to support her lifestyle had to come from somewhere.

The same for Kurniawan, who in a short time went from working in a golf pro shop to setting the rare wine market on its ear with his multimillion-dollar expenditures. Kurniawan's Asia-based brothers charged millions of dollars on American Express cards linked to Kurniawan's card, all paid off from his domestic Wells Fargo bank account along with his own hefty bills, including $40 million for wine in a five-year period. Was this a way of laundering dirty money hidden away by his uncles and cleansed by Kurniawan's wine sales in America? In 2002, according to an FBI source, Kurniawan told an auction house employee that buying and reselling wine was a "great way to launder money."

For five years, Kurniawan and John Kapon were entwined as drinking buddies and business partners. When it all unraveled, an unavoidable question arose: Did Kapon know or suspect that Kurniawan was counterfeiting the very wines that he was himself hawking at Acker auctions? A nonverbal and purely subjective answer to that question confronted me in Kapon's office a few weeks after Kurniawan's arrest. I was working on a profile of Kapon for *Wine Spectator*. A final interview was scheduled. Kapon could have canceled it but didn't. His publicist called me before the interview to warn me that no questions would be permitted relating to Kurniawan.

We met in a windowless conference room above Acker's retail shop. Kapon was at one end of a long table, I at the other. He fielded my not very exciting queries. At the end of the interview, we rose. It was time to say good-bye—almost.

"John, I know I'm not supposed to ask you about Rudy, but I'll ask a question anyway that you don't have to answer." When I felt his eyes lock with mine, I asked: "Do you feel that Rudy betrayed you?"

The question evaporated Kapon's normally breezy, even insouciant, manner. He said nothing, but his stricken expression seemed to say it all. The look on a person's face may not be proof of what is going on in his head, but at this moment, I was persuaded that Kapon did not know that Kurniawan was counterfeiting wine. I also believe that he didn't want to know. "To me, there is nothing better than aged wine," Kapon has written. It follows that for him there is nothing worse than counterfeit aged wine, so deftly made that he took it for real.

⚘

Kurniawan will always be infamous for his fakery. But it bears repeating that fairness requires crediting him for the stupendous real wine he poured unstintingly. One particular evening in spring

2005 is venerated in the memory of Paul Wasserman. It featured old to ancient wines purchased by Kurniawan directly from the cellar of Bouchard Père & Fils, an august Burgundian firm founded in 1731. Bernard Hervet, former wine director at Bouchard, arranged the transaction. Wasserman delivered the wines himself to Patina, a deluxe restaurant in downtown Los Angeles where they were to be poured. Many of them were superb, none more so than an 1865 Volnay Santenots, which acted on Wasserman the way a madeleine acted on the emotions of Marcel Proust. His tasting note, more like a long reverie, evokes not only this 140-year-old pinot noir but also the elusive thing that every passionate wineola hopes to experience:

> I grew up with old, if not particularly fine, furniture. Ever open a really old linen cupboard? I mean early 19th or 18th century? This is exactly what the Santenots smells like. The smell of old wood itself. The dust in the nooks you can't reach. Centuries of beeswax. Even the traces of old muslin sachets of lavender, no longer used, but there, somewhere. [And] blackberry liquor . . . is here, too. Not obliterating but crystalline and assertive. The palate. . . . You spend your life, as a member of the trade, assessing young wine, wine that is not quite ready, wine that is past its peak, wine that is caught before its peak, wine that is gorgeous but with a little something, a slight edge of tannins, too much fruit for the tannins, too much alcohol, etc. And then there is this. You never see this. You have faith, you believe in its existence, but it's a mythical creature. . . . Oh it's not a big wine. It's so light you can turn it around in your mouth, testing all angles, caressing for asperities. You will find none. . . . It's a mathematical equation. Both sum and subtraction and the result is both infinite and zero. . . . It's certainly fading. But fading is different from past its

peak. . . . I don't think this will ever dry out, it's just going to vanish one day. You'll wake up one morning and it will be gone.

After the event, he wrote: "Rudy is . . . Wow. Thanks. Speechless. Here are the keys to my house, you can use it as a garden shed. I'll sleep with the shovels."

❦

Kurniawan's last hope was that on appeal, the warrantless search of his home by the FBI would be ruled illegal. The abundant evidence found that morning might then be suppressed at a retrial. In December 2016, a three-judge panel of the US 2nd Circuit Court of Appeals heard Mooney argue that Kurniawan's Fourth Amendment rights had been violated by the search. But Mooney, who had flown in from Los Angeles for the hearing, was cut off by the judges before he could complete his presentation.

Appellate panels can be slow in rendering a decision. But in Kurniawan's case, less than three weeks passed before this panel issued a summary order rejecting his appeal. "We assume, as the district judge did . . . that the protective sweep of Kurniawan's home was illegal," the three-judge panel wrote. Therefore, "the evidence observed in plain view by the agents during the sweep should not have been included in the subsequent search-warrant affidavit." But, even without that evidence, "there was still probable cause to issue the search warrant." That probable cause was based on the detailed evidence of Kurniawan's counterfeiting activities collected by the prosecution and the FBI before the arrest.

Reflecting on the decision, Mooney told *Wine Spectator*, "I sort of expected this result, but I didn't expect it this terse and this quick."

Over his years of incarceration, first in Brooklyn and then in Taft, California, I wrote to Kurniawan five times asking if he would agree to an interview. He never responded. At Kurniawan's request, Judge Berman had arranged for him to be sent to a prison within a few hours' drive from Arcadia so that his mom could conveniently visit. From what I'd heard about this matriarch, she was imposing despite her small size. Jerry Mooney, Kurniawan's lawyer, told me, "She was always in the distance, but when she was unhappy about something, I would hear about it from her other sons in Asia." Would Mrs. Tan be willing to speak to me about Kurniawan, offering insights that only a mother can? Mooney told me that she and Kurniawan spoke often by telephone. Would she tell me how he was handling prison life? She might welcome the chance to defend her son.

Through the Chinese American Equalization Association, an Arcadia-based activist group, I found a seventeen-year-old Mandarin interpreter, Karen Zhang. We met in front of a busy Asian super-market in Arcadia on a Saturday morning in November 2016. We walked a few blocks south along East Naomi Avenue, lined with a mix of old and new homes, then turned down the cul-de-sac to Mrs. Tan's neatly kept two-story house. A three-car garage dominated the street level of the facade. We entered through a low gate on the side leading to a recessed entrance portico. Two ceramic dragons flanked the front door. All the windows, even tiny ones on the sec-ond floor, were shuttered. If Mrs. Tan was home, she might as well have been entombed. We buzzed and waited and buzzed again. No answer. Next door, the neighbor was just backing his SUV out of his garage. Speaking in Chinese, he told Karen that he rarely saw Mrs. Tan except when she went shopping. He added that he hadn't seen Rudy Kurniawan for quite a while, apparently unaware of the current residence of his neighbor. Karen agreed to return the next day.

After lunching on a Chinese-style seafood burrito, I walked back to the house alone. All the windows were still shuttered. I rang the bell anyway. If Mrs. Tan answered, there was sure to be a moment of awkward silence, but at least I would get a look at this mom who had lived with her son in a wine-counterfeiting workshop. That didn't happen. About to walk away, I noticed narrow windows head-high on the doors of the garage. On tiptoes, I peered in. A car occupied the left bay. The middle bay was partly empty. Spilling into it from the right bay were heaps of wine cases and cartons. Just under my eyes were several cases marked "Grand Vin de Château Latour." Farther back were cartons marked "Sotheby's" and others that bore US Customs stickers—signs of Kurniawan's overseas wine purchases. Apparently, Mrs. Tan had cleared this mountain of wine packaging from her house, left behind once the FBI had taken away the evidence that it wanted.

Though I had never entered this house, I did know one thing that was within, as told to me by Jerry Mooney, who had once visited. Upstairs, Mrs. Tan has laid out her son's pajamas on his bed, awaiting his return. Sadly for mother and son, that won't happen.

Two weeks earlier, Kurniawan had turned down my latest request to visit him, made through the warden at Taft Correctional Institution. I still hoped to be allowed to visit the prison. But I was informed that "due to security concerns, our Warden has declined your request for a tour of our facility." That did not foreclose me from checking out Taft with my own eyes. And maybe even catching a glimpse, somehow, of Kurniawan. Torrential rain followed me as I left Arcadia and headed north on I-5. It tailed off as I approached the "Grapevine," the high pass leading down from Los Angeles County to the south end of the San Joaquin Valley. Even in late November, the slopes above me were covered with snow. The turnoff to Taft, on single-lane Route 33, took me along miles of orange groves. I passed through sad little Maricopa, its main drag dead except for Tina's Diner. It was dusk as I approached the outskirts of Taft (population 9,300). Oil rigs nodded on the ridges. Oil is what birthed Taft. On March 10, 1910, a stupendous oil blowout occurred at a drilling site between Maricopa and Taft. Known as the Lakeview Gusher, it spewed out nine million barrels of heavy oil over the next eighteen months. Lots of oil is still left under Taft.

Half a mile outside town, I turned onto Cadet Road. In the distance, isolated by sagebrush-strewn flatlands, lay the low, flat-roofed, gray concrete buildings of Taft Correctional Institution, illuminated now by intense white light from atop tall poles. Double-coiled barbed-wire fences sparkled in the light.

I parked in front of the pleasingly landscaped reception building. Inmate visiting hours were long since over and mine was the lone car in the visitors' section. Inside, two inmates were emptying trash cans and tidying up. A trim young guard in a khaki uniform, whose name tag said "E. Madrid," was on duty. I explained to her that I'd come to Taft because I was writing a book about an inmate. I wanted to learn what kind of place he would be calling home for years to come. And I mentioned Kurniawan's name.

"I know who he is," Officer Madrid said brightly. No surprise there, given that among Taft's more than two thousand prisoners Kurniawan was the sole wine counterfeiter—the only one, in fact, in any federal prison.

"I was hoping for a tour of the facility, but was turned down."

"Then you shouldn't be here," said Officer Madrid. "You're on federal property. You should leave now. If you come back, you could be arrested."

"If that happens, could my bunkmate be Rudy?"

It was a joke, but Officer Madrid did not laugh.

After checking in at Taft's new Best Western Plus, I went to Black Gold Brewing Company on Center Street, the town's main retail strip, where I found proprietor Mike Long sitting outside with friends. Long told me of the correctional facility's most famous pair of graduates: Tommy Chong, half of the pot-addled comedy team Cheech and Chong, and stock scammer Jordan Belfort. As "cubie" mates (there are no barred cells at Taft), Chong encouraged Belfort to write the tale of his dissolution. The result was a book and movie, *The Wolf of Wall Street*, starring Leonardo DiCaprio.

The original name of Taft was Moron. A local history explains that it was changed "for obvious reasons." The former Taft State Bank, now a pub, is the handsomest building I saw in town, but Taft's most imposing edifice is the elaborate Oil Workers Monument, a full-scale model of a drilling derrick and muscular workers cast in bronze. On my way out of town, before stopping one more time at the prison, I pulled in at the West Kern Oil Museum. A volunteer guide told me that inmates from Taft once regularly arrived to assist with museum repairs. They even created a display about the Yokuts Indians, who were the first to use local oil products before they were abused to near extinction. "The inmates had a guard with them," the grandmotherly volunteer said, "but they couldn't have escaped if they wanted to, because we fed them a home-cooked lunch and they ate so much that they could barely walk." After local people complained that the inmates were taking away work that should go to them, further service by inmates was banned. If Kurniawan were permitted to do community service, Taft could have had a gifted teacher of wine appreciation.

On this Sunday afternoon, the families visiting inmates were mostly Mexican. The guard at the desk was friendly, but looked at me blankly when I mentioned Kurniawan's name. I was hoping that Dale Patrick, the prison's media relations officer who had twice turned down my request for a tour, might be on the premises. Face to face, maybe he would change his mind. But Patrick was not there.

Leaving Taft's parking lot, I looked back at a running track and soccer field visible behind the compound fence. Gaggles of inmates, dressed in desert drab, were walking or jogging the track. I pulled over and pointed my binoculars at the scene. My hope was to spot Kurniawan, but he wasn't there. Nor could I spot him in a sheltered area where visitors were huddling with inmates. And so I headed back to Los Angeles in post-Thanksgiving traffic. I'd gone to Taft in a spirit of defiance against the authorities who had told me I couldn't, but also in the spirit of nothing ventured, nothing gained. By some fortunate fluke, maybe I'd come in contact with Kurniawan. If I could have asked him only one question, it would have been: "Why did you mess up the one thing that, other than your mother, you truly loved and honored?" Now that the whole unlikely affair was history, maybe he would have unburdened himself. But the chance was slim. For Rudy, truth always seemed to be on lockdown.

That day, Karen Zhang texted me to say that she had returned to Mrs. Tan's house at the end of the cul-de-sac. When she buzzed this time, Mrs. Tan appeared at a window. "She greeted me, and turned on her outdoor light. However, after I introduced myself and mentioned about her son and the reasons for being there, she turned off her light. I stayed in front of her door for a couple more minutes for any reply and rang her doorbell again, but she stopped responding."

❧

On January 9, 2021, Kurniawan will have served out his sentence. Awaiting him at the prison door will be Immigration and Customs Enforcement agents, who will detain him. As an undocumented immigrant and former felon, he will be deported on the first available flight to Jakarta. Left behind will be his several legacies. One is a lesson that applies to us all, even teetotalers: A masterly con man, like the one who chatted me up long ago at a Paris curbside, will always be one step ahead of us. He will push the right emotional buttons when the moment is right, and we will do his bidding. Our confidence in our invulnerability is the weakness he will profit from.

As for collectors who bend the knee to old wine, Kurniawan has bequeathed them a hangover of pleasure-destroying doubt each time they pull a crumbly cork. And then there is the actual, significant residue of fake bottles still lurking in serious cellars all over the land. Downey estimates that they number in the thousands. What exactly is in them? Retired FBI agent Jim Wynne called these creations "Frankenstein wines."

Invoking the monster in Mary Shelley's great horror novel is apt. Dr. Victor Frankenstein assembled him out of spare body parts, while Dr. Conti assembled his creations out of spare wine parts. But then they diverge. At the end of the novel, the monster "was soon borne away by the waves, and lost in darkness and distance."

The last of Kurniawan's creations will not be borne away for a very long time.

Afterword

"Everyone loves to pat themselves on the back and say, 'Oh, I knew Rudy was a fraud from the beginning,'" said Tim Kopec, wine director of the late New York restaurant, Veritas. Those were the days when Kurniawan would arrive with a client at 5 p.m., order a $7,000 white sipper, and be gone by 6. "I will say from the front lines, working the floor at Veritas: He tricked everybody."

The last known rich collector to have been tricked by Kurniawan—and the only one besides Bill Koch to go public by suing him (among other defendants)—is the Oxford-educated, Singapore-based investor Stephen Diggle. The timing and the magnitude of the con to which Diggle fell victim shines a light on how Kurniawan doubled down on fakery instead of backing away as the FBI closed in on him. Court documents from Diggle's lawsuit became available too late to include in the first edition of this book, and they reveal previously hidden details of how Kurniawan adaptively plied his trade when he could no longer do it under his own sullied name.

In the spring of 2011, Kurniawan—scarce on the wine scene, although apparently still busy in his home workshop—got in touch with Richard Brierley, a business contact from his glory days. Brierley, by then a wine specialist at Vanquish (a London firm specializing in selling champagne to nightclubs), had previously cut a sharp figure in Manhattan wine circles as head of Christie's North American wine department. "I met Rudy Kurniawan in or around the end of 2002," Brierley wrote in an affidavit obtained by Diggle's lawyers.

"This was the first of numerous meetings and business dealings that I had with Mr. Kurniawan during my time at Christie's."

That relationship would come as a surprise to Kurniawan's watchers, who were only aware of his high-profile bond with John Kapon's Acker Merrall & Condit during those same years. At Vanquish, Brierley had already done "somewhere between five and ten deals" with Kurniawan.

Now Kurniawan was pitching another deal—a big one. He was looking to sell 132 bottles, many of them oversized, that bore the labels of his specialty: Mythic vintages of the two greatest Burgundian appellations, Romanée-Conti and La Tâche. To offer single bottles of these wines would have been a triumph for other dealers. Kurniawan was offering some in case lots—two cases plus twelve magnums, actually, of 1962 Romanée-Conti. Brierley huddled with Vanquish's co-owner, Jimmy Metta, who "acknowledged that Mr. Kurniawan had gained a reputation for selling wine that was likely counterfeit," according to Brierley. Still, both men were ready to hawk the proffered wine. "I trusted in my ability to address issues of authenticity upon inspection of the bottles," Brierley wrote.

His confidence was challenged when, a few years later, Maureen Downey—the government's authentication expert at Kurniawan's trial—turned her thumbs down on all 132 bottles, for which Diggle had paid $2.45 million. Downey's "firm professional belief [was] that Mr. Kurniawan made these counterfeit wines."

Not all shared that belief in toto. One person in particular was Geoffrey Troy, the burgundy expert who had first inspected the wines on Diggle's behalf, and who'd rejected only a minority. Another was Aubert de Villaine, co-proprietor of the Domaine de la Romanée-Conti. When Diggle took a sampling of the trove back to their source in the quiet village of Vosne-Romanée, de Villaine's verdict was less than definitive: "Each bottle or magnum shows elements that tend to be doubtful regarding the authenticity of the labeling and other elements that seem to conform to the original labeling. Not one can escape this double observation."

De Villaine had good reason to hedge, given Kurniawan's multiple methods of craft. Presented with an authentic bottle that had been refilled and resealed with the original cork and capsule, how could de Villaine or anyone else pronounce it fake with certainty? The wine may be fake, but it is locked in the bottle—and it truly could be from the winery, if not from the listed vintage. For example, Kurniawan purchased from a Manhattan dealer most of its inventory of mediocre 1994 vintage Château Pétrus, then apparently converted the bottles into far more desirable—and expensive—vintages, such as 1989. It remains Pétrus.

Diggle might have backed away from the transaction had he known the true identity of the seller. But he was merely told that it was a "male, elderly, wealthy wine collector who had health problems and wanted to sell a portion of his vast collection." And then it was hinted that this collector was Don Stott, the retired Wall Street exec and voracious collector of rarest burgundy. When the wines were shipped for their initial inspection to Wine Cellarage in the South Bronx, Kurniawan hid behind the name of one of his brothers, Dar Saputra. Writing from dscellar@gmail.com, and listing a Hong Kong address, "Saputra" wrote: Pls keep bottles on their sides as always. Richard will be there to help me inspect all on Thursday morning. Just let me know the cost and I'll pay accordingly. Thx much. DS.

"If I had known the wine came from Rudy," said Geoffrey Troy, "I'd have walked out of there immediately."

Diggle's lawsuit, filed in New York, was settled before the case went to trial in 2018. Nondisclosure agreements bind all parties. Diggle declined my request to be interviewed. I failed to learn what happened to those 132 bottles.

Even now, years after Kurniawan was locked away, his shadow can still darken transactions. This, a North American wine dealer learned in the spring of 2018 as he prepared to sell seven bottles of burgundy representing the apex of collectability.

Each was a methuselah holding the equivalent of eight regular bottles. Each was from a venerated appellation of Domaine de la Romanée-Conti. Each was from the splendid 2005 vintage. Production ranged from six to fifteen individually numbered examples. After 2008, the giant bottles got rarer yet. That was when the Domaine permanently halted all methuselah production. Aubert de Villaine found it increasingly distasteful that purchasers were all too often buying them to "flip" rather than to uncork; flipping is for houses in a hot real estate market, not for rare formats of wines raised from France's most venerated soil with something akin to fierce parental love.

The methuselahs at hand, each in its own pine crate, were kept in a perfectly cooled and humidified cellar. Their original owner, an heiress, had purchased them directly from the authorized importer, whose stampings were on each crate along with those of the Domaine. They had not been moved for ten years. Early in 2018, a buyer in Hong Kong—represented in a private sale by a major auction house—agreed to buy the septet for $1.25 million. Given its impeccable provenance, the transaction should have gone smoothly. Instead, it percolated with suspicion.

A wine department specialist for the auctioneer descended into the cellar. He photographed each crate, before the fiberglass banding that secured them was cut. Then he photographed each methuselah and inspected the labels with a jeweler's loupe at 10x magnification. Certain letters on the label on one of the "meths" gave him pause due to a slight blue penumbra around the edges of certain letters—a so-called double strike. Was that a sign of fakery?

The dealer didn't think so; this bottle was one of the least expensive of the septet. If you were a counterfeiter, he argues, why not go for the top bottle: Romanée-Conti itself? Once the bottles were returned to their crates, the original bands were reconnected with tape where they'd been cut. The specialist and dealer each signed the tape at the junctures, so that the banding couldn't be re-cut without detection.

Weeks passed before the auction house approved the sale on behalf of its client. Had its due diligence been excessive? The head of the auction house (who, like the dealer, asked not to be named) told me: "We won't be involved with any sale unless we have no doubt whatsoever about authenticity." Both he and the dealer agreed that Kurniawan's legacy beclouded this sale. Kurniawan was no stranger to the Domaine's methuselahs. One that he'd crafted—a 1971 Romanée-Conti—had been purchased at an Acker auction for $85,000 by real estate mogul Michael Fascitelli, in 2006. Seven years later, it was exhibited to the jury at Kurniawan's trial.

While the 2005 vintage arrived too late in the game for Kurniawan himself to counterfeit, others have carried on his legacy. "I have seen examples of Romanée-Conti 2005 bottles with fake capsules made in a factory and labels very nearly resembling the originals," authenticity consultant Michael Egan told me. Egan also saw an infestation of 2010 and 2011 DRC wines. "With these younger wines, the labels are expected to look pristine, so the counterfeiters don't have to work at antiquing them," he said.

The latest challenge for counterfeiters is to mimic high-tech security features now arming labels and bottles at medium-to-high price points. A common line of defense is to put proof tags on neck capsules. Their unique visual and numeric codes can be checked against a web database to indicate whether or not the bottle is genuine. A burgeoning weapon against wine counterfeiting, Chai Vault, takes its cue from Bitcoin by establishing an allegedly impregnable blockchain system that details a bottle's life history.

Not all effective anti-counterfeiting measures are electronic. Many wineries now print microtext on their bottles, too tiny to be seen by the naked eye. The owners of a prized Pomerol producer include the names of their children in microprint on capsules. Labels are also being printed with ultraviolet ink that glows under a black light. Some inks are spiked with a chemical marker detectable only by a dedicated handheld scanner. Holograms are also used. Bottle glass may be etched with tiny serial numbers, like that of Château d'Yquem. Years ago, Ann Colgin planted a wet kiss on the labels of her cult Napa Valley wine, leaving a lipstick print—and her DNA.

In this century, not only technology changes the new vintages; the wine itself—though still fermented grape juice—has also changed. Global warming brings with it riper grapes, which translates to wines with higher alcohol content and more sensory impact. Advances in production—such as high-speed optical sorting machines for wine grapes, and precise temperature control during fermentation—can result in wines that seem as sleekly engineered as an iPhone.

Where does that leave the extant bottles from deep in the last century that were made by un-credentialed vignerons who never imagined such fakery would threaten them? Do they still merit a collector's passion? Certainly some will be too enfeebled to deliver pleasure. Yet others can bring rewards that are unobtainable from modern wines, no matter how alluring with their deftly calibrated fruit. The most special of these survivors still have wisdom to whisper.

If only collectors could be certain they are not being whispered a lie.

A final note: In a letter to me following my book's publication, Aubert de Villaine wrote that he had "only one criticism regarding the book. It is when you compare Rudy's story to Gatsby's. I understand your idea, but frankly, it is much too flattering to Rudy!!" Rereading the tale of Jay Gatsby, I continue to find many parallels with Kurniawan, including one previously omitted—both men used names that differed from their birth names. That said, my eyes are open to de Villaine's important point: Gatsby, unlike Kurniawan, ended up a tragic hero. Now I'm confident that de Villaine and I can agree on one thing. As the myriad guests partied away the nights in West Egg, Gatsby would never have served them fake wine.

Notes

Unless otherwise noted, interviews and direct observation by the author are the sources of the statements and conversations reported in this book. Much information throughout the text was drawn from testimony, filings, and rulings in the proceedings of *United States v. Kurniawan*, No. 12 Cr. 376 (RMB) (S.D.N.Y.), available at pacer.gov. The trial was held December 9–18, 2013.

INTRODUCTION

xiii   **The average price paid . . . eight dollars.** The exact average price in January 2017, as supplied by Adam Polonski of Impact Databank, was $7.68.

xv   **Baron Philippe de Rothschild, proprietor . . . ripening that year.** Michael Broadbent, *Michael Broadbent's Vintage Wine: Fifty Years of Tasting Three Centuries of Wines* (New York: Harcourt, 2002), 42–43.

xv   **Of this wine, decades . . . Mount Etna.** Ibid.

xv   **In 1950, Sherry Wine . . . $2.25 per bottle.** "About Us," Sherry-Lehmann: Wine and Spirits Merchants Since 1934, accessed March 21, 2017, sherry-lehmann.com/about-sherry-lehmann-wine-and-spirits.

xvi   **Ten bottles of well-credentialed . . . in May 2016.** Jamie Ritchie (CEO and president, Americas and Asia, Sotheby's Wine), interview with author, December 2016.

xvi   **The highest price ever paid . . .** Ibid.

xix   **The phases were laid . . . Peynaud (1912–2004).** "Ask Dr. Vinny," *Wine Spectator*, October 12, 2015, winespectator.com/drvinny/show/id/52197.

xx   **In the late 1960s, Michael Broadbent . . . chilly cellars.** Broadbent, *Michael Broadbent's Vintage Wine*, 216.

xxi   **In 2002, Broadbent sampled . . . Wilfred Jaeger.** Ibid., 63, 422.

xxiii   **Serena Sutcliffe, long . . . become a pestilence.** Interview with author. Also see: James Suckling, "Q&A with Serena Sutcliffe: An Expert on Old Wines Talks About Counterfeits," *Wine Spectator*, December 15, 2009, winespectator.com/magazine/show/id/41143.

CHAPTER 1

1   **A camera recorded Rudy . . . wines in his lap.** *Sour Grapes*, documentary film, directed by Reuben Atlas, Jerry Rothwell, a Met Films and Faites un Voeu production, 2016. Footage of Kurniawan by Vince Cariati circa 2004.

2   **A *Wine Spectator* review . . . spice and sage."** James Laube, "Another Winner," *Wine Spectator*, November 15, 1999, winespectator.com/magazine/show/id/8397.

2   **They were gathered at . . . connected to wine.** Corie Brown, "$75,000 a Case? He's Buying," *Los Angeles Times*, December 1, 2006, latimes.com/nation/la-et-rudy1-story.html.

4   **Émile Peynaud argued that . . . aid of reasoning."** Émile Peynaud, *Le goût du vin: Le grand livre de la degustation* (Paris: Dunod, 1980), 21.

6   **The priciest wine auction . . . since the 1930s.** Peter D. Meltzer, "Doris Duke Cellar Nets $3.8 Million at Auction," *Wine Spectator*, June 7, 2004, winespectator.com/webfeature/show/id/Doris-Duke-Cellar-Nets-38-Million-at-Auction_22032.

7   **"As is so often the case . . . Thank you, Rudy."** Posting by Paul Wasserman on the Mark Squires Bulletin Board hosted on eRobertParker.com, March 4, 2005, archive.robertparker.com/forum/archives/bulk-archive-2005-2008/58190-jadot-chevalier-demoiselles-and-musigny-vertical.

10   **In his application for asylum . . . in Indonesia."** Kurniawan's 2000 application for asylum was denied in 2001. His appeal of that decision to the Board of Immigration Appeals was rejected in 2003. See Complaint as to Rudy Kurniawan in *United States v. Kurniawan*, No. 12 Cr. 376 (RMB) (S.D.N.Y.), ECF No. 109.

10   **In May 2002 . . . California coast.** Benjamin Wallace, "Château Sucker," *New York Magazine*, May 13, 2012, nymag.com/news/features/rudy-kurniawan-wine-fraud-2012-5.

12   **When in 2006 a *Los Angeles Times* . . . my family."** Corie Brown, interviewed in *Sour Grapes*.

12   **One person who . . . documentary about Kurniawan.** *Criminels 2.0*, episode 3/6, "Rudy Kurniawan, l'escroc aux grand crus," dailymotion.com/video/x4m3vtg.

12   **The next day, at . . . even $3,000.** Government Trial Exhibit 26-2, *United States v. Kurniawan*, No. 12 Cr. 376 (RMB) (S.D.N.Y.).

13   **Reality for one Meyer . . . California, house.** Samantha Brooks, "Ultimate Home 2008: Belle of Bel Air," *Robb Report*, April 1, 2008, robbreport.com/home-and-design/ultimate-home-2008-belle-bel-air.

14   **In July 2005, he purchased . . . 405 freeway.** Purchase information from Don Cornwell's unpublished "Historical Highlights—Rudy Kurniawan's Counterfeiting Career," graciously provided to me by the author.

15   **One sold in Hong Kong in 2015 for $221,000.)** Wei Gu and Dean Napolitano, "Hermès Birkin Bagged for Record Price at Christie's Hong Kong Auction," *The Wall Street Journal*, June 1, 2015, wsj.com/articles/hermes-birkin-bagged-for-record-price-at-christies-hong-kong-auction-1433149955.

16   **But in his *Wine Spectator* report . . . at my table."** Bruce Sanderson, "A
      Special Patch of Burgundy," *Wine Spectator*, January 3, 2006, winespectator.
      com/webfeature/show/id/A-Special-Patch-of-Burgundy_2888.

17   **Though his name was absent . . . to be sold.** Acker Merrall & Condit,
      Cellar I and II catalogs.

19   **In a scene in *Sour Grapes* . . . wine carousers.** *Sour Grapes.*

20   **It was dubbed . . . "THE Cellar."** Acker Merrall & Condit sale catalog 08-
      04, 135.

20   **The catalog specified . . . insulated basket.** These conditions were stated,
      for example, in the 1960 catalog titled "Sous le Signe des Fruits de la Terre
      de France."

23   **The venerated chef Fernand . . . bottle of ink."** Fernand Point, *Ma
      Gastronomie* (Wilton, CT: Lyceum Books, 1974), 53.

23   **As laid out in his 1863 . . . single cask.** From Thomas George Shaw, *Wine,
      the Vine, and the Cellar*, collected in Alexis Bespaloff, *The Fireside Book of Wine*
      (New York: Simon & Schuster, 1977), 243.

24   **Wine importer Kermit Lynch . . . region of Bordeaux.** Kermit Lynch,
      Adventures on the Wine Route: A Wine Buyer's Tour of France (New York:
      Farrar, Straus and Giroux, 1988), 61–62.

25   **That was the reckoning . . . Manhattan hotel.** Tyler Colman, "Blind
      Tasting Is Tough—Tasting Bordeaux 2005 with Robert Parker," *Dr. Vino*,
      October 2, 2009, drvino.com/2009/10/02/blind-tasting-bordeaux-2005-
      robert-parker.

CHAPTER 2

28   **It had dished out . . . end of 2007.** Tomoeh Murakami Tse and
      Renae Merle, "The Bonuses Keep Coming," *Washington Post*, January
      29, 2008, washingtonpost.com/wp-dyn/content/article/2008/01/28/
      AR2008012802561.html.

28   **Huge sums were still . . . *Big Short*.** Michael Lewis, *The Big Short* (New
      York: W. W. Norton, 2010), xv–xvi.

30   **As far back as 1733 . . . expensive wine.** Allen D. Meadows, *The Pearl of the
      Côte: The Great Wines of Vosne-Romanée* (Winnetka, CA: Burghound Books,
      2010), 264.

30   **After claiming that he . . . dueling La Tâches.** Posting by Rudy
      Kurniawan on the Mark Squires Bulletin Board hosted on eRobertParker.
      com, October 24, 2004 at archive.robertparker.com/forum/archives/bulk-
      archive-2004-and-older/42770-last-weekend-where-i-tried-to-kill-john-
      kapon-with-legendary-wines.

33   **Acker's catalog billed . . . Rarest Champagne."** Acker Merrall & Condit
      sale catalog 08-4, April 25, 2008.

33   **Rosania's champagne sold . . . $2.6 million.** Peter D. Meltzer, "Auction
      Highlight," *Wine Spectator*, April 25, 2008, at winespectator.com/
      auctionhighlight/show/id/518.

36   Kapon's text painted . . . Praise the Lord!" Acker Merrall & Condit sale
      catalog 08-4, 135.

37   He found "no evidence . . . up to it!" Alun Griffiths, email correspondence
      with author, spring 2008.

38   Clive Coates, a British . . . in bottle." Clive Coates, "Roumier," Clive
      Coates MW, accessed March 24, 2017, clive-coates.com/tastings/domaine/
      roumier.

40   Three weeks after . . . secure his loans. Government Trial Exhibit 24-2,
      United States v. Kurniawan, No. 12 Cr. 376 (RMB) (S.D.N.Y.).

40   It would obtain a signed . . . $10.6 million. *Acker, Merrall & Condit v. Rudy
      Kurniawan*, Affidavit of Confession of Judgment of Rudy Kurniawan, Index
      No. 08115871, filed in New York State Supreme Court, November 25, 2008.

CHAPTER 3

43   "Lower-end brands don't . . . Rolexes!" Chloé Pilorget-Rezzouk, "La
      technologie la plus pointue contra les contrefaçons," *Liberation*, August
      24, 2014, liberation.fr/societe/2014/08/24/la-technologie-la-plus-pointue-
      contre-les-contrefacons_1086184.

44   The domaine's origin . . . William Ponsot. "History," Domain Ponsot,
      accessed March 24, 2017, www.domaine-ponsot.com/History.

46   During a domaine visit . . . fully appreciated." Remington Norman, *The
      Great Domaines of Burgundy* (New York: Henry Holt, 1993), 50.

48   Its tiny village . . . and Chambolle-Musigny." Ibid., 38.

50   In the aftermath of the dinner . . . Los Angeles." John Kapon, "Big Boy
      Does Los Angeles," *Vintage Tastings*, April 12, 2008, vintagetastings.com/
      all/2008-4-12_00080.html.

54   After several messages . . . to get healthy." Peter Hellman, "Domaine
      Ponsot Proprietor Halts Sale of Fake Bottles," *Wine Spectator*, May 16, 2008,
      winespectator.com/webfeature/show/id/Domaine-Ponsot-Proprietor-Halts-
      Sale-of-Fake-Bottles_4131.

55   Dear Rudy, . . . With warm regards, Laurent Ponsot. Government Trial
      Exhibit 36-17, *United States v. Kurniawan*, No. 12 Cr. 376 (RMB) (S.D.N.Y.).

CHAPTER 4

61   This chapter draws on the author's article, "Play Hard, Work Harder," *Wine
      Spectator*, June 30, 2012, winespectator.com/magazine/show/id/46804.

62   In a 1930s newspaper ad . . . for $1.70. Reproduced in Acker Merrall &
      Condit sale catalog 11-2, March 19, 2011.

65   Kapon somehow always . . . *Vintage Tastings*. Gil Lempert-Schwarz,
      introduction to *The Compendium*, by John Kapon (London: Fine Wine
      Editions, 2012), 8.

65   One weekend in 2011 . . . Saturday auction. John Kapon, "Chicago
      Recap," *Vintage Tastings*, November 2, 2011, vintagetastings.com/all/2011-
      11-2_00015.html.

69   **He was riled . . . David Molyneux-Berry.** "Taste3 Conference: David
      Molyneux-Berry" YouTube video, 20:02, from the Taste3 Conference
      in Napa in May 2007, posted by "Taste3," May 22, 2007, youtube.com/
      watch?v=HFnOSx6Ow1w.

71   **Greetings from Hong Kong . . . truly great.** Posting by John Kapon on
      the Mark Squires Bulletin Board hosted on eRobertParker.com, August
      15, 2007, archive.robertparker.com/forum/archives/bulk-archive-2005-
      2008/143972-david-molyneux-berry-on-fake-wines/page3.

73   **In *The Compendium*, his . . . same case!"** Kapon, *The Compendium*, 13.

CHAPTER 5

77   Much of the information in this chapter, including emails and credit
      card expenditures, is drawn from exhibits submitted in *United States v.
      Kurniawan*, No. 12 Cr. 376 (RMB) (S.D.N.Y.).

77   **The term *confidence man* . . . on city streets.** Jean Braucher and Barak
      Orbach, "Scamming: The Misunderstood Confidence Man," *Yale Journal of
      Law & the Humanities* 27, no. 2 (2015), 250.

78   **In David Maurer's 1960 . . . have to steal."** David Maurer, *The Big Con:
      The Story of the Confidence Man* (New York: Anchor Books, 1999), 1.

78   **Two candid photos . . . as Dr. Conti.** *United States v. Kurniawan*, No. 12
      Cr. 376 (RMB) (S.D.N.Y., Government Exhibit 14-1, images 8174 and 8315).

79   **Acknowledging that this . . . voice of Burgundy."** Meadows, *The Pearl of
      the Côte*, 326.

80   **Brian, . . . all the rare wines you have.** *United States v. Kurniawan*, No. 12
      Cr. 376 (RMB) (S.D.N.Y.). Email correspondence between Brian Devine
      and Leny Tan was attached as Exhibit D to a May 23, 2014, submission to
      the government. In an affidavit dated July 29, 2014, Brian Devine explained
      his dealings with Leny Tan and stated his losses. He included a summary of
      thirty-four checks paid to Lenny Tan totaling $5,320,602.50.

81   **But Devine did "know" Leny . . . in an affidavit in June 2014.** Ibid.

81   **Along with a return to owner . . . stuff in the parcel."** Ibid.

84   **She told *Wine Spectator*'s Esther . . . merlot."** Esther Mobley, "The
      Authenticator," *Wine Spectator*, November 30, 2015, winespectator.com/
      magazine/show/id/52225.

85   **In 2012, . . . World War II period."** John Tilson, "The Sordid Story
      of Wine Manipulation & Wine Fraud Covering over 40 Years of
      Tasting Old Wines," *The Underground Wineletter*, January 10, 2012,
      undergroundwineletter.com/2012/01/the-sordid-story-of-wine-
      manipulation-wine-fraud-covering-over-40-years-of-tasting-old-wines.

86   **"Where Hardy Rodenstock . . . prior to 1945."** Michael Broadbent,
      *Michael Broadbent's Vintage Wine: Fifty Years of Tasting Three Centuries of
      Wines* (New York: Harcourt, 2002), 38.

86   **In a tasting note, he wrote . . . this is it."** Posting by Paul Wasserman on
      the Mark Squires Bulletin Board hosted on eRobertParker.com, October 11,
      2003, archive.robertparker.com/forum/archives/bulk-archive-2004-and-
      older/28099-petrus-1921-1966-very-long.

86   **The British wine critic Harry . . . burgundy bottles!"** Frank J. Prial, "A
        Long-Lasting Champion of Good Taste," *The New York Times*, December 5,
        2001, nytimes.com/2001/12/05/dining/wine-talk-a-long-lasting-champion-
        of-good-taste.html.

88   **I have known this collector . . . storage of his wines.** Acker Merrall &
        Condit sale catalog 069.

88   **At the British dealer . . . in case lots.** Interview with Southwick proprietor
        George Rhys.

89   **But Kurniawan also purchased . . . quality.** Ibid.

89   **On his lively blog . . . Let that be a relief!"** Matthew Hayes, "A Message
        to You Rudy . . ." *Legless in Burgundy*, December 22, 2013, leglessinburgundy.
        com/2013/12/22/a-message-to-you-rudy.

90   **Just three months after . . . 1945 Romanée-Conti.** *United States v.
        Kurniawan*, No. 12 Cr. 376 (RMB) (S.D.N.Y.), Government Exhibit 31-1.

91   **Twenty days after that . . . to Kurniawan.** Ibid. See Twellman Affidavit,
        Government Document 135-1.

91   **Fascitelli wired payment of $5.5 million.** Ibid., Government Document
        136-1.

92   **Kurniawan had one more . . . of just $30 million.** Ibid., Government
        Exhibit 122-1.

93   **One hard-knuckled loan . . . $6.75 million.** Ibid., Government Exhibit
        24-10.

95   **According to FAC loan officer . . . through Acker.** *United States v.
        Kurniawan*, No. 12 Cr. 376 (RMB), (S.D.N.Y), p. 79.

95   **That month, he spent . . . charter services.** Ibid., Government Exhibit
        26-3.

96   **On January 18 . . . other illnesses.** Ibid.

96   **One week after the faux . . . star client.** Ibid., Government Exhibit 24-2.

96   **He also agreed to pledge . . . loans.** Ibid.

96   **Seven months later, both . . . scheme.** Ibid.

97   **This was when Acker compelled . . . $10.4 million.** *Acker Merrall &
        Condit v. Kurniawan*, ECF No. 99, Affidavit of Confession of Judgment,
        Index No. 08115871, filed in S.D.N.Y. on November 25, 2008.

97   **Most sensational was . . . Pomerol.** *The Evening Sale: Finest and Rarest
        Wines*, Los Angeles: Christie's, April 27, 2007. Auction catalog, sale 1899.

97   **Robert Parker called 1982 . . . ever tasted."** Robert Parker, *Bordeaux: A
        Comprehensive Guide to the Wines Produced from 1961 to 1997* (New York:
        Simon & Schuster, 1998), 902.

99   **In spring 2009, the $2.2 million . . . Christie's New York.** See
        "Complaint as to Rudy Kurniawan," signed by FBI Special Agent James
        P. Wynne and US Magistrate Judge Ronald L. Ellis in S.D.N.Y., March 5,
        2012.

100   **But he didn't yet know . . . year earlier.** Ibid.

100   **For his Christie's sale of Gordon's . . . encumbrances."** Ibid.

100   **On August 20, a new consignment agreement . . . held by Gordon."** Ibid.

100   **Now it stated: "Acker also holds liens on the property."** Ibid.

100   **Hours before the auction, he wrote . . . did it anyway."** Case 1:12-cr-00376-RMB, Affidavit in Support of a Search Warrant, Document 18-7, paragraph 35, p. 26.

101   **Yet here was Christie's . . . betrayed Kurniawan's handiwork.** NYWinesChristie's Fine and Rare Wines sale catalogs, September 12, 2009, and October 15, 2009.

102   **That sum was split . . . Kurniawan's wines.** Ibid.

CHAPTER 6

103   This chapter draws on "The Crusade Against Counterfeits," *Wine Spectator,* June 30, 2009, winespectator.com/magazine/show/id/41140, written by the author and Mitch Frank.

103   **What could bring sudden . . . TV show *20/20*?** Megan Chuchmach and Brian Ross, "What Makes a Billionaire Cry? Bill Koch Duped by Wine Fakes," ABC News, June 13, 2014, abcnews.go.com/Blotter/makes-billionaire-cry-bill-koch-duped-wine-fakes/story?id=24111774.

104   **Instead, Koch mobilized . . . shadowy foe.** Bill Koch and Brad Goldstein, multiple interviews with author.

104   **Opening a scientific front . . . cesium-137.** Ibid.

105   **When the final lot . . . $21.9 million.** Peter D. Meltzer, "Sotheby's Scores Big with Bill Koch's $21.9 Million Wine Auction," *Wine Spectator,* May 24, 2016, winespectator.com/webfeature/show/id/Sothebys-Koch-53198.

105   **He laced up their . . . anger.** Daniel Schulman, *Sons of Wichita: How the Koch Brothers Became America's Most Powerful and Private Dynasty* (New York: Grand Central, 2014), 1.

106   **Despite an attack . . . his glory days.** Peter Hellman, "Behind the Scenes at Bill Koch's Big Night," *Wine Spectator,* May 19, 2016, winespectator.com/webfeature/show/id/53183.

109   **He called the triumph . . . thousand orgasms."** Ibid., 3.

109   **Reportedly, Koch also . . . rival craft.** Ibid., 190.

110   **The previous evening, two magnums . . . for $79,625.** Guy Collins, "Petrus 1961 Magnums Lead Sotheby's New York Wine Auction," Bloomberg, December 9, 2014, bloomberg.com/news/articles/2014-12-09/petrus-1961-magnums-lead-sotheby-s-new-york-wine-auction.

110   **In 1985, a single Jefferson bottle . . . intense excitement.** Benjamin Wallace, *The Billionaire's Vinegar: The Mystery of the World's Most Expensive Bottle of Wine* (New York: Crown, 2008), 76.

110   **Broadbent had written . . . little bit of history."** Christie's Finest and Rarest Wines sale catalog, December 5, 1985.

111   **He had relied on the assurances . . . no proof."** Ibid.

111   **A researcher there responded . . . 1787 vintages."** Patrick Radden Keefe, "The Jefferson Bottles," *The New Yorker,* September 3, 2007, newyorker.com/magazine/2007/09/03/the-jefferson-bottles.

111   **The tale told by their purveyor . . . being demolished.** Ibid.

112   **He pronounced it . . . completely removed."** Ibid.

112   **"Admittedly, there is no . . . Jefferson ordered."** Christie's Finest and Rarest Wines sale catalog, December 5, 1985.

113   **Years later . . . two engravers.** Described in *Koch v. Christie's.*

113   **Having nailed down . . . orchestrated the fraud.** *Koch v. Rodenstock,* Case No. 1:06-cv-06586-BSJ-DCF, S.D.N.Y. Filed August 31, 2006.

113   **The next year, Koch sued Chicago . . . Jefferson bottle.** See *Koch v. Chicago Wine Co.,* No. 08-L-3458 (Ill. Ct. Cl. filed March 23, 2008). See also Mitch Frank, "Collector Accuses Chicago Companies of Wine Fraud," *Wine Spectator,* April 1, 2008, winespectator.com/webfeature/show/id/Collector-Accuses-Chicago-Companies-of-Wine-Fraud_4066.

113   **And he sued Royal . . . from Rodenstock.** Case No. 1:13-mc-00260-P1 *Koch et al v. Royal Wine Merchants, Ltd., et al,* S.D.N.Y. Filed July 22, 2013.

113   **Koch next took aim . . . Romanée-Conti.** Peter Hellman, "Billionaire Wine Collector Bill Koch Settles with Acker Merrall & Condit," *Wine Spectator,* July 17, 2014, winespectator.com/webfeature/show/id/50279.

114   **"We go to extreme lengths . . . any purchaser's money."** Christopher Faherty, "Billionaire Sues Wine Auction House," *New York Sun,* April 25, 2008, nysun.com/new-york/billionaire-sues-wine-auction-house/75326.

114   **The next year, Koch directly . . . those bottles.** Mitch Frank, Peter Hellman, and Jacob Gaffney, "Billionaire Sues Major Collector," *Wine Spectator,* September 11, 2009, winespectator.com/webfeature/show/id/40637.

114   **The following year, Koch . . . wines."** *Koch v. Christie's International LLP,* US Court of Appeals, 2nd Circuit, No. 11-1522-cv. See also: Mitch Frank and Peter Hellman, "Koch Sues Christie's over Alleged Counterfeit Wines," *Wine Spectator,* March 30, 2010, winespectator.com/webfeature/show/id/42425.

114   **"That would have resulted . . . fakes of any kind."** Ibid.

115   **From the other side . . . "an absolute bully."** Peter Hellman and Mitch Frank, "Counterfeit Suit Targets Christie's," *Wine Spectator,* June 15, 2010, winespectator .com/magazine/show/id/42621.

115   **Koch had bought them . . . $3.7 million.** Peter Hellman, "Alleged Counterfeit Wines Go on Trial," *Wine Spectator,* March 25, 2013, winespectator.com/webfeature/show/id/48192.

116   **In *Koch v. Greenberg* . . . entrepreneurial spirit.** Ibid.

117   **Greenberg angrily emailed . . . unsuspecting others."** Email dated May 25, 2004. *Koch v. Greenberg,* Case 1:07-cv-09600-JPO-DCF, Document 35-17, filed May 14, 2012.

120 **Veteran British wine writer . . . 1948.** Stephen Brook, *The Complete Bordeaux: The Wines, the Châteaux, the People* (London: Mitchell Beazley Wine Library, 2007), 504.

120 **As for 1929 Romanée-Conti . . . in 1968.** Michael Broadbent, *The Great Vintage Wine Book* (New York: Knopf, 1980), 198.

123 **"This was a litigation of choice . . . Oetken wrote.** *Koch v. Greenberg*, Case 1:07-cv-09600-JPO-DCF, Document 508, filed March 31, 2014. See also: Peter Hellman, "Judge Slices Bill Koch's $12 Million Verdict in Counterfeiting Lawsuit," *Wine Spectator*, April 1, 2014, winespectator.com/webfeature/show/id/49771.

CHAPTER 7

125 This chapter draws on the author's article "Catching Dr. Conti," *Wine Spectator*, November 15, 2015, winespectator.com/magazine/show/id/52224. The emails and credit card expenditures cited are extracted from the trial record.

125 **One spring day . . . Radden Keefe.** Patrick Radden Keefe, "The Jefferson Bottles," *The New Yorker*, September 3, 2007, newyorker.com/magazine/2007/09/03/the-jefferson-bottles.

127 **In an art fraud case . . . Knoedler & Co.** Graham Bowley, William K. Rashbaum, and Patricia Cohen, "Dealer at Center of Art Scandal Arrested on Tax Charges," *The New York Times*, May 21, 2013, nytimes.com/2013/05/22/arts/design/dealer-at-center-of-art-scandal-arrested-on-tax-charges.html.

127 **But Knoedler's president . . . by eleven experts.** Knoedler & Company fax transmission, "Letter to Laura De Sole," from Ann Freedman to James Kelly/James Kelly Contemporary, December 11, 2004.

128 **"Among the mysteries . . . documented provenance."** Colin Moynihan, "Knoedler Gallery Director Settles Lawsuit over Fake Rothko," *The New York Times*, February 7, 2016, nytimes.com/2016/02/08/arts/design/knoedler-gallery-director-settles-lawsuit-over-fake-rothko.html.

130 **In his autobiography, *Caveat Emptor* . . . art cop."** Ken Perenyi, *Caveat Emptor* (New York: Pegasus, 2012).

132 **The total for that month . . . Wells Fargo checking account.** *United States v. Kurniawan*, No. 12 Cr. 376 (RMB) (S.D.N.Y.), Government Exhibit 26-2.

132 **Yet when Kurniawan was asked . . . I *love* to travel."** *Sour Grapes*, documentary film, directed by Reuben Atlas, Jerry Rothwell, a Met Films and Faites un Voeu production, 2016.

133 **When two bottles arrived broken . . . wanted to keep."** *United States v. Kurniawan*, No. 12 Cr. 376 (RMB) (S.D.N.Y.), ECF No. 101, Government Exhibit 13-13.

135 **Emails from 2007 . . . village of Meursault.** Ibid., ECF No. 107, Government Exhibits 13-15, 13-16, and 13-29.

135 **"I'll take them all," Kurniawan responded.** Ibid., ECF No. 109, Government Exhibit 13-16.

137   **The plan was to "make a proverbial . . . for Vanquish.** Jason Boland and Richard Brierley, "Welcome to the Evening Sale," *The Evening Sale: An Auction of Rarities,* London: Spectrum Wine Auctions/Vanquish, February 8, 2012.

138   **(Buy Musigny Blanc, Robert Parker . . . profoundness.")** Robert Parker, *Burgundy: A Comprehensive Guide to the Producers, Appellations, and Wines* (New York: Simon & Schuster, 1990), 426.

139   **His first post began: "In the last . . . in London."** Don Cornwell, "Rudy Kurniawan & Global Wine Auction Fraud Thread" post #1, Wine Berserkers, February 4, 2012, wineberserkers.com/forum/viewtopic.php?t=61172.

139   **Instead of stonewalling . . . unloaded on Cornwell.** Cornwell, "Rudy Kurniawan & Global Wine Auction Fraud Thread" post #210, Wine Berserkers, February 6, 2012, wineberserkers.com/forum/viewtopic.php?f=1 &t=61172&start=200#p811983.

140   **"These lots have been . . . told the audience.** Reported to me by audience member Emilia Terracciano on the following morning.

141   **Yet Boland's response . . . bottles being offered.** Spectrum Wine Auctions and Vanquish, Luxury Drinks Specialist, "The Evening Sale: An Auction of Rarities" sale catalog.

142   **On March 5, 2012, less than . . . New York.** Complaint, March 5, 2012, *United States v. Kurniawan,* No. 12 Cr. 376 (RMB) (S.D.N.Y.), ECF No. 1. The complaint was heard by US magistrate judge Ronald Ellis.

148   **Q: Why washing bottles . . . A: That's not possible.** Ibid., Document 18-6.

CHAPTER 8

153   This chapter draws on the author's reporting for *Wine Spectator* on pretrial hearings in 2012 and 2013 and on the trial in December 2013, in partnership with *Wine Spectator* news editor Mitch Frank, and is supplemented by interviews with prosecution and defense attorneys. Quotations from emails are from trial filings. Trial testimony as quoted in this chapter has been edited for flow and concision.

163   **Hardy testified . . . in Bordeaux.** *United States v. Kurniawan,* No. 12 Cr. 376 (RMB) (S.D.N.Y.), ECF No. 99, beginning on page 127.

163   **"I am fuckin . . . lafleur!!"** Ibid., Government Exhibit 13-11.

164   **"I was sitting at my desk . . . smiles from the jurors.** Ibid., ECF No. 103, 549.

166   **Cru's wine director, . . . RK"** Ibid., Government Exhibit 13-13.

168   **"Of the bottles sourced . . . not clearly fraudulent."** Douglas E. Barzelay, "The Rise and Fall of a Wine Counterfeiter," June 18, 2012, oldvinenotes. com/2012/06/18/the-rise-and-fall-of-a-wine-counterfeiter.

173   **The result has been personally . . . and me."** Affidavit of Susan Twellman, filed July 18, 2014, *United States v. Kurniawan,* No. 12 Cr. 376 (RMB) (S.D.N.Y.), ECF No. 135.

183   **Since 1984, federal sentencing . . . punishment.** The *Guidelines Manual* is available on the website of the United States Sentencing Commission, www. ussc.gov/guidelines.

184 **Mooney's presentencing memo . . . were rife.** *United States v. Kurniawan,* No. 12 Cr. 376 (RMB) (S.D.N.Y.), Document 119, filed May 1, 2014.

187 **Dear Judge Berman, . . . Respectfully submitted, Rudy Kurniawan.** Ibid.

190 **Yet his credit card . . . $11,000.** Ibid.

190 **"I was surprised when . . . contrary of an attraction."** Aubert de Villaine, email correspondence with author, January 23, 2017.

CHAPTER 9

193 **This chapter draws** from the author's reporting in various articles published by *Wine Spectator.*

193 **In a May 2009 report . . . radicchio salad.** Sharon Labi, "Rockpool Bar & Grill Offers $89,510 Wine Bottle and Free Meal," *Daily Telegraph,* May 9, 2009, dailytelegraph.com.au/for-wine-but-meals-free/news-story/cc49d263ec813e29b03f3a8382609bba.

194 **He told a local newspaper . . . Kurniawan.** Huon Hooke, "Rockpool's David Doyle Stung by Wine Fraudster," *Good Food,* September 9, 2014, goodfood.com.au/drinks/rockpools-david-doyle-stung-by-wine-fraudster-20140905-3ezn2.

194 **In 1980, the late wine critic . . . of the best."** Robert Finigan, *Private Guide to Wines,* January 7, 1980, quoted at Domaine Leroy, accessed March 25, 2017, domaine-leroy.com/homepage.

195 **In May 2013, fourteen months . . . Rockefeller Center.** *Fine and Rare Wines: Featuring Selections from the Historic Cellar of Richard Gill and Ristorante Barolo,* New York: Christie's, May 31, 2013, 52–53. Auction catalog, sale 2704.

195 **Though it started out . . . with fragrance."** Broadbent, *Michael Broadbent's Vintage Wine,* 232.

196 **"It has been years since . . . have matured."** Parker, *Burgundy,* 662.

196 **In a Wine Berserkers blog post . . . previous year.** Don Cornwell, "Rudy Kurniawan & Global Wine Auction Fraud Thread" post #4936, Wine Berserkers, May 26, 2013, wineberserkers.com/forum/viewtopic .php?f=1&t=61172&start=4935.

197 **Looking further into the story . . . Arizona.** Peter Hellman, "Christie's Pulls Burgundy from Auction After Authenticity Questioned," *Wine Spectator,* May 29, 2013, winespectator.com/webfeature/show/id/48501.

198 **De Villaine said nothing . . . not authenticate it."** Aubert de Villaine, email correspondence with author, spring 2013.

199 **She declared each . . . be fake.** *United States v. Kurniawan,* No. 12 Cr. 376 (RMB) (S.D.N.Y.), Government Exhibit 148-1. See also Peter Hellman, "Firm Alleges Rudy Kurniawan Sold It $2.45 Million in Fake Burgundy, and Wine Merchants Helped," *Wine Spectator,* May 24, 2016, winespectator.com/webfeature/show/id/Firm-Alleges-Rudy-Kurniawan-Sold-Fake-Burgundy.

200 **Though shamed and jailed . . . Burgundy.** Peter Hellman, "Wine Counterfeiter Rudy Kurniawan's Stake in Burgundy Vineyards Is Sold," *Wine Spectator,* February 29, 2016, winespectator.com/webfeature/show/id/52802.

200   It took the form of . . . Côte d'Or. Letter from Etienne & Partners to
      Judge Berman, dated November 19, 2014, *United States v. Kurniawan*, No. 12
      Cr. 376 (RMB) (S.D.N.Y.), ECF No. 179.

205   That year, the Hospices de Beaune . . . holdings to him. Don and Petie
      Kladstrup, *Wine and War: The French, the Nazis, and the Battle for France's
      Greatest Treasure* (New York: Broadway, 2001), 76.

206   But in November 2015, it morphed . . . "Rudy wines." Peter Hellman,
      "Rudy Kurniawan's Last Wine Auction," *Wine Spectator*, December 16, 2015,
      winespectator.com/webfeature/show/id/52507.

208   "The sugars and nitrogen . . . Texas Disposal Systems. Interview with
      author in "Unfiltered: Rudy K's Fake Wines Get the Death Penalty," *Wine
      Spectator*, December 10, 2015, winespectator.com/webfeature/show/id/52489.

EPILOGUE

212   "FAC has consulted . . . wealth and reputation." Fine Art Capital
      executive summary recommending loan to Kurniawan, January 14, 2008,
      United States v. Kurniawan, No. 12 Cr. 376 (RMB) (S.D.N.Y.), Government
      Exhibit 23-3.

212   Topmost on the tree is . . . in the 1960s. All information about
      Kurniawan's extended family is from Leo Suryadinata, *Southeast Asian
      Personalities of Chinese Descent: A Biographical Dictionary* (Singapore: Institute
      of Southeast Asian Studies, 2012), 920.

215   I was working on . . . *Spectator*. Peter Hellman, "Play Hard, Work
      Harder," *Wine Spectator*, June 30, 2012, winespectator.com/magazine/show/
      id/46804.

216   I grew up with old . . . it will be gone. Posting by Paul Wasserman on the
      Mark Squires Bulletin Board hosted on eRobertParker.com, June 1, 2006.
      archive.robertparker
      .com/forum/archives/bulk-archive-2005-2008/56147-tn-one-in-a-lifetime-
      bouchard-back-to-1864.

222   Awaiting him at the prison . . . detain him. Rachael Yong Yow
      (public affairs officer, Immigration and Customs Enforcement), email
      correspondence with author, December 13, 2016.

Acknowledgments

During eight years of covering Rudy Kurniawan for *Wine Spectator*, news editor Mitch Frank was my partner. While a few of our stories shared a byline, Mitch was a deft shaper of them all. Before Kurniawan came into the picture, I was tutored on the slippery subject of wine auctions by Peter Meltzer, *Wine Spectator*'s auction correspondent. Bruce Sanderson, the magazine's senior editor who covers Burgundy and Italy, has always been ready to share his expertise. The person who persuaded me to go forward with this book is Esther Mobley, then a young editor and writer at the magazine, now the wine editor of the *San Francisco Chronicle*.

I was alerted to Kurniawan's story by wine merchant Geoffrey Troy. He spent countless hours answering my arcane queries in words and statistics. A trio of wine authenticators also shared their expertise with me. One was Michael Egan, based in Bordeaux but equally adept at nailing fakes from Burgundy. Maureen Downey, a tigeress in defense of authentic wine, generously granted me access to her website winefraud.com. As for Don Cornwell, there are almost no words. How Don manages to juggle two careers—corporate lawyer and tracker of minutiae related to fake wine—remains a mystery to me.

Bill Koch's battalion of lawyers and investigators might well erect a statue in gratitude to their benefactor. As a journalist, I'd chip in. Only Koch, among the titans who Rudy victimized, was willing to step forward. His aide-de-camp, Brad Goldstein, supplied me with key documents and insider tales concerning the global investigations that he directed on behalf of this Koch brother.

I thank Burgundians Erwan Faiveley, Etienne de Montille, Christophe Roumier, Jeremy Seysses, Aubert de Villaine, and the indomitable Laurent Ponsot. Thanks also to Bordeaux defenders Alun Griffiths, formerly of Berry Bros. & Rudd, and Fiona Morrison MW. On this side of the pond, Allen Meadows, aka Burghound, and Douglas Barzelay were generous with their deep knowledge of Burgundy and offered astute insights on Kurniawan. Additional contributions came from Patrick Farrell MW, Wilfred Jaeger, John Kapon, Jefery Levy, Dave Parker, Rob Rosania, Samantha Sheehan, Paul Hayes Tucker, Paul Wasserman, and Josh Wertlieb. Robert Bohr evoked the free-spending Cru restaurant era as only he could. Interior designer Jerry Meyer shed light on a different side of Kurniawan. Dr. Karen Strassler was generous with her expertise on ethnic Indonesian Chinese culture. My thanks go, too, to Wahyu Dhyatmika, a journalist with feet on the ground in Jakarta. Others who offered their insights into Kurniawan asked not to be named.

On the law enforcement front, Asssistant U.S. Attorney Jason Hernandez and FBI Special Agent James Wynne (both have moved on) were the lynchpins of the investigation into Kurniawan. Had they not shared with me details of their work, this book would have been stillborn. Lynzey Donahue, public affairs officer of the US Marshals, delivered essential information and images. I also thank Rachael Yong Yow, public affairs officer in the New York office of US Immigration and Customs Enforcement. Senior Federal District Judge Richard Berman could have been aloof from a writer's documentation needs but was not.

From the defense side, Michael Proctor, Kurniawan's lawyer in the pre-trial phase, counseled me on the issues relating to the FBI's initial search of Kurniawan's house. Kurniawan's principal trial lawyer, Jerry Mooney, patiently explained broad and fine points of the defense. I thank Jerry Rothwell and Reuben Atlas, codirectors of the fine documentary film *Sour Grapes*, for sharing their research with me. Producer and videographer Vince Cariati, the sole person to have filmed Kurniawan extensively, also contributed vivid insights.

The extraordinary Matthew Lore, founding publisher of The Experiment, committed to this book when it was a far-from-finished manuscript. He entrusted its editing to Nicholas Cizek, who was often patient beyond human norms. The book is much the better for Nick's refining of it. Nick told me that I couldn't have hoped for a better copy editor than Anne Horowitz, and after she corrected and tweaked my manuscript, I am a believer. Thanks also to the rest of the Experiment team, including Jeanne Tao, Pamela Schechter, Sarah Smith, Sarah Schneider, Chloe Texier-Rose, and the indefatigable, ever-resourceful Jennifer Hergenroeder.

For the creation of a bright and shiny new personal website featuring this book, I am grateful to my daughter, Kate Miller. And finally, Susan Cohen, who has journeyed with me these thirty-eight years, applied her disciplined mind and raptor-sharp eye to honing and clarifying the text.

Photo Credits

1. "Rudy Kurniawan poses with Burgundy's venerated Aubert de Villaine . . ." *Courtesy of the US Department of Justice*

2. "Kurniawan holds up his paddle . . ." *Courtesy of Mel Hill*

3. "Good times! . . ." *Courtesy of the US Department of Justice*

4. "Laurent Ponsot, fourth-generation winemaker . . ." *Courtesy of Jean-Louis Bernuy*

5. "Billionaire Bill Koch on the cover . . ." *Courtesy of* Wine Spectator

6. "Los Angeles lawyer and amateur French wine label detective Don Cornwell . . ." *Courtesy of Joe Schmelzer*

7. "The first sight federal agents would have seen . . ." *Courtesy of the US Department of Justice*

8. "On a shelf in Kurniawan's house . . ." *Courtesy of the US Department of Justice*

9. "Labels were being soaked off bottles . . ." *Courtesy of the US Department of Justice*

10. "A close-up of the drainer . . ." *Courtesy of the US Department of Justice*

11, 12, 13. "Kurniawan's Domaine de la Romanée-Conti wax and cork stamps and stencil . . ." *Courtesy of the US Department of Justice*

14. "A drawer full of wine labels . . ." *Courtesy of the US Department of Justice*

15. "Here, Kurniawan has created a blank frame . . ." *Courtesy of the US Department of Justice*

16. "To most eyes, this label would appear to be correct. . . ." *Courtesy of the US Department of Justice*

17. "Printing instructions in both English and Indonesian . . ." *Courtesy of the US Department of Justice*

18. "Assistant US Attorney Jason Hernandez . . ." *Courtesy of the US Department of Justice*

19. "Wine authenticator Maureen Downey . . ." *Courtesy of Maureen Downey/ winefraud.com*

20. "This bottle, vintage 1945 . . ." *Courtesy of Maureen Downey/winefraud.com*

21. "This methuselah . . ." *Courtesy of Maureen Downey/winefraud.com*

22. "Defendant Kurniawan listens as victim Bill Koch is questioned . . ." *Courtesy of Jane Rosenberg*

23. "Assistant prosecutor Joseph Facciponti . . ." *Courtesy of Jane Rosenberg*

24. "At a Texas recycling facility . . ." *Courtesy of the US Department of Justice*

About the Author

PETER HELLMAN, a New York–based journalist and author, has been a contributor to *Wine Spectator* for more than a decade. His work has also appeared in *The New York Times*, *The Wall Street Journal*, *New York* magazine, and numerous other publications. His books include *When Courage Was Stronger than Fear*, *Chief!*, and *Fifty Years After Kitty Genovese*. He and his wife, Susan, live in New York City, where they raised their children, Jacob and Kate.